MW01026032

Forensic
Science

VISIT ONLINE

OXFORD QUICK REFERENCE

The most authoritative and up-to-date reference books for both students and the general reader.

Many of these titles are also available online at www.oxfordreference.com

A Dictionary of

Forensic
Science

SUZANNE BELL

OXFORD

UNIVERSITY PRESS

Great Clarendon Street, Oxford OX2 6DP

Oxford University Press is a department of the University of Oxford.
It furthers the University's objective of excellence in research, scholarship,
and education by publishing worldwide in

Oxford New York

Auckland Cape Town Dar es Salaam Hong Kong Karachi
Kuala Lumpur Madrid Melbourne Mexico City Nairobi
New Delhi Shanghai Taipei Toronto

With offices in

Argentina Austria Brazil Chile Czech Republic France Greece
Guatemala Hungary Italy Japan Poland Portugal Singapore
South Korea Switzerland Thailand Turkey Ukraine Vietnam

Oxford is a registered trade mark of Oxford University Press
in the UK and in certain other countries

Published in the United States
by Oxford University Press Inc., New York

British Library Cataloguing in Publication Data
Data available

Library of Congress Cataloging in Publication Data
Data available

Typeset by
SPI Publisher Services, Pondicherry, India
Printed in Great Britain on acid-free paper by
Clays Ltd, Elcograf S.p.A

ISBN 978-0-19-959400-9

10 9

Contents

Preface

Forensic science is a diverse discipline that incorporates everything from computers to death investigation. As such, no one volume can do it justice. What I have attempted to do is capture the breadth of forensic science as opposed to focusing on one or two aspects such as crime scenes or toxicology for example. Appendix 4 lists additional reading for those who wish to explore further.

There is a perception that forensic science has never been more popular, but that is not necessarily the case. The 'CSI effect' (see the entry for more information) is a new term for an old phenomenon. When M. J. B. Orfila gave his dramatic testimony at the LaFarge trial in 1840, he cemented his status as the premier forensic toxicologist of his day. Students flocked to study with him and this early group of students became the first generation of what we recognize today as forensic scientists. The stories of Sir Arthur Conan Doyle launched another flurry of fascination with forensic investigations. Other books and now movies and television shows have contributed to the public's fascination with forensic science. This volume is designed to assist those sharing that fascination to learn more about the subject.

You will note that some words are preceded by an asterisk. This indicates that there is an entry for that word in the Dictionary. Where there are multiple accepted terms for a concept, there are signpost entries directing you to that term. Some entries are accompanied by web links which can be found on-line.

Enjoy.

S.B.

May 2011

ABI Profiler and COfiler kits Commercial reagent kits made by Applied Biosystems (now under Life Technologies Corporation) that are used for *DNA typing. The Profiler Plus kit amplifies nine of the thirteen STR loci currently typed in the United States. The COfiler kit amplifies the remaining six loci.

ABO blood group system A blood group system discovered by Karl Landsteiner in 1900. The ABO system consists of antigens found on the outer surfaces of red blood cells (also called erythrocytes and commonly abbreviated to RBCs) and corresponding *antibodies in the serum. The approximate frequencies (UK and USA) are A: 42 per cent; O: 44 per cent; B 10 per cent; and AB 4 per cent. A significant proportion of individuals (~80 per cent) are *secretors, meaning that the antigens present in their blood are also found in other body fluids such as saliva. Prior to wide adoption of DNA typing, the ABO blood group system was the key element of forensic serological examination of blood and body fluids. *See also* ABSORPTION-ELUTION AND ABSORPTION-INHIBITION; LATTES, LEON.

abrasion A scraping-type injury to the skin that typically occurs as a result of friction or rubbing. The injury is limited to the upper layers of the skin.

absorbance A measure of the amount of electromagnetic energy that is absorbed by a given sample. The amount of energy absorbed will depend on the concentration of the sample, the amount of sample through which the energy travels, and a constant called the molar absorptivity coefficient (ε). This coefficient depends on the structure of the sample molecule and the wavelength of the energy. This relationship is summarized as the Beer–Lambert Law: $A = \varepsilon bc$ where ε is the molar absorptivity, b is the path length and c is concentration. Many spectrophotometric techniques used in forensic science take advantage of this relationship to determine the concentration of a sample. In other cases, such as *infrared spectroscopy (IR), the pattern of absorbance across many wavelengths is used to help identify the compounds present in a sample.

absorption-elution and absorption-inhibition Two tests that were used to type blood and *body fluids for *ABO and other *blood group systems. Absorption-inhibition was developed in 1923 in Italy by Vittorio Siracusa and absorption-elution followed in the 1930s. Many modifications and variations have occurred, and the general procedures were applied to other blood group systems. Absorption-inhibition works by reducing the strength of an antiserum based on the type and amount of antigens present in the stain. Conversely, absorption-inhibition is based on the reduction in strength of an antiserum when that antiserum is in the presence of antigens that will bind with it. As a result of the binding, the strength of the antiserum is reduced. *See also* CULLIFORD, BRIAN.

accelerant The flammable material that is used to accelerate the propagation of an intentionally set fire. Accelerants can be solids, liquids, or gases, with petrol (gasoline) being the most commonly used. Solid accelerants include paper, fireworks, road flares, and black powder. Butane (cigarette lighter fuel), propane, and natural gas are examples of gaseous accelerants, which do not leave any chemical residue at a fire scene.

AccessData A company headquartered in Utah that provides a number of widely used software tools applied in computer and digital forensic investigation and analysis. This includes FTK software (forensics toolkit), decryption software, and software for mobile devices.

accidental characteristics Physical markings and features in a material that are acquired by wear or by some accidental or other non-repeatable circumstance during manufacture. Tyre treads, bullets, shoe soles, plastic bags, glass, and a host of other materials of forensic interest can acquire accidental characteristics when they are manufactured. For example, glass that is made by pouring molten material into a mould may develop bubbles which would be considered an accidental characteristic.

accident reconstruction A type of forensic engineering investigation involving the study of automobile accidents and related accidents involving motorcycles, trucks, pedestrians, bicycles, boats, buses, trains, and other vehicles. Reconstructions can be used in civil or criminal cases and can become crucial when there are no witnesses. Points of investigation in traffic accidents commonly include speed of the car(s), car positions, direction(s) of travel, braking, and point(s) of impact.

accounting, forensic The application of accounting techniques to criminal and civil matters. Forensic accountants study financial records

and other financial evidence, prepare analyses and reports, and assist
in investigation.

accreditation The process of assuring that a forensic laboratory
follows procedures and protocols as set forth by a professional
organization such as ISO or ASCLD/LAB. Gaining accreditation
involves examinations of policies, procedures, staff education and
training, and general laboratory operations. This review is undertaken
by the organization that would grant the accreditation status and
usually involves a site visit. Accredited laboratories may be audited by
the accrediting body to check compliance.

accuracy One of many *figures of merit used in *metrology (generally)
and in quantitative forensic analysis. The accuracy of a result is a
quantitative measure of how close the result of a given analysis is to the
correct or true value. While a true value can never be known, there are
materials such as certified reference materials in which the reported
composition can be accepted as a true value, along with an *uncertainty.
Accuracy is a function of the *precision and the *trueness associated
with the analysis.

(⊕) SEE WEB LINKS

• A European organization of analytical chemists; the website has many useful
documents and definitions. Last accessed May 2011.
• A working group site with many useful metrological definitions applicable to
forensic analysis. Last accessed May 2011.
• This links to the International Vocabulary of Metrology kept by the Bureau
International de Poids et Mésures in Paris, France. Last accessed May 2011.

acid **1.** Arrhenius definition: A compound that dissociates in water to
produce H^+ which forms H_3O^+ and the conjugate base A^-:

$$HA \xrightarrow{H_2O} H_3O^+ + A^-$$

2. Brønsted–Lowry theory views an acid as a compound that donates
a proton (H^+) and a base as a compound that accepts a proton. This
framework is commonly used related to the definition of acidic and basic
drugs in *seized drug analysis and *toxicology.
3. In Lewis acid/base theory, an acid is a compound that accepts an
electron and a Lewis base donates an electron.

acid/base extraction A chemical separation procedure that
exploits changes in pH and relative solubilities to effect the separation.
These extractions are typically performed using *liquid/liquid extraction
(LLE) and *solid phase extraction (SPE).

acid phosphatase (AP, ACP, EAP) *See* ERYTHROCYTE ACID PHOSPHATASE.

acid salt 1. A salt (combination of an *anion and *cation) that forms from a partially deprotonated, multi-protic acid. For example, the diprotic acid H_2CO_3 can be partially deprotonated to form H^+ and HCO_3^-. The acid salt forms from the anion; an example being $NaHCO_3$.

2. In the forensic context, the term is occasionally used to describe salt forms of drugs. An acid salt of a drug formed from a basic drug in a protonated form and a counter ion such as chloride (Cl^-) or sulphate (SO_4^{2-}). An example is the hydrochloride salt of cocaine, symbolized as cocaine•HCl. Cocaine has an *ionizable centre that can be protonated to become a positively charged cation that can form the salt as shown. The acid salt of a drug molecule has different characteristics, including solubilities from the unprotonated drug molecule.

Formation and structure of cocaine•HCl

acrylic Chemical compounds (*polymers) incorporated into paints, fibres, and other coating and resin materials. The monomers are compounds such as acrylic acid in which a key structural feature is a carbon-carbon double bond (an unsaturated bond). An example of this class of polymer is Plexiglas, also known as Perspex in the United Kingdom.

action (of firearms) The mechanical process by which a *cartridge is loaded and secured into a firearm before firing and how it is removed afterward. For example, a pump-action shotgun ejects a spent cartridge and loads a new one by means of manual pumping. In terms of pistols and revolvers, the term single action means that by pulling the trigger the firing pin is driven into the primer to fire the weapon (single action only or SAO). Double action means that pulling the trigger cocks the firing pin back and releases it (DA or DAO). If the weapon is a revolver, a double action design also causes the cylinder to rotate when the trigger is pulled.

ACE-V In the evaluation of fingerprint or other types of pattern evidence, an abbreviation for a four-step process: analysis, comparison, evaluation, and verification. It is pronounced as 'ace vee'.

adenine (A) One of four *nucleotide bases that comprise DNA and RNA. Due to its molecular structure, adenine will associate with thymine (T), and the two are referred to as complements of each other.

adiabatic flame temperature The calculated theoretical maximum temperature at which combustion of a fuel occurs. The condition of the fuel and presence of oxygen (or other oxidant) will determine actual flame temperature. Although there are two conditions for which adiabatic conditions are defined (constant volume and constant pressure), forensic applications are usually based on the assumption of constant pressure.

adipocere A greyish wax-like substance that forms as a result of post-mortem hydrolysis of body fat. The word comes from a combination of the Latin words for fat (or adipose tissue) and wax, and the consistency of adipocere is very much like soap. Adipocere formation is most common in bodies found in damp environments such as mud, wet soil, swamps, or in water.

ADME The process that occurs once a person ingests a drug or poison (or any other *xenobiotic compound or substance). In order the steps are: absorption, distribution, metabolism, and elimination. The xenobiotic can enter a person's system by many *modes of ingestion; and once this has occurred, the substance is absorbed into the bloodstream. It is then distributed to the different tissues in the body as metabolism begins to occur, principally in the liver. The final stage is elimination, primarily but not exclusively through urine.

admissibility and admissibility hearings The process of determining what evidence and expert testimony will be heard by a court or trier of fact. The standards that courts use to determine admissibility of evidence vary among and within nations. Example standards that have been and still are used include variations of 'general acceptance', meaning that the scientific method used is generally acceptable to a significant proportion of the scientific discipline to which they belong. In other jurisdictions, the judge acts as the 'gatekeeper' and decides, using a variety of tools such as standards, peer-reviewed publications, error rates, and other metrics, whether scientific evidence and testimony is to be admitted and heard.

adulterant A compound that is added to an illegal drug as a diluent. An adulterant is pharmacologically active and often produces physiological effects grossly similar to the drug. An example adulterant would be caffeine (a stimulant) added to *cocaine (also a stimulant).

adversarial system A system based on competing arguments. The legal system in most countries is based on the adversarial system in which each side presents arguments before the trier of fact, the entity that renders a decision based on the perceived merits of the arguments.

AFIS (IAFIS) (Integrated Automated Fingerprint Identification System) Computerized systems for searching *fingerprint databases and identifying suspects in the United States. Although IAFIS is the full abbreviation, the term 'AFIS' is frequently used to represent the same database. The database holds approximately 55 million records and is managed in the Federal Bureau of Investigation, Criminal Justice Information Services (CJIS) Division. *See also* IDENT1.

age-at-death estimation A determination of the approximate age of a deceased person. Common methods of age determination are based on skeletal development and measurements, and dental development and condition. Given that skeletal and dental formation follows a known and consistent pattern of development, estimates based on these techniques are reliable to within a year for younger people. Once growth and development are complete, estimates become more difficult and, in general, the older the person is, the larger the uncertainty of the age estimates.

agglutination Clumping of biological particles. For example clumping of red blood cells that occurs when cells with one type of antigen on their surface are placed into a solution that contains *antibodies to that antigen, resulting in an antigen-antibody reaction or immunological reaction. For example, when red blood cells from a person with Type A blood are placed into a solution containing anti-A antibodies, the cells will clump together. The agglutinin is the antibody and the agglutinogen is the antigen. *See also* ABO BLOOD GROUP SYSTEM.

agonist A compound that binds to a site on a cell and causes a physiological response generally identical to that produced by an *endogenous compound. Many drugs are agonists.

algor mortis Post-mortem cooling of a body. Many variables affect the cooling rate including ambient temperature, how much fat the victim has, and amount of exposed surface area.

alkaline phosphatase An enzyme that causes the removal of phosphate (PO_4^{3-}). It is produced in several locations in the body including the liver. It is active in basic environments, in contrast to acid phosphatase (*see* ERYTHROCYTE ACID PHOSPHATASE).

alkaloids A class of chemical compounds that are extracted or obtained primarily from seed plants. The pure compounds are usually colourless and bitter tasting, and are encountered in forensic work as drugs or *poisons. Example alkaloids are drugs in the *opiate family and *cocaine. The characteristic chemical feature of alkaloids is an ionizable centre containing an amine group (RNH_2), so the term 'nitrogenous base' is also used.

allele Alternative form of a gene or base pair sequence that occurs on a chromosome. The allele frequency is defined as the percentage or alternative form of a gene (an allele) present in a given population, a term often simplified to the frequency.

allelic ladder A method for standardizing the interpretation of *DNA typing procedures based on *short tandem repeats (STRs). To create a ladder, a mixture is created that contains all known variants of each typed *locus that is analysed along with the case samples. The ladder provides a size-based reference that facilitates identification of alleles as well as detection of new variants.

alligatoring A charring pattern seen in burned wood that resembles alligator skin.

allozyme The allelic form of an enzyme which is determined by a given gene.

alternative light source (ALS) Illumination sources other than ambient room light or sunlight. An ALS is used to make objects or impressions that cannot be otherwise seen visible. An ALS unit typically provides several different selectable wavelengths of light that are chosen based on the application. An ultraviolet source can induce *fluorescence in materials such as semen or treatments applied to bloodstains, allowing them to be seen.

alu repeat 'Jumping genes' or sequences of DNA that are widely distributed and may be found in many areas of the genome of humans and primates.

ambient data Information on a computer or related device such as a mobile phone that is not stored in typical formats or in typical and easily accessible portions of the storage media. This can include data that has been partially overwritten or erased. Recovery of ambient data may require specialized tools and software.

amelogenin A genetic locus that can be used in conjunction with *DNA typing to identify a person's sex. The gene codes for tooth pulp, but the basis of the sex determination is the variation in the length of this locus between males and females. The female pattern is shorter than the male pattern. Because this locus is found on the X and Y chromosome, two differences are seen in the DNA profile: the male (XY) will exhibit two peaks, one larger than the other while a female's DNA will yield one peak.

amido black A reagent used to help visualize latent prints. It is a dye that stains proteins present in the fingerprint residue.

amino acids The molecular building blocks of proteins including DNA. All of these molecules have at least one acidic site (functional group) as well as an NH_3 ('amino' as in ammonia) group. Proteins are polymers of amino acids, meaning they are built by linking many ('poly') amino acids together in a long chain.

ammonium nitrate (NH_4NO_3) A salt used as a fertilizer that can also be used in drug synthesis and for the making of improvised explosives like ANFO (ammonium nitrate-fuel oil). Such an explosive was used in the 1995 bombing of the Murrah Federal Building in Oklahoma City in the United States. ANFO is also used commercially and militarily.

ammunition In modern firearms, ammunition consists of a projectile and a *cartridge case containing *propellant and the *primer that ignites it. The function of ammunition is to exploit the chemical energy stored in the propellant by first igniting it. The powder burns rapidly, releasing heat and rapidly expanding hot gases that are trapped behind the projectile in the breach and barrel of the weapon. When sufficient pressure is built up, the pressure accelerates the projectile forward and out of the barrel.

amphetamine (amfetamine) A central and peripheral nervous system stimulant that produces elevated heart rate and blood pressure and, at higher doses, effects such as hallucinations, convulsions, prickling

of the skin, unpredictable emotional swings, extreme aggression, and
death. Amphetamine is a basic drug that is often encountered as the *acid
salt amphetamine•HCl. Amphetamine and related stimulants are
abused worldwide. Medically, amphetamine has been used as an
appetite suppressant and it is also known by the names Dexedrine and
Biphetamine.

Amphetamine

amplicon In *DNA typing, a segment of DNA, typically a *short tandem
repeat (STR) created by amplification during the polymerase chain
reaction (*PCR) step.

amplification The process of creating multiple copies (*amplicons) of
segments of DNA for typing purposes. Amplification is typically carried
out by polymerase chain reaction (*PCR).

**amplified fragment length polymorphism (AFLPs,
AmpFLPs)** In current *DNA typing methodology, relatively small
segments of DNA, also known as mini-satellites, are the target of typing
procedures. These loci consist of *variable number of tandem repeats
(VNTR) that are amplified using polymerase chain reaction (*PCR)
procedures and subsequently typed. These loci are highly polymorphic,
leading to their utility in forensic DNA typing.

amylase An enzyme that catalyses the breakdown of starches;
α-amylase is found in saliva and is the basis of an older *presumptive
test for its presence.

Amy model A probability model for fingerprint comparisons
introduced by L. Amy in the 1940s. It was one of many early attempts to
develop a statistical model applicable to *fingerprints and *friction ridge
patterns.

anabolic steroids A class of synthetic steroids related to the male sex
hormone *testosterone. These compounds have androgenic properties
that promote the development of secondary male characteristics such as
increased muscle mass, improved muscle tone, and deepening of the
voice. Dangers of anabolic steroid misuse include kidney and liver
damage, liver cancer, masculinization, and infertility in women,

impotence in men, and unpredictable emotional effects including mood
swings and extreme aggression. Some of these effects are irreversible.

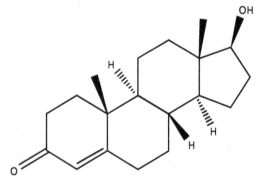

Testosterone

anaesthetic A drug or substance that causes a loss of sensation. A
general anaesthetic causes loss of consciousness and awareness while a
local anaesthetic affects a small area and causes numbness. *Cocaine and
related compounds can be used as local anaesthetics. Propofol® is an
example of a general anaesthetic.

anagen phase The active growth phase in the life cycle of a hair, which
can last for several years. The length of this phase varies, but generally falls
between three and eight years. The phase of a hair may be important in
that hair in the *telogen phase is shed naturally whereas hair in the other
two growth stages (anagen and *catagen) may be forcefully removed.
Typically, well over half the hairs on the scalp are in the anagen phase
at a given moment.

analgesics A class of drugs that relieves or reduces pain by depressing the
central nervous system (CNS). Aspirin and paracetamol (acetaminophen or
Tylenol®) are common over-the counter (OTC) analgesics. Many narcotic
drugs, including opium alkaloids such as *morphine and *codeine are
powerful analgesics with a high potential for abuse.

analyser 1. Generically, an instrument or device used in a
measuring process.
   2. In *polarizing light microscopy (PLM), one of two polarizing filters
used is placed after the sample and before the eyepiece in the optical train.

analyte The substance, compound, or element that is the target of a
given test or analysis.

androgens Hormones that directly affect the growth and development of the male reproductive system. *Testosterone is androgen.

androlone A metabolite of *testosterone, also known as stanolone or DHT (dihydrotestosterone). This steroid cannot be converted to estradiol and as a result, is considered to be a pure androgenic steroid (one which influences male secondary sexual characteristics). It is abused as a performance-enhancing substance.

angle of acceptance The angle that describes the image-forming cone of light that enters a lens of a microscope. It is related to the numerical aperture (*NA) of the lens used in the microscope objective.

(((🌐))) SEE WEB LINKS

• An excellent general reference for microscopy. Last accessed May 2011.

angle of impact **1.** In blood spatter, the angle of impact is formed by the trajectory of blood when it strikes a surface. As shown in the figure, a drop of blood striking at a 90° angle will be essentially circular. As the angle becomes more oblique, the resulting spot becomes more elongated and the amount of elongation can be used to estimate impact angle.

2. The term is also used analogously to describe *wound biomechanics and bullet trajectory.

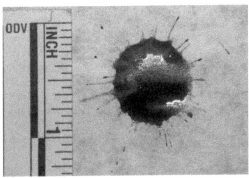

Impact of a blood droplet travelling perpendicular to the paper

anion An atom or group of covalently bonded atoms (called polyatomics) carrying a negative charge (for example, Cl^- or chloride, NO_3^- or nitrate).

anisotropic An optical property of some crystals and fibres useful in the forensic analysis of evidence such as dust, soil, and fibres. A material that is *isotropic for a given optical characteristic will have the same value of that characteristic regardless of the direction from which the light is coming. In contrast, anisotropic materials have a non-uniform distribution of such characteristics. Solid materials that are made up of molecules that are randomly placed or molecules that are not symmetrical will be isotropic. Many types of glass are also isotropic. Other kinds of crystals and many polymers (which consist of ordered subunits bonded together) are anisotropic. The term *birefringence is also used to describe anisotropy.

annealing In *DNA typing procedures, the step in which *primers are added to the DNA after it has been denatured. The DNA primers, which are specific for certain DNA regions, bind to the intact DNA and prepare it for addition of bases that will complete the copying operation. Annealing is sometimes also referred to as *hybridization.

anode The electrode with a positive charge or potential that will attract negatively charged species. The most common forensic application of this term is in electrophoresis in which the negatively charged species (*anions) are drawn toward the anodic end of the system.

ante-mortem Prior to or before death. Ante-mortem dental records for example can be used to identify the victims of mass disasters such as plane crashes.

anthrax A deadly disease caused by bacteria that was sent through the US mail during October and November of 2001, resulting in five deaths. It also recently appeared in heroin samples found in Scotland, resulting in at least ten deaths. This outbreak appears to have been the result of accidental contamination. The bacteria (*bacillus anthracis*), is found in soil and occasionally infects domesticated animals such as sheep and cattle. The spores of the bacteria can lie dormant in soil for years and infect humans; the spores can also be manipulated to form a potent biological weapon. The US incident, also called 'Amerithrax', helped raise awareness of bioterrorism threats worldwide and sped the development of bioforensics, a discipline that studies biological weapons and threats in much the same way forensic toxicologists study chemical poisons. The investigation was closed in 2010 after the FBI determined that Dr Bruce Ivins (1946–2008), a scientist working at Fort Detrick, Maryland, acted alone in the crime. Ivins committed suicide in 2008.

anthropology, forensic The analysis and study of skeletal remains that are or become involved in legal procedures. Anthropology is a diverse field that studies many aspects of human culture and existence from its earliest roots. The discipline can be divided into cultural anthropology and physical anthropology, the branch that examines, among other things, osteology. Osteology is the study of the variability, development, growth, and evolution of the human skeleton. Forensic anthropology emerged primarily from osteology and physical anthropology. Forensic anthropological methods are often used for identification of remains, *age-at-death estimations, and sex determination.

anthropometry The use of body measurements to identify individuals. Most often the term is associated with a system of body measurements developed by *Bertillon and used for identification purposes until replaced by fingerprinting in the early 1900s. Anthropometric measurements are still used in forensic *anthropology, where measurements of bones or bone fragments can be used to estimate properties such as the height and stature of a deceased person.

antibody, antigen, and antiserum Collectively, terms related to immunological reactions that play a role in forensic toxicology and forensic biology. An immunological reaction involves the combination of an antigen with an antibody. An antigen is a substance that provokes production of an antibody; a material recognized as foreign by an organism. As an example, a person's *ABO blood type is determined by the type of antigen found on the surface of their red blood cells (RBC). A person with Type A blood has A antigens on the surface of their red blood cells and anti-B antibodies in their plasma. An antiserum is a serum that contains antibodies specific to a given antigen or antigens. In early blood transfusions, little was known about blood types resulting in many cases of severe immunological responses and death that occurred when the wrong type was transfused. If a person with type A blood (A antigens, anti-B antibodies) is given type B blood (B antigens on the RBC, anti-A antibodies), the anti-A antibodies bind with the A antigens on the cell surface, causing *agglutination reactions that can be life threatening. Antigen-antibody reactions are also an integral part of screening tests in forensic toxicology and are called collectively *immunoassays. *See also* LANDSTEINER, KARL.

anti-forensic In *computer forensics and cybercrime investigation, a term referring to tools and techniques used to erase, destroy, or make data unrecoverable.

antimony (Sb) A chemical element that is one of three elements considered characteristic of *gunshot residue (GSR). It is also found as an ingredient in copier toners, and occasionally as a poison.

apocrine gland A sweat gland associated with hair follicles that secrete oily fluid rich in cholesterol and fatty acids.

archaeology, forensic Although often considered interchangeable with forensic *anthropology, forensic archaeology is emerging as a separate but related discipline. In general, forensic anthropologists concentrate on the analysis of skeletal remains while forensic archaeologists focus on the location and excavation of these remains. Archaeological procedures are well suited for processing clandestine graves and for crime scene analysis and reconstruction, particularly when the scene goes undiscovered for long periods of time. Forensic archaeology is also employed in cases of mass graves that often accompany wars or other large-scale conflicts. Forensic archaeologists assist in locating grave sites via tools such as aerial photography, surface site disturbance, ground penetrating radar, and physical probing. Once a potential gravesite is identified, methodical excavation methods are employed to recover evidence and its context. An important aspect of interpretation involves the stratigraphy (layering) found during the excavation.

arsenic (As) A heavy metal that was widely used as a poison until advancements in forensic toxicology in the mid-1800s allowed toxicologists to detect it in body tissues. Arsenic is a metal and is found in the same chemical family as *antimony, also used as a poison. Arsenic exists in many forms, all of which are toxic to varying degrees. The first reliable chemical test for arsenic was the *Marsh test, made famous by the *LaFarge case in 1840. Arsenic persists in hair, nails, and to a small extent in bone, so it is possible to detect cases of arsenic poisoning even in skeletonized remains.

arson The act of purposely setting a fire with criminal intent. In the United Kingdom, the latest available statistics state, more than 2,200 fires are intentionally set each week, resulting on average in about 60 injuries and 2 deaths. In the United States, more than 50,000 fires were intentionally set from 2003 to 2006, causing 377 civilian deaths, over 100 injuries, and nearly $900 million in property damage. The conviction rate for arson is typically low, around 6 per cent in the United States. Fire investigators determine if a fire can be assigned to natural causes, accidents, arson (incendiary), or indeterminate causes. In the case of incendiary fires, the usual motive is profit in the form of insurance fraud. The role of the forensic chemist in arson investigation focuses on detection of *accelerants, *explosives, and *incendiary devices.

Car burning as a result of an intentionally set fire. The point of origin is inside the vehicle.

art, forensic Application of drawing, sculpture and other visual tools to forensic casework. Areas within forensic art include composite imagery, in which interviews and witness statements are used to generate a sketch of a missing person or suspect; image enhancement; ageing progressions, in which images are generated to indicate what a child will look like as he or she grows, or how an adult's appearance will change as he or she ages; post-mortem drawings; superimposition, in which computers are used to superimpose photographs of a person's face over the computerized representation of a skull, also for identification purposes; *facial reconstruction; and preparation of graphical or visual information for courtroom presentation.

arterial spurt When an artery is punctured by a knife, gunshot wound, or other injury, the arterial spurt produces a distinctive wavelike pattern that correlates with blood pressure. The pattern can be produced as long as the heart is beating.

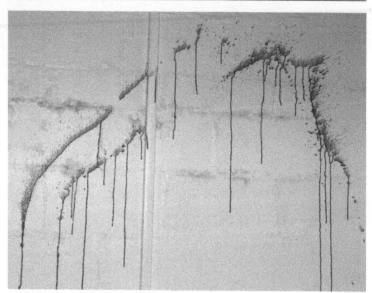

Arterial spurt bloodstain pattern

ASCII Abbreviation for American Standard Code for Information Exchange, a file format used for text storage and display in computers. Most computers and related devices support ASCII formatting.

asphyxia Death caused by lack of oxygen to the brain, also called anoxial death. It is a *mechanism of death that can be caused in many ways such as suffocation, strangulation, drowning, crushing of the airway, or swelling of the airway in response to injury. Suffocation can occur when the airway is blocked by an object (choking or smothering with a pillow) or in confined spaces where oxygen is depleted or displaced by another gas such as nitrogen or carbon dioxide.

There are several types of asphyxia encountered in forensic death investigation including positional, in which the person has got into a position in which breathing is impaired; crush asphyxia, in which crushing injuries impair breathing; autoerotic asphyxia in which a neck ligature is used; and strangulation. Chemical asphyxiation (anoxia) occurs when the mechanism of oxygen transport is impaired in the body such as can occur in the presence of high concentrations of carbon monoxide.

assessment, crime scene An initial evaluation of a crime scene to determine scale, scope, dimensions, and other information essential to evaluating potential hazards, determining what types of personnel and

resources will be needed and gathering information for planning
subsequent evaluation, documentation, and processing steps.

atavistic criminal personality A concept that arose from early
evolutionary and natural selection theories toward the end of the 19th
century. A person with an atavistic personality was considered to be
less highly evolved than normal and, as a result, was more likely to
engage in criminal behaviour.

atomic absorption (AA) An instrumental technique used for
elemental analysis. In forensic science, target elements include lead (Pb),
barium (Ba), antimony (Sb), and copper (Cu) in suspected *gunshot
residue (GSR). Heavy metal poisons such as *arsenic can also be detected
and quantitated using AA. Other terms used to describe this technique
include flame absorption spectrophotometry (FAS) and atomic absorption
spectrophotometry (AAS). In place of a flame, a graphite furnace can be
used for heating and atomization.

atomic emission (AE) Instrumental techniques for elemental analysis
that detect *electromagnetic energy emitted by metal atoms in the excited
state. This typically occurs under conditions of extremely high
temperatures. The instrument most commonly used in forensic
applications relies on an *inductively coupled plasma torch to induce
emission, and the technique is referred to as ICP-AES for inductively
coupled plasma atomic emission.

atomic spectroscopy Spectroscopic methods designed to detect
specific atoms or elements via characteristic absorbance or emission of
*electromagnetic radiation (EMR), typically in the UV/visible range. In
both cases, the samples are typically prepared by dissolution in acids and
introduced to an extreme heat environment that causes de-solvation and
atomization of the sample. In atomic absorption (AA), a sample is
aspirated into a flame through which wavelengths of light are directed that
are specific for the element of interest. If the element is present, light is
absorbed, resulting in a decreased signal at the detector compared to if
none of the element was present. In lieu of a flame, a graphite furnace may
be used for heating. In modern atomic emission spectroscopy (AES), a
sample is directed into an *inductively coupled plasma (ICP) that is hot
enough to excite the atoms. As the atoms return to the ground state,
energy characteristic of the element is given off and detected.

attenuated total reflectance (ATR) A variation of *infrared
spectroscopy (IR) widely used in drug analysis and the analysis of trace
evidence such as *paint and *fibres. ATR differs from traditional IR in that
the sample is in direct and tight contact with the ATR objective, which can

a

be made of materials such as diamond or salts of zinc and cadmium. The radiation interacts with the sample at several points before being directed to the detector.

audit A comprehensive review of a laboratory's procedures, personnel, and practices typically conducted by an outside and independent entity. Audits are integral to laboratory *accreditation.

autoignition temperature The lowest temperature at which a material such as an *accelerant will ignite under normal atmospheric conditions without an external source of ignition. The temperature of the surrounding environment must be high enough to supply the *energy of activation necessary to start the combustion process.

autolysis The post-mortem breakdown of cells caused by enzymes in the cells. This process is sometimes referred to informally as 'self-digestion' and is part of the decomposition process.

autopsy The post-mortem medical examination (also referred to as a necroscopy) that involves a thorough external examination of the body, dissection, sample collection, histological examinations, and toxicological testing. The purpose of the autopsy is to determine the cause of death and to the extent possible, the circumstances surrounding the death. The word 'autopsy' is derived from Greek and is roughly translated as 'to see for one's self' or 'to see with one's own eyes', but the term has evolved to the current usage referring to a post-mortem dissection. Autopsies are usually performed when a death is suspicious, unattended, or otherwise unexplained.

autoradiogram (autorad) An X-ray image that reveals labelled DNA fragments produced during *restriction fragment length polymorphism *DNA typing procedures, a method that preceded current methods. To produce an autorad, the DNA *probes were labelled with radioactive material (or sometimes a luminescent material) and allowed to react with DNA that has been separated using electrophoresis and transferred to a membrane. After the probes bind to DNA on the membrane, the pattern can be visualized by placing the membrane next to X-ray film. The bound probes irradiate the film, producing the autorad.

autosome Any chromosome that is not one of the sex chromosomes. Humans have 23 pairs of chromosomes of which one pair determines sex. The remaining 22 are **autosomal**.

auxochrome A chemical functional group attached to a *chromophore that alters the wavelength(s) of light that can be absorbed by that chromophore. Examples of auxochromes are carboxylate ($-COOH$) and

amine ($-NH_2$) functional groups. In forensic science, auxochromes are
important in dye chemistry, paints, inks, and in *ultraviolet light
spectroscopy.

average man standard A legal term that is sometimes employed as
a comparative value. For example, in a case where negligence is an issue,
the question could be phrased such as 'did the defendant take the same
level of care and caution as would be expected of the average man?'

azides A chemical functional group consisting of two nitrogens linked
by a triple bond. In forensic science, azides are encountered in
explosives and as part of the *primers used in firearm *ammunition.
One of the most common is lead azide, $Pb(N_3)_2$.

aziridine (C_2H_5N) A triangular chemical structure with bonds under
considerable strain found in some molecules of forensic interest, such
as by-products of methamphetamine synthesis.

azo dye (azo linkage) A type of chemical bond frequently seen in dyes
and in the products of *presumptive colour tests. The linkage is made via
two nitrogen atoms in the form $-N=N-$.

Azostix A pre-packed test strip used to detect urea in blood. It works by
detecting a pH change when urea is catalytically converted to CO_2 and
ammonia. Forensically, these sticks can also be used to detect the
presence of urine, which contains a high concentration of urea.

B

back spatter A type of *bloodstain pattern that occurs when blood is projected backwards relative to the direction of a force. For example, a gun fired at close range to a victim may collect back spatter, with the blood travelling backwards relative to the path of the bullet.

Baeyer, Friedrich (1835–1917) A German chemist who won the Nobel Prize in chemistry in 1905. His full name was Johann Friedrich Wilhelm

Dr Friedrich Baeyer

Adolf von Baeyer and his advances in drug and dye chemistry had significant, if indirect, impact on the future practice of forensic chemistry. He discovered barbituric acid, the precursor of the *barbiturates; synthesized the dye indigo; and discovered *phenolphthalein, a compound used in the most common presumptive test for blood.

ballistics, forensic   Although the term is used generically to describe the scope of forensic firearm examination, ballistics strictly defined is the study of projectiles in motion. Forensic ballistics examines the motion of projectiles fired from weapons and is described by a number of different terms. **Internal ballistics** includes the motion occurring inside the weapon and barrel; **intermediate ballistics** deals with the transition from internal to external at the muzzle end of the barrel; **external ballistics** applies while the projectile is in flight to the target; and **terminal ballistics** is used when the projectile impacts the target. The latter is related to the topics of *distance determination and *wound ballistics.

ball powder   A *smokeless powder particle that is manufactured into a spherical shape. The ingredients are mixed in a solvent base and allowed to form small spherical particles that are then allowed to dry. The spheres can be further processed by pressing into disks.

Balthazard, Victor (1852–1950)   A French forensic scientist who served as the medical examiner for the city of Paris and helped advance scientific crime investigation and in particular firearms and *bloodstain pattern analysis. In 1910 he, along with Marcelle Lambert, wrote the first comprehensive book on hair analysis entitled *The Hair of Man and Animals* (translation). In it, they stressed the importance of microscopic examination and the careful evaluation of microscopic structures, still standard today. Balthazard also developed an advanced photographic method of comparing markings on bullets and in 1912 testified in a case using photos and point comparison techniques to identify bullets involved in a fatal shooting. He was also among the first to note other distinctive markings in firearms including firing pin impressions and fabric impressions that result when a soft lead bullet passes through woven fabrics. In 1911, he proposed what came to be known as the Balthazard model for fingerprint description and classification. This model assigned probabilities to minutia patterns, and was historically important as the foundation for modern approaches to fingerprint comparison. In the realm of bloodstain pattern analysis, he published a key paper in 1939 describing how the length and width of blood drops are affected by angle and height of origin. This information remains central to bloodstain pattern analysis practices today.

Dr Balthazard in his laboratory

barbiturates   A class of drugs based on barbituric acid that act to
depress the central nervous system (CNS) and are therefore classified as
CNS depressants. Administered primarily by ingestion of pills,
barbiturates produce a general feeling of well-being and promote sleep.
Friedrich *Baeyer first synthesized barbituric acid in 1863, possibly
naming the compound after a woman of his acquaintance. It was not until
1903 that the first derivative (Veronal) was marketed as a sedative, and
several others followed. Barbiturates are classified by how long lasting
they are; with pentobarbital and secobarbital being short-acting,
amobarbital intermediate, and barbiturates such as phenobarbital being
long-acting. Abuse of barbiturates can lead to dependence, and an
overdose can kill by altering the pH of the blood and disturbing the system
that regulates breathing. Since barbiturates are acidic, overdoses can
cause inflammation of the stomach lining and small intestine, where
absorption takes place.

barium nitrate (BaNO₃) A salt used in primers in *ammunition. It serves as an oxidizer.

baseline (baseline measurement) A technique used in crime scene documentation to accurately record the location and orientation of evidence. In this approach, a baseline is established using a tape measure or similar device. The length and orientation (NSWE) is also recorded. The location of evidence is then recorded as a function of the straight line distance from the baseline to the object. The baseline method can be extended to a grid system with four lines and the location recorded as a function of its rectangular coordinates (x, y) within the grid. Baselines can also be utilized with *polar coordinates if appropriate to the scene.

base pair Complementary amino acids that form hydrogen bonds that lend shape to molecules such as DNA and RNA. In DNA, the complementary base pairs are adenine and thymine (A-T) and guanine and cytosine (G-C). Thymine is replaced by uracil in RNA replication.

bathochromic shift A shift of an absorbance band to a longer wavelength (lower) energy due to a change in the composition of a molecule or *chromophore; also referred to as a red shift.

Bayesian statistics A statistical approach to analysis that involves comparing hypotheses (theories) that takes into account prior knowledge and modifies it using information gathered from evidence. This contrasts with frequentist methods, which rely on traditional statistics and (usually) a normal distribution. The key feature of Bayesian methods is the concept of prior probabilities which is incorporated in a general expression such as:

$$Pr(H_m|N, n, m) = \frac{Pr(m|H_m, n, M)Pr(H_m|N)}{\sum Pr(m|H_m, n, N)Pr(H_m|N)}$$

Where Pr is probability, H_m is the hypothesis based on m, and n is the sample size. The prior probability is expressed as $Pr(H_m|N)$. The challenge in applying Bayesian methods usually arises out of difficulties in expressing the likelihood ratio in an objective rather than subjective manner. In forensic science, Bayesian methods have been applied to sampling and to the interpretation of many types of evidence from drugs to DNA to trace evidence.

Becke line (Becke line method) A method used in microscopic analysis to determine the relative differences in refractive index of two adjacent media, such as a particle and the surrounding mounting media. The Becke line appears as a bright halo of light surrounding a specimen that is immersed in a liquid. When the *refractive index (RI) of a

The Becke line (indicated by the arrow) moves as the focus is adjusted. The left and right columns show crystal in two different refractive index media and movement of the line is seen as the focus is adjusted.

specimen is the same as the refractive index of the liquid, the Becke line vanishes. This phenomenon can be further exploited by moving the specimen relative to the objective of the microscope. The Becke line method is used in the analysis of particulates such as glass, minerals, and fibres. The line will move into the media with the higher refractive index.

beginning stroke The initial stroke of a pen or other writing instrument, a characteristic that can be studied as part of *questioned document examinations.

benzodiazepines One of the most widely prescribed drug classes in the world, benzodiazepines are used principally as mild tranquillizers and as anticonvulsants. Benzodiazepines produce a sense of well-being and reduce anxiety but, unlike *barbiturates, do not generally cause as much sleepiness. The most famous member of this family is probably Valium (diazepam); other examples include lorazepam (Ativan), Xanax, Halcion, and Klonopin. Benzodiazepines can induce physical and psychological addiction and have been used in *drug facilitated sexual assaults. Diazepam was introduced in the early 1960s and quickly became one of the most prescribed drugs ever produced. Molecularly, the benzodiazepines are characterized by the presence of halogens such as chlorine in the structure.

Bertillon, Alphonse (1853–1914) A French forensic scientist who developed the first systematic *biometric method for the identification of suspects and criminals, setting the stage for fingerprinting, which ultimately replaced it. The system, called anthropometry or **Bertillonage**, used eleven body measurements along with descriptive information and photographs stored on a card, similar to modern fingerprint cards.

bertrand lens An accessory lens used in microscopy, typically *polarizing light microscopes but also in transmitted light microscopes. The lens can be used as part of the *Kohler illumination alignment procedure or as a tool to identify interference patterns in crystalline materials.

bias A *figure of merit related to *accuracy and *trueness. The bias of a measurement is the total *systematic error associated with that measurement. Bias is the inverse of trueness; a high bias implies low trueness.

bicomponent fibres Synthetic fibres that consist of two components that have different chemical or physical properties. A common arrangement is to have a core of one component surrounded by a sheath of the other. Other arrangements include side-by-side and layered.

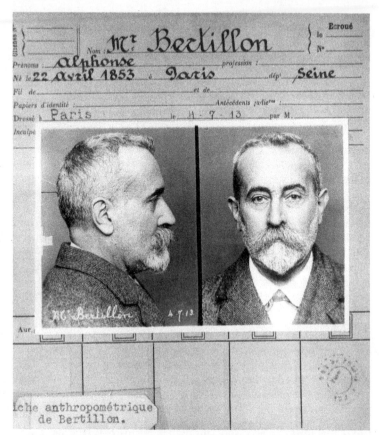

Bertillon appearing on an example of one of his identification cards

bindle (bindle wrap) A paper packet created by folding, used to store drugs such as cocaine. *See also* DRUGGIST'S FOLD.

bioavailability (F) The amount of an ingested drug that survives *first pass metabolism and is available for distribution to the body and tissues through the bloodstream. Morphine has a bioavailability of approximately 25 per cent, meaning that if a dose is taken orally, 75 per cent is lost before entering the bloodstream. Drugs ingested by smoking or intravenous injection are essentially 100 per cent available.

biological dragnet (mass screening) A law enforcement operation in which DNA samples are collected from most or all people in a selected area in an attempt to find a perpetrator or source of biological evidence. A biological dragnet was utilized in the first DNA case involving the murder of two young girls by Colin Pitchfork in the United Kingdom. *See also* NARBOROUGH MURDERS; JEFFREYS, SIR ALEC.

biological profile Another term used for DNA profile.

biology, forensic The analysis of evidence for biological composition or characteristics using biological and biochemical techniques. Forensic *serology was an early example of forensic biology, although the latter term was not widely used until after *DNA typing emerged. Forensic *entomology is also part of forensic biology although in common usage, the term forensic biology usually means DNA typing.

biometrics The use of physiological features and measurements as a form of identification. One of the earliest forms of biometrics was *Bertillonage in which bodily measurements were taken and recorded to assist in criminal investigation. *Fingerprints are based on biometrics, as are hand geometry, vein patterns in the eyes (or arms), and facial features.

biopolymer A polymer produced by living organisms. Cellulose is a biopolymer based on glucose and proteins are biopolymers based on amino acids.

biotransformation A conversion that occurs in a biological organism after a substance is ingested. *Metabolism is an example of biotransformation, as is *conjugation.

Birch method (**Birch reduction**) A method used to make *methamphetamine and related compounds in *clandestine laboratories. Technically, the Birch reduction refers to a generic process in synthetic organic chemistry in which ammonia (NH_3) and a Group I metal such as sodium (Na) or lithium (Li) is used to reduce an aromatic ring by breaking double bonds and adding hydrogen. In clandestine labs, the Birch method, also called the Nazi method, uses ephedrine or pseudoephedrine as a starting material (or precursor).

bird's eye view A perspective frequently used for sketches and drawings of crime scenes. The perspective is looking down on the area of interest from a point directly above.

birefringence In a material such as a crystal or fibre with two refractive indices, birefringence is the difference between the two. Birefringence is determined using a *polarizing light microscope (PLM) and is a common forensic application in fibre analysis. The *refractive index (RI) of the fibre can be different when observed parallel to the long

Birch method
Ephedrine reacts with anhydrous ammonia and a Group I metal
(here lithium Li) in THF to produce a reactive intermediate that rapidly forms
methamphetamine. The solution initially should be a deep blue colour which
gradually turns greyish brown as methamphetamine is produced.

axis of the fibre than when observed perpendicular to it. The calculated
difference between these two values is the birefringence of the fibre.

bite marks A type of *impression evidence that can be left in the skin of
a person or animal, but also in other surfaces or substrates such as food,
chewing gum, and even in pencils and pens. The variables within dental
structure include angles between teeth, missing teeth, fillings and other
dental work, and wear patterns. As a result, a bite mark has been
considered to be individually unique. Bite marks in victims are common in
sexual assaults, homicides, domestic assaults, and child abuse cases. In
general, bite marks are compared to the actual dental structure via
overlays of digital images.

bit mapping *See* DISK MIRRORING.

bit stream back-up A technique used to back up data stored on
computers and related devices such as hard drives, removable media, and
mobile phones. As with *bit stream imaging, every bit is copied, whether it
is currently being utilized to represent data or not. This type of back-up is
also referred to as a mirror image back-up.

bit stream imaging A tool used in *computer forensics investigations
in which the data stored on a hard drive or other storage media is copied

one bit at a time. The technique, also called disk imaging, captures every bit, even if it is not being used to represent data.

black powder *See* GUNPOWDER.

Blandy, Mary (1721–52) An English woman convicted for the murder of her father by poisoning with arsenic who was executed in 1752. Her case was notable for a measure of scientific investigation pre-dating the *Marsh test.

As part of the investigation, medical investigators compared the white powder recovered from the scene with known arsenic to testify that arsenic had been used. They also testified to detecting a garlicky odour on heating the powder and on the well-preserved state of the father's organs, symptoms of arsenic. Mary testified in her own defence, admitting using the powders but maintaining that she thought they would soften her father's attitude toward a suitor named Captain William Henry Cranstoun. Her father had thrown Cranstoun out of the household when it was learned that he was already married. Supposedly Cranstoun instructed Mary to give her father some calming powders. She did so, providing small doses of the white powder later identified as arsenic in her father's supper over several weeks. He became gravely ill, as did household servants who ate leftovers. Mary burned incriminating letters from Cranstoun and tried to get rid of the remaining powder, but some was saved by a household servant. She was arrested, tried, and convicted while Cranstoun escaped to France.

blank A type of *quality control sample that is prepared such that it does not contain any detectable amount of the target compound or analyte. It is used to check that procedures, instruments, and equipment are clean and to prevent the occurrence of *false positives.

blasting cap A device that is part of an *explosive chain used to initiate *detonation of *high explosives. The detonator contains a low explosive that is ignited typically by a burning fuse or by an electrical charge.

blast wave *See* DETONATION.

blind sample A quality assurance/quality control (QA/QC) sample used to check that the results reflect what would be expected for case samples and that the sample does not get preferential treatment.

blood An extracellular fluid (a fluid found outside the cells) that is a complex mixture of organic and inorganic materials including electrolytes such as sodium, proteins, fats, and several different kinds of cells. The characteristic red colour of blood comes from the complex bond formed between *haemoglobin (Hb) in red blood cells (RBCs) and oxygen. By spinning a blood sample in a centrifuge, it can be separated into a

MISS BLANDY *at the place of Execution near Oxford, attended by the Revᵈ Mᵉ Swinton*

The execution of Mary Blandy

cellular component (approximately 45 per cent of the total volume)
and a non-cellular component called plasma, which makes up the
remaining 55 per cent. *Presumptive tests for blood such as the
*Kastle–Meyer test, are based on the detection of haemoglobin.

Plasma can be further subdivided into serum and fibrinogen, the
material that forms clots. Serum, a clear straw yellow liquid, carries
electrolytes, with the sodium ion (Na^+) and the chloride ion (Cl^-) being
the most concentrated. Proteins (albumins and globulins) are also carried
in the serum. The word *serology, associated with forensic serology, is
derived from 'serum'.

The cellular portion of blood can be divided into three types of cells: red
blood cells (RBCs, also called erythrocytes); white blood cells (WBCs,
leucocytes); and platelets (thrombocytes). RBCs, which transport oxygen
and bicarbonate, are the most numerous and are unique in that they lose
their nucleus before entering into the circulatory system. WBCs (several
types exist) are the next most numerous and are active in fighting diseases.
Platelets are needed for clot formation.

All portions of blood contain *genetic marker systems that have been
exploited in forensic biology. Serum contains serum blood group systems
such as *haptoglobin (Hp) and *group-specific component (GC). Within
the cellular component, WBCs contain the *human leucocyte antigen
(HLA) system that contains many different factors and types. Both the
serum blood group systems and HLA system were difficult to type in stains
and were not routinely used in forensic casework.

Unlike red blood cells, the white blood cells have a nucleus, which is the
source of DNA used in *DNA typing. The thirteen loci that are usually
typed in current practice can also be classified as genetic markers since
they are inherited and polymorphic. Red blood cells are the richest source
of non-DNA genetic marker systems that were once widely used in
forensic serology. These cells (erythrocytes) have on their surface the
antigens that make up blood group systems such as ABO and Rh. Within
the cell are found the *isoenzyme systems such as phosphoglucomutase
(*PGM) and *esterase D (ESD) as well as variations of the haemoglobin
molecule. The ABO blood group and isoenzymes were the most used in
casework prior to the advent of DNA typing.

blood alcohol (BAC) The concentration of ethanol (generically
referred to as alcohol) detected in a blood sample and reported as grams
per decilitre (g/dl) or as a volume/volume percentage. The legally
allowable limit varies worldwide, typically in the range of 0.02 to 0.1 per
cent. Ethanol is a *psychoactive substance that crosses the blood brain
barrier, causing behavioural changes and impaired motor skills. Anyone
with a BAC level greater than the legal limit is considered to be legally

intoxicated. The blood alcohol test is considered an evidentiary test, meaning the results can be used as evidence in a prosecution; in contrast, field tests produce approximate results only and are used only to determine if a BAC test should be performed. In the laboratory, BAC levels in blood are usually determined using a *headspace method coupled to *gas chromatography (GC) with a flame ionization detector (FID). Two GC columns are used to confirm the identification.

blood group systems Systems of protein types in blood that are based on antigens that are *polymorphic. The ABO system is the best known, however many more exist, including the Rh, MNSs, Kidd, Duffy, P, Kell, and Lewis systems. None is easy to type in stains and none is as persistent as the A and B antigens of the ABO system. Research into typing techniques for forensic work was largely abandoned once typable *isoenzyme systems were identified such as *PGM. In turn, isoenzyme systems have given way to *DNA typing. *See also* CULLIFORD, BRIAN.

bloodstain patterns (blood spatter patterns) These are stains found on objects, bodies, or at crime scenes. Often the stains are clearly visible, but occasionally stains must be visualized using reagents such as *luminol (e.g. if the stain is on a dark surface). The patterns of these stains can be useful in reconstruction of events that produced them. Spatter patterns have been classified by the force, measured in feet per second, required to produce the drop or droplets which strike the wall, ceiling, floor, or other stained objects. Types of spatter include *cast-off, *back spatter, forward spatter, *blow back, bubble rings (*vacuoles), and *arterial spurting. In crime scene reconstructions, the likely point of origin for each stain is identified and used to construct a likely sequence of events that produced them.

blow back 1. A *bloodstain pattern created by close range gunshot wounds. If a weapon is discharged in contact with the victim's body, blood and tissue can be deposited on the weapon.

2. A principle exploited in modern semi-automatic and automatic firearms. When such a gun is fired, the forward expansion of gases also forces the *cartridge case backwards into the *breech block. Some of the expanding gas from the burning propellant is directed into a piston chamber, which operates an extractor that grabs the empty cartridge and ejects it from the breech area.

blow flies An insect that can live out its life cycle on a corpse; as a result, blow flies are used in forensic *entomology to assist in death investigations. The forensic information that may be determined includes time of death and when a body was placed in a given location.

blunt force trauma An injury or injury pattern inflicted by an object or surface that lacks sharp edges such as a hammer or bat. This contrasts with injuries produced by weapons such as a knife. The injury results from excessive and often violent compression. This results in bruising (contusions) on the surface of the skin and haemorrhaging beneath. Blunt force trauma can also create rips or tears in the skin, but these can be distinguished from cuts or stab wounds (*incised wounds) based on appearance. In some cases, the injury pattern reflects the weapon that is used, such as a small circular bruise from a hammer blow.

Bodle, John An English man suspected of arsenic poisoning and whose case was instrumental in leading to the development of the *Marsh test for arsenic by chemist James *Marsh. In 1832, Bodle had been accused of poisoning his grandfather and Marsh was asked to assist in the case by testing the stomach contents for the presence of arsenic. He used a method that involved extraction of the arsenic and formation of the yellow sulphur salt. Unfortunately, the salt was not stable and had degraded by the time it was to be presented as evidence in the case. Bodle was acquitted and bragged about it, driving Marsh to develop the improved test that was to bear his name.

(((⊕))) SEE WEB LINKS

- This website has an excellent section on arsenic and arsenic poisonings. Last accessed May 2011.

body fluids A type of evidence that can be analysed using serological and immunological techniques and in some cases, *DNA typing. Body fluids and body fluid stains encountered as evidence include saliva, semen, sweat, urine, faeces, vomit, vaginal fluid, and human milk. By 1932 it was understood that there was an inherited characteristic that determined if a person secretes substances such as the A and B antigens of the *ABO system into body fluids. Approximately 80 per cent of the Caucasian population are secretors, which means that their body fluids (saliva, semen, and vaginal fluids) can be typed using the same techniques used to type blood. With the advent of DNA typing, secretor status has become less critical. *See also* HOLZER, FRANZ JOSEPH.

boldenone An *anabolic steroid used and abused in athletics and body building.

bolt action A type of firearm design in which the bolt (the part of the firearm that contains the burning propellant) is manually operated. A familiar example is a bolt action hunting rifle in which a round is fired, then ejected by manual manipulation of the bolt. This action also loads the next cartridge.

bone Along with teeth, the components of the body that persist the longest post mortem. Bone is the primary tool of forensic *anthropologists and can be used for identification, determination of sex, estimation of age at death, and estimation of stature. The study of bones generally is called osteology.

bore In firearms, the open cylindrical portion of the barrel. The nominal bore diameter is equivalent to the *calibre of handguns and rifles.

Borkenstein, Robert (1912–2002) An American toxicologist best known for invention of the breathalyzer and as an instructor in the area of alcohol intoxication. Borkenstein began his career as a police officer in 1930 and moved into the position of director of the Indiana State laboratory. His experience with investigation of traffic accidents led him to focus on alcohol as a public safety hazard. Eventually he went to the Indiana University where he headed the forensic program for many years. He invented the breathalyzer in 1954. Courses in alcohol detection and highway safety were launched in 1958 and are still offered today.

(⊕) SEE WEB LINKS

• A website describing courses offered in forensic toxicology and intoxication. Last accessed May 2011.

botany, forensic A branch of forensic biology focusing on plant and plant-derived physical evidence. Examples include pollen, fungus, moulds, plants, stems, and leaves. Plant matter has been used in civil and criminal cases and has been applied to tasks such as estimation of a time of death and the *post-mortem interval (PMI), identification of plant matter in stomach contents to characterize a last meal, identification of plant poisons, linking of a suspect to an outdoor scene, determining if a body has been moved, determination if a person was alive or dead when placed in water, and detection of clandestine graves.

boundary, crime scene *See* PERIMETER, CRIME SCENE.

breath alcohol (BrAC) Content of ethanol (referred to generically as alcohol) detected in exhaled breath. After ingestion and distribution through the bloodstream, ethanol can evaporate from the blood into exhaled air deep in the lungs. As such, exhaled air contains a concentration of alcohol that is proportional to the concentration of alcohol in the blood. The concentration is governed by *Henry's law, which states that when a fluid such as blood is in equilibrium with a gas such as air, the concentration of a volatile substance (ethanol) in the gas will be proportional to the concentration in the fluid, as long as the temperature remains constant (as it does in the body). For ethanol in blood in contact with air at body temperature (98.6 °F or 37 °C), that ratio is about 2300:1, meaning that there will be 2,300 times as much alcohol in the blood as in the air. Since this ratio is known, it is possible to mathematically relate breath alcohol concentration to blood alcohol concentration.

breech face markings Markings produced on the base of a *cartridge case as a result of firing a gun. When the trigger of a firearm is pulled, the firing pin strikes the *primer, igniting it and then the *propellant. The rapid expansion of gas accelerates the bullet down the barrel, but it also drives the cartridge case backwards into the breech block. Since the breech block is a machined or filed surface, it possesses a pattern of markings that can be transferred to the cartridge case as a form of *impression evidence if it collides with sufficient velocity.

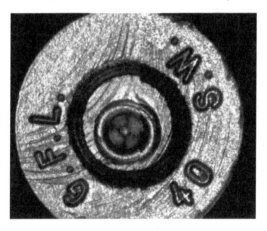

Example breech face markings on a fired cartridge. The indentation in the centre is the firing pin impression.

Brides of Bath case A 1915 case in England that involved Sir Bernard *Spilsbury in his most famous case. George Smith stood accused of murdering three young women that he allegedly courted and married. Shortly thereafter, each died in the bathtub. Once suspicion was raised, all three bodies were exhumed. Spilsbury determined that all had died by drowning. Through experimentation, Spilsbury showed that Smith had managed to yank the women by the feet while they lay reclined in the tubs. A strong violent jerk, he demonstrated, could cause the victim to become immediately unconscious. They drowned without struggle. While doing the experiments, Spilsbury's willing subject, a nurse, passed out and had to be revived. The story only added to Spilsbury's fame.

brisance The shattering power of an explosive, as opposed to pushing power. In general, the faster an explosive builds a pressure wave during *detonation, the higher the brisance.

bubble ring *See* VACUOLE.

buffer In *computer forensics, a term that refers to a region of memory that is used to temporarily store data for rapid access. For example, if an image file is sent to a printer, much of the data is first temporarily stored in a buffer before being sent in smaller batches to the printer.

buffers Aqueous solutions prepared in such a way as to stabilize the pH. Buffers are prepared by combining a weak acid with its salt. For example, a phosphate buffer can be prepared by combining phosphoric acid (H_3PO_4) and sodium phosphate (Na_3PO_4).

bulk sample Typically, the individual item or parent item within a forensic exhibit. If a kilogram of white powder is received at a laboratory packaged in plastic, this kilogram is the bulk sample. Subsamples are typically taken for subsequent analysis, leaving most of the bulk sample behind.

bullet trajectory The path taken by a bullet from the time it leaves the barrel of the gun until it stops or is stopped. This time frame is governed to a large extent by *external ballistics considerations. Bullets may strike multiple surfaces such as going through a wall or ricocheting off metallic surfaces, all of which will affect the flight path. With bullet holes in stable surfaces such as a wall in which the hole can be discerned, the ratio of the *minor axis divided by the *major axis can be used to estimate the impact angle. This same strategy is used in *bloodstain pattern interpretation in which the angle of impact of blood drops can be estimated by this same measurement.

bullet wipe *See* BULLET WOUNDS.

bullet wounds Distinctive injuries that are produced by firearms. When a bullet strikes flesh, the skin is stretched and then broken as the projectile penetrates. As it enters, material on the surface of the bullet such as dirt and dust, lubricants, powder and primer residue, and lead will be wiped onto the skin in a pattern called bullet wipe or smudge ring. The bullet will also scrape off skin cells and cause other surface trauma, creating an injury called a contusion (bruise) ring. These features may be obscured or altered by the presence of clothing, and in some cases the bullet wipe pattern may obscure the contusion ring. The shape of the bullet wipe and contusion ring can provide information about the relative positions of the shooter and victim. In the case of straight-on shooting, these features will be roughly circular but can be more oval shaped if the shot comes from an angle or is offset from centre. Beyond the bullet wipe and contusion ring there will be a dispersed deposit of *gunshot residue that is referred to as stippling. The concentration of these residues and how much they are spread out will depend on the distance between the shooter and the victim.

buoyant flame (buoyant plume) A flame in which temperature differences drive the flow of less dense materials upwards relative to more dense materials. This is an example of normal convection.

burden of proof The responsibility for presenting evidence and testimony to support a position. In most Western legal systems, the burden of proof is on the prosecution, meaning that the prosecution must prove the charges are true. If the burden of proof were on the defence, it would mean that the defendant would be responsible for disproving the charges.

burn patterns (fire patterns) Patterns on a surface such as a wall or ceiling created during a fire. The patterns can be made by differences in colour and in texture and can be used to reconstruct the course of events that occurred during the fire.

button rifling A common method used to machine *lands and grooves into the barrel of a firearm. A hardened steel plug (button) is forced into the unmarked barrel and high pressure applied to generate the markings.

cache In a computer or related device, a location where data is temporarily stored to facilitate rapid access. In computers, caches are typically located on a hard drive.

calibre Originally, the diameter of the barrel of a rifled pistol or rifle; the term can also refer to the size of *cartridges used in firearms. Calibre is measured from the top of the *lands and is given in hundredths or thousandths of an inch or in millimetres. Common calibres include .22, .38, .40, .45 inches, and 9 mm for pistols and .22 and .30-06 for rifles. The calibre of a gun is considered to be a nominal measurement, meaning that the actual barrel diameter may vary slightly from the calibre measure to describe it.

calibration The process of using known reliable standards under set conditions to relate an experimentally observed quantity with a true value along with uncertainties. As examples, an analytical balance can be calibrated using a set of calibration weights and a pH meter can be calibrated using solutions of known pH. A calibration curve establishes a relationship between an instrumental response (voltage, area counts, etc.) that results from the introduction of a known amount of a sample, compound, or element. Calibration curves are usually characterized by a linear fit to generate a linear expression in the form of $y = mx + b$. This equation can then be used to calculate the concentration of an unknown sample based on the response obtained.

cannabinoids Typically, compounds that contain 21 carbons and that are found in the cannabis (marijuana) plant. The best known of these is *THC, delta-9-tetrahydrocannabinol, which is the *psychoactive substance in marijuana. Other cannabinoids include CBD (cannabidiol) and CBN (cannabinol). Recently, there have been numerous synthetic compounds introduced that have similar psychoactive effects to THC; collectively these are referred to as cannabinomimetic compounds.

cannelures Small grooves imprinted by rolling on the base of a bullet or near the top of a *cartridge case. For bullets, cannelures can hold lubricant or they can be used as a seat around which the throat of the cartridge case can be crimped closed. In cartridge casings, the cannelures prevent the bullet from being forced backwards into the cartridge case.

capillary electrophoresis (CE) A group of instrumental techniques widely applied in forensic science, including in *DNA typing. The techniques evolved from electrophoresis conducted on horizontal slabs of gel or other media, and share the same basic principles. Many types of capillary electrophoresis exist; the ones used most in forensic science are capillary zone electrophoresis (CZE), capillary gel electrophoresis (CGE), and micellular electrokinetic capillary chromatography (MEKC or MECC). The common element in all of these techniques is the use of a narrow capillary tube filled with a conductive, water-based media such as gel or buffer. As in traditional gel slab electrophoresis, separation of the individual compounds in the sample occurs as these molecules move under the influence of an applied electrical field. Molecules with a net negative charge will move towards the anode (positively charged end) of the capillary, while molecules with a net positive charge will move towards the cathode. Neutral molecules move along with the *electroosmotic flow established in the capillary. Although separation mechanisms vary, CE is based principally on size/charge differentiation. As applied to DNA typing, the instrumentation is based on gel-filled capillaries and fluorescence-based detection. CE has also been applied in forensic *toxicology and in the analysis of *propellants and *explosives.

carbonic anhydrase (CAII) An *isoenzyme system that is polymorphic in black populations and was used occasionally in forensic *serology prior to the advent of *DNA typing.

carbon monoxide (CO) A compound generated during *combustion, the amount of which depends on conditions such as the *fuel/air ratio and temperature. Carbon monoxide binds to haemoglobin more strongly than oxygen, forming *carboxyhaemoglobin. If enough oxygen is displaced, this can cause death by means of chemical *asphyxia (suffocation). CO gas is colourless, odourless, tasteless, and also highly flammable. It is a leading cause of accidental and intentional poisoning worldwide.

carbon powder A fine powdered material that can be used to assist in the visualization of *latent fingerprints. The composition is as the name implies.

carboxyhaemoglobin The complex formed between *haemoglobin and *carbon monoxide, the presence of which in the bloodstream is indicative of CO poisoning.

cartridge cases Also called shells or simply 'casings', the cartridge is the part of a round of ammunition that contains the *propellant. The bullet is seated at the forward end and the *primer at the base of the cartridge case. Casings are usually made of brass (which can be reloaded), nickel-coated brass, or aluminium, which is not designed to be reloaded. Given the composition, cartridge casings are often referred to generically as 'brass'. In *shotgun ammunition, the cartridge case is made of plastic or cardboard and crimp-sealed at the top.

Example cartridge cases. The smaller casing on the right is a *rimfire design; the rest are *centrefire.

case law Generically, the body of legal decisions that form the precedent for current decisions.

casting A technique to preserve and replicate *impression evidence in soft material such as soil, tissue, or snow. Casts can be made of *tyre prints, *shoe prints, *bite marks, and *toolmarks. When done properly, casting produces excellent positive replicates of the impression, but they are not exact duplicates. Dental stone is frequently used for impressions in soil; epoxy-like materials for toolmarks, and Snow Print Wax® for impressions in snow.

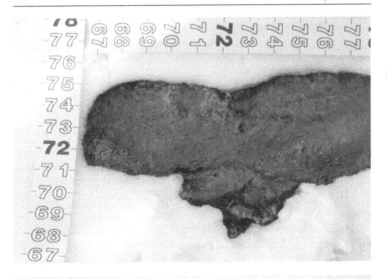

On the top, a casting being made in snow and on the bottom, the resulting cast

cast-off pattern A *bloodstain spatter pattern created when a bloody weapon or a limb such as a fist is swung or otherwise moved fast enough to eject blood. As shown in the photo, this cast-off blood impacts surfaces in a characteristic pattern that depends on the speed and angle of the impact. This information can be used in crime scene analysis and reconstruction.

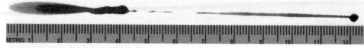

An example of a cast-off pattern

catagen stage The intermediate stage of a hair growth cycle. It is the transition state between active growth (*anagen) and dormancy (*telogen) phases.

cathode In an electrical system or instrument such as an electrode or a *capillary electrophoresis (CE) system, the electrode or zone toward which positively charged species are drawn; *cations move toward the cathode.

cation A positively charged ion, be it a single atom or group of atoms.

cause of death The immediate cause of a death; the action or injury that most directly caused a person to die. In criminal matters, a medical cause of death is not necessarily the legal cause. For example, if a victim is stabbed and dies as a result of complications such as infection, the legal cause of death remains the stabbing and the case remains a homicide even though the immediate cause of death was infection. Cause of death is also distinct from the circumstances of death, which comprise the situation and conditions that led up to the fatal event. Determining the cause of death in questionable deaths is typically the responsibility of a *Medical Examiner (ME) or coroner.

cellulose A *biopolymer made of glucose subunits. Cotton fibres are based on cellulose, which is seen in forensic science as fibre evidence and in *guncotton. It is a type of glucose polymer that cannot be digested by humans, in contrast to starch, which is also composed of cellulose but because of a different type of linkage, is not digestible by humans.

cellulose nitrate A form of *cellulose in which a portion of the $-OH$ groups are replaced with $-NO_3$. This material has many uses including as *guncotton.

cellusolve A generic term referring to a group of solvents (*vehicle) widely used in inks. Examples are ethyl cellusolve (2-ethoxyethanol) and butyl cellusolve (2-butoxyethanol). Spellings with 'cellosolve' are also used.

centralites A group of compounds used as stabilizers in *propellants and energetics (*explosives). The two most common are methyl centralite (1,3-dimethyl-1,3-diphenylurea) and ethyl centralite (1,3-diethyl-1,3-diphenylurea).

central pocket loop A friction ridge pattern found in *fingerprints; one that has and continues to be part of fingerprint classification systems.

centrefire cartridge A type of firearm *ammunition in which the *primer is centred in the base of the *cartridge. Most small arms ammunition (> 0.22 calibre) is of the centrefire design.

certification A process employing written and laboratory testing that ensures the proficiency of forensic analysts and the reliability of the data and results they produce. Typically, individual analysts are certified in their forensic discipline while laboratories are *accredited.

certified reference standard (certified reference material (CRM)) A substance, sample, or material that has been analysed and characterized for one or more property or component using reliable and validated methods. A CRM is provided with a certificate attesting to the characteristics of interest along with uncertainties.

chain of custody Procedures and documentation used to ensure the integrity of evidence from collection to courtroom presentation and through to final disposition or destruction. The paramount goal of the process is to avoid any breaks in the chain, which would bring into question the reliability of the evidence and the link between the evidence and the scene or person from which it was obtained. Electronic methods may also be incorporated in the chain of custody. An example would be the use of bar codes.

chamber and chamber marks The chamber of a firearm is that portion at the rear of the barrel where the cartridge is placed before firing. Chamber marks can be imparted to a *cartridge when it is loaded, ejected, or when it expands during firing.

Chamot, Emile (1868–1950) An American microscopist who along with *Mason, authored what is still considered to be the classic text in chemical microscopy, *Handbook of Chemical Microscopy*, first published in 1930–1931.

Emile Chamot

chasing the dragon Ingestion of a drug such as heroin by smoking; the drug is typically placed on a substrate such as foil and heated to generate the smoke, which the user inhales.

check digit In computer and related applications, a check digit is a number that is typically found in the last field of a larger number or string of numbers. This digit is calculated or derived from all of the other digits in the string and, as a result, any changes in the string of numbers will result in a change in the value of the check digit.

check washing *See* CHEMICAL ERASURE.

chemical enhancement The use of chemical reagents to visualize and enhance patterns in *latent fingerprints. Examples include *DFO and *ninhydrin.

chemical erasure The use of chemicals such as solvents, bleach, or commercial products such as brake fluids to obliterate printing or writing on a document. When this process is used to remove original or commercial printing, it is called 'check washing'.

chemical microscopy The use of a microscope, usually but not exclusively a *polarizing light microscope (PLM) to observe the results of chemical reactions conducted on a microscope slide or other small container. *Crystal tests are the best-known applications of chemical microscopy currently used in forensic science. *See also* CHAMOT, EMILE; McCRONE, WALTER.

chemiluminescence A process in which an energy releasing chemical reaction releases that energy via emission of light rather than heat. *Luminol assists in the visualization of blood via a chemiluminescent reaction. The spelling 'chemoluminescence' is also seen.

chemistry, forensic The application of the principles and techniques of chemistry, particularly analytical chemistry, to legal and law enforcement situations. Forensic chemistry is usually considered to incorporate *seized drug analysis and *arson, with *toxicology and *explosives sometimes included. Other areas of forensic chemistry include analysis of trace evidence such as glass, fibres, *paint, and *gunshot residue.

chiral Molecules that have non-superimposable mirror images are termed 'chiral molecules'. The classic example is the hand; the reflection of a hand in the mirror cannot be superimposed on the hand itself because the orientation is different. A chiral centre in a molecule, typically a carbon atom, is one that has four different groups attached, which leads to **chirality** of that molecule. Mirror image compounds that result from one or more chiral centres are called *enantiomers.

chitin A *biopolymer based on glucose that forms the exoskeleton of insects. Because of the bonding within the polymer, the structure is very strong and rigid, but cannot expand. This leads to insects shedding the exoskeleton to facilitate growth.

chloroform A common solvent ($CHCl_3$) once widely used in laboratories and in medicine as an anaesthetic. Use has decreased since the compound was identified as a carcinogen. It was also once used as a poison and as a method to disable someone, although the latter is not as simple and common as depicted in the media.

choke The constriction in the barrel of a *shotgun. The greater the degree of choke, the smaller the dispersal pattern of the shot pellets.

christmas tree stain A staining technique used to visualize sperm cells, so named because the different parts of the sperm cell take up different colours, simplifying microscopic identification. The tail shows as a yellow-green and the head shades of red and pink. The staining proceeds in two parts using a dye (nuclear fast red) and picroindigocarmine made from picric acid and indocarmine dye.

chroma In the *CIELAB and *Munsell colour systems (among others), the perceived intensity or purity of a colour.

chromaticity (chromaticity diagram) A graphical method of expressing colour that starts by obtaining a spectrum using a *colorimeter. A series of mathematical operations is used to represent the spectrum through two chromaticity coordinates (x, y). These coordinates are then plotted on the chromaticity diagram, which are useful for colour comparisons. The disadvantage of the chromaticity coordinate approach is that the colour space is not symmetric. This means that the region of uncertainty or variation around a given point is not the same across all of the space; thus the *CIELAB system is generally preferred for colour comparisons.

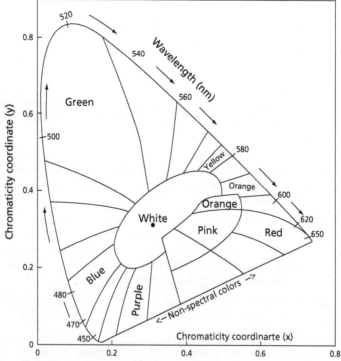

The calculated x and y values are plotted in this space

chromatography The term chromatography means literally 'colour writing', and has evolved to describe a class of separation techniques used extensively in forensic science. The name colour writing originated from early development work in which plant pigments were separated into their components, producing bands of colour in the separation column, a process called column chromatography. Similar colour bands can be seen in *thin layer chromatography (TLC) used for drug and ink analysis. All chromatographic separations are based on *partitioning, although the mechanisms vary based on the specific application. A **chromatogram** is the printed or digital output of a chromatographic instrument. A chromatogram is a plot of the response of the detector as a function of time and peaks are initially characterized by the retention time.

chromophore Broadly defined, the portion of a molecule or compound that is responsible for its perceived colour. Specifically, the chromophore is the atoms or group of atoms in which an electronic transition occurs that allows for interactions in the visible range of the electromagnetic spectrum. The term can also be used generically to refer to interactions in other regions of the spectrum, not just in the visible range.

CIELAB (CIE L*A*b*, CIE LAB) A colour mapping system used for colour comparisons. The system was introduced in 1976 by the

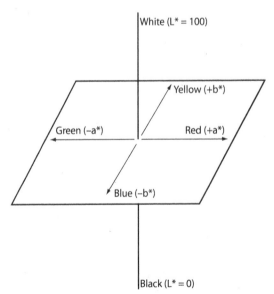

The CIE space can be thought of as cylindrical about the black-white axis

International Commission on Illumination (CIE) as an alternative to systems such as those based on *chromaticity coordinates. The disadvantage of chromaticity diagrams is that the spaces are not symmetrical; the green spaces are larger than the red spaces as an example. The CIELAB colour space is symmetrical. The mathematic derivation of CIE coordinates is based on the same general approach as that used to obtain chromaticity coordinates.

ciphers A method of encoding a message (digital or other) in which the words or letters are rearranged or altered based on instructions found in a cipher key. In computers or related devices, information can be encoded by inputting it to a cipher program which generates ciphertext. This text is decoded by inputting it into a reverse cipher routine. The cipher key is required for both encoding and decoding.

circle search *See* SPIRAL SEARCH.

circumstance of death *See* CAUSE OF DEATH.

clandestine laboratory Illicit laboratories established to manufacture or process illegal drugs. Although the types of drugs made vary by country, region, and by current availabilities, the most common types of clandestine labs are those making *methamphetamine, *amphetamine, and PCP (*phencyclidine).

Clarke's Handbook of Drugs A two-volume set (or computer disks) published by Pharmaceutical Press, widely used in forensic *toxicology as a standard reference. It was previously published as *Clarke's Isolation and Identification of Drugs*.

class characteristics Those characteristics that describe a discrete group or subgroup of items (or individuals) that are similar. In the forensic context, this similarity usually arises due to reproducible processes used to create the characteristic. Classification of evidence is a process of assigning it to these groups or categories. Members of a given class will share the same class characteristics, while evidence that can be individualized will possess characteristics that make it unique. Class characteristics are central to *fingerprints and other types of pattern evidence but are used throughout forensic science. For example, a drug might be successively classified as opiate-heroin and a red stain as blood-human.

clearance rate The rate at which a drug or poison is removed from the body. The clearance rate depends on factors such as lipid/water solubility and is related to the *half-life ($t_{1/2}$). The term refers to all mechanisms of removal including through the urine, exhalation, faeces, etc.

club drugs A group of illegal drugs frequently used in clubs, bars, nightclubs, and at parties. Examples include *ecstasy (MDMA) and *ketamine.

coagulation The process of clotting in blood. Degree of clotting can provide useful information in *bloodstain pattern analysis and *death investigation.

cobalt thiocyanate test (Ruybal test) A *presumptive test used principally for cocaine, although the reagent will react with other drugs. The reagent will form an insoluble ion pair in the presence of cocaine which precipitates out as a silvery turquoise blue solid. There are three common variations of the test. In the first, the reagent is prepared by dissolving cobalt thiocyanate (CoSCN) in distilled water, sometimes with additional ingredients such as ammonium thiocyanate or glycerine. When this is added to cocaine powder, a blue solid (blue precipitate) is formed. To increase the specificity of the test, a variation called the Scott or Ruybal test has been used in which three reagents are employed. The first is a cobalt thiocyanate solution containing glycerine, the second is a hydrochloric acid solution, and the third is chloroform, an organic solvent that does not mix with water. If cocaine is present, addition of the first reagent will cause the blue precipitate to form and the addition of the second will cause the blue to turn to a clear pink colour. Adding the final reagent, chloroform, will cause two layers to form in the test tube, the aqueous layer (the water-based solution), and the chloroform layer. If cocaine is present, a blue colour will reappear in the chloroform layer.

cocaine A powerful central nervous system stimulant derived from the leaves of the coca plant (*Erythroxylon coca*). Cocaine can also be synthesized, but the process is difficult and expensive and so far has not replaced the coca plant as the primary source in the illegal drug market. The coca plant grows in the Andes Mountains and in some parts of Asia, and the largest source of raw coca is South America, principally Columbia.

coca paste An intermediate form of cocaine generated from the leaves of the coca plant. Typically the leaves are crushed or otherwise macerated and then are treated with a basic material to form the pasty material.

codeine An opiate alkaloid that is found naturally in *opium at concentrations of approximately 0.7–2.5 per cent. Codeine is taken orally as an *analgesic and as a cough suppressant, and it is usually synthesized from morphine rather than extracted from opium.

CODIS (Combined DNA Indexing System) A national program in the United States coordinated by the FBI that assists state and local labs in establishing DNA databases from unsolved crimes, missing persons, and convicted offenders. As of June 2010, the CODIS system held more than eight million offender profiles.

codon A series of three base pairs found in DNA (or RNA) that code for a specific amino acid.

coincidental match A match or linkage that is indicated by evidence but that occurred by chance and not as a result of criminal activity or contact.

cold shock A reflexive reaction that can occur when a person is suddenly immersed in cold water, resulting in sudden death.

colorimetry A form of *spectrometry that operates in the visible region (~400–700 nm) of the electromagnetic spectrum. Because the eye can be used as a detector, colorimetry was one of the first forms of spectrophotometry developed. In modern instruments, instrumental detectors replace the eye with devices that convert light to electrical current that can be displayed or further manipulated. Colorimetry is occasionally used to describe *ultraviolet light spectrometry as well as visible spectroscopy. *See also* CHROMATICITY; CIELAB; COLOUR SPACES; MUNSELL COLOUR SYSTEM.

colourant A substance or formulation that when applied to a surface imparts colour. Examples are *inks and *paint and the main colouring ingredients are *dyes and *pigments.

colour spaces Graphical spaces used to represent colours and colour differences in an easily interpretable and object manner. Examples include the *CIELAB space, *Munsell, and *chromaticity coordinates. The starting point for translating a colour to a point in a colour space is a visible light spectrum that is mathematically processed and reduced down to two or three plotted points.

colour tests *See* PRESUMPTIVE TESTS.

combustion The chemical reaction broadly defined as burning which occurs when a hydrocarbon (a compound containing only carbon and hydrogen) or an oxygenated hydrocarbon is combined with oxygen at elevated temperatures. At the simplest level, a combustion reaction is one that takes place between a fuel and an oxidant. Heat is important, both as a product of the reaction and to ensure that the reaction has enough energy to be self-sustaining. The oxidant is usually (but not always) atmospheric oxygen. The generic reaction for combustion of a hydrocarbon is given by:

$$\text{Hydrocarbon(g)} + O_2(g) \Rightarrow CO_2(g) + H_2O(g)$$

In reality, a complex mixture of products is produced based on fuel, temperatures, ratio of combination, and many other factors. For example, *carbon monoxide can be produced in significant quantities if the mixture is oxygen-poor (in other words, a rich mixture) and/or the combustion temperature is relatively low. Combustion in air always produces some nitrogen-oxygen compounds as well.

comparison microscope A microscope that consists of two compound light microscopes linked together in such a way that two different objects can be examined side by side. The analyst looking through the viewer sees a field of view divided down the middle by a thin line, with the image from the left microscope stage on the left and the image from the right on the right of the viewer. There are two types of comparison microscopes, differentiated by the type of lighting used. For comparing objects that are opaque such as bullets, a vertical or reflected light source is needed while for objects that transmit light such as fibres, a transmission light source is employed. *See also* GODDARD, CALVIN.

An example view of two cartridge cases as seen through a comparison microscope.

compartment model Mathematical algorithms and programs used in pharmacology and toxicology to model how an ingested substance moves through the body. Different tissues or fluids are defined as compartments such as the blood, urine, or liver, and mathematical and experimental models can be used to describe a drug's distribution amongst the different compartments. Compartments are usually shown as linked boxes.

competitive assay A type of *immunoassay in which two or more antigens compete for an antibody binding site. Typically, the two antigens are the same compound, with one labelled and one unlabelled. The unlabelled version is a drug and the labelled version is that same drug with a fluorescent, radiochemical, or other type of label bonded to the molecule.

composite sample A sample, such as derived from a large drug seizure, that is made by combining several separate samples and mixing thoroughly before taking one or more portions for analysis.

compression algorithms Computer programs designed to reduce the size of a file; particularly photographs. There are two general types: lossless algorithms such as ZIP files in which the original file can be recovered in exactly the same form it was prior to compression. Lossy methods involve conversions that cannot be undone. An example of a lossy compression would be converting a scanned image in a TIFF format to a JPEG file.

computer forensics A term used to describe several types of forensic analysis applied to digital devices such as computers, mobile phones, and storage devices. The term digital evidence is sometimes used to describe the type of evidence involved in these investigations, in contrast to physical evidence. One of the unique aspects of forensic computing is that it is often difficult to identify the original evidence given that copies are easily and frequently made. A computer may be central to the commission of a crime or peripherally involved as a place where planning documents are stored and web searches are conducted (for example). The goal of forensic computing investigations is in the broader sense the same as any forensic practice, the recovery of evidence in context without damage.

concentric cracks A series of cracks in physical evidence, often *glass, which consists of a series of roughly circular cracks. Where cracks begin and end can provide information on how the glass was broken and from what side.

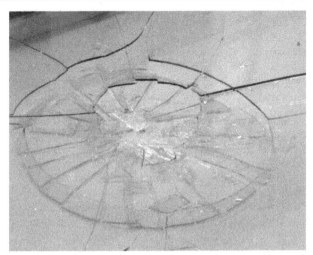

Concentric cracks circle the point of impact

concept search   In forensic computing investigations, the process of searching a large collection of electronic evidence such as documents and webpages to identify ideas and concepts as opposed to isolated words or phrases. A key part of such searches is identifying the context in which words and phrases are found and using this information to extract information relevant to an investigation from the much larger collection.

confirmation bias   A tendency, whether conscious or not, to draw conclusions from data or tests that confirm a pre-conceived idea or expectation.

conflagration   A very rapid burning or combustion reaction, but one in which the flame front is moving at less than the speed of sound.

coning and quartering   A method used to homogenize powdered materials prior to taking a sample. The powder is mixed on a clean flat surface, pushed into a tall conical pile, and then divided into four sections that are then mixed thoroughly one pile at a time. The four parts are pushed together, mixed, and the process repeated as needed.

conjugation   A reaction in which a drug or metabolite is bonded to a polar structure such as glucuronic acid. The conjugates are more water soluble and thus are more likely to be eliminated in the urine. Prior to analysis, it is often necessary to break down conjugates using a basic compound or an enzyme.

contact wound A gunshot wound that results from direct contact of the barrel of the weapon and the skin. The characteristics of a contact wound can include burning and searing, *stellate patterns and large amounts of residual unburnt powder and *gunshot residue (GSR).

control chart A method used to chart an experimental measurement over time to gauge the performance of instrumentation, equipment, and analysts. A control chart is often used as part of a determination of *uncertainty. The chart typically includes upper and lower warning limits (UWL, LWL) and upper and lower control limits (UCL, LCL) around the quantity of interest. These ranges are usually established from the standard deviation of replicate measurements of the quantity of interest over time. When a measurement falls outside these ranges, some type of corrective action is called for.

Controlled Substances ACT (CSA) In the United States, drugs and related substances are regulated at the Federal level as controlled substances. There are five Schedules into which a drug can be placed based on accepted medical use and addictive potential, with Schedule I substances having the highest potential for abuse and Schedule V having the least.

contusion A bruise; damage that results from a blow that breaks blood vessels. This can occur beneath the skin as well as on the surface; if beneath, skin discoloration can result.

cordite 1. A group of *smokeless powders developed in England.
    2. A form of smokeless powder combined with materials that allow the substance to be wound in brown twine-like cords.

coroner Latin for crown, an elected or appointed official who is charged with determining the cause of death in cases where the death appears to be the result of foul play, was unattended, or occurred under questionable or suspicious circumstances. The position of coroner was a remnant of Roman law instituted in England during the 12th century. The modern coroner is a judicial officer that is elected or appointed, but whose tasks are mainly administrative. The job of the coroner is to determine the cause of death using whatever resources are necessary, which can include ordering an autopsy by a pathologist or forensic pathologist.

Coroners Act (1877) A law passed in England to standardize and improve death investigation. The act was driven in part by homicides committed by *poisons.

correlated techniques **1.** Analytical techniques that produce information based on the same fundamental chemical principles. For example, analysis of a sample by *thin layer chromatography (TLC) and *gas chromatography (GC) would be correlated because both separate compounds based on the same mechanism of selective partitioning.

2. In weighing samples, correlation refers to a relationship between weighing operations. For example, obtaining the weight of powder in a bag could be accomplished by weighing the bag full, emptying the powder, and weighing the empty bag. The weighing events are correlated to an extent.

correlation A definable mathematical relationship such as found in *calibration curves. Instrument responses are calibrated based on the correlation between concentration and response. In many, but not all cases, the correlation is linear over some range, meaning that the relationship between two variables can be described using a linear equation.

cortex The central portion of a hair in which features such as *pigments and the *medulla are found.

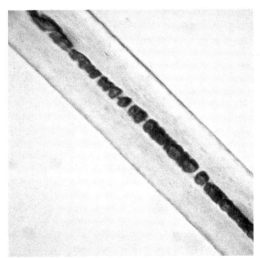

The darkened area of the hair is the medulla, which is embedded within the cortex.

cortical fusi Vacuoles (air pockets) found in the *cortex of hair.

Cotton, Mary Ann (1832–73) A famous poisoner who is
suspected of killing at least fifteen people, including her mother,
several children and stepchildren, three spouses, and one lover, all for
insurance money. Her last victim was allegedly her stepson, Charles.
The attending physician used the *Reinsch test to detect arsenic in
the dead boy's tissues. Mary maintained that arsenic vapours
emitted from wallpaper killed the child but the jury rejected this,
found her guilty, and sentenced her to death. The execution was
postponed to allow her to give birth to another child.

(🌐) SEE WEB LINKS

• An extensive source of information about the crime and its aftermath. Last
  accessed May 2011.

Mary Ann Cotton

Coventry case One of the earliest cases in which blood typing and
*secretor status were involved. The case occurred in 1939 in England.
Pamela Coventry was an 11-year-old found viciously raped and murdered

after disappearing on her way to school. The key piece of evidence was a cigarette found on her body. The case was handled by Bernard *Spilsbury, assisted by serologist Roche Lynch. Lynch knew of the recent discovery of secretion of blood group antigens into body fluids and attempted to type the saliva on the cigarette butt and compare it to body fluids found on a handkerchief owned by the primary suspect. Lynch was unable to type the saliva on the cigarette since, as it turned out, the suspect was a non-secretor. Despite the negative results in this particular case, an important precedent was set for the use of serological tests into the 1990s.

crash and shoot An informal term referring to the dilution of a sample such as blood or plasma with an organic solvent such as acetonitrile. The 'crash' refers to the resulting precipitation of proteins out of solution followed by injection (shooting) of a portion of the sample into an instrument.

creatine and creatinine Creatinine is a natural component of urine, a product present as a result of muscle action. As a result, it is usually present in reasonably stable amounts from day to day. Creatine is used as an energy source by muscles and is sold as a supplement. Creatine breaks down to creatinine, resulting in elevated levels in the urine. Levels of these compounds are sometimes monitored to detect potential doping or dilution of urine as part of drug testing.

crime Generally, an act in violation of the law of a state (be it nation or state within a nation); a violation of a code or written law that was created to protect society. Crimes can be classified in many ways that are jurisdiction dependent. Examples include crimes against property (burglary for example), crimes of omission (failing to stop and aid victims of an accident), crimes of passion, crimes of violence, and white-collar crime such as fraud, bribery, and software piracy.

crime scene The location at which a crime occurred. This can be as small as a room or a car or much more complex and some complex crimes may have more than one scene. For example, if a person is killed in an apartment and then their body is transported in a car and then buried in a remote location, there are three scenes. The death scene is the primary crime scene, the car a secondary scene, and the burial site a tertiary scene. There is no one set way to process a crime scene but typically any scene is first secured and then documented via photography, video, and written records. Evidence collection is also thoroughly documented. Crime scene reconstructions, a recreation of the events immediately before, during, and after the commission of a crime, are occasionally undertaken to determine the most likely sequence of events that occurred during the commission of the crime. The reconstruction is primarily based on a combination of physical evidence, deduction, and witness testimonies. Reconstructions can determine a likely series of events or can refute them. *See also* BLOODSTAIN PATTERNS.

crime scene documentation *See* DOCUMENTATION, CRIME SCENE.

crime scene integrity *See* SCENE INTEGRITY.

criminal anthropology An idea that developed in the late 19th century that criminals differed sufficiently from 'normal' people that simple measurements of body features could be used to identify them. The concepts of criminal anthropology influenced forensic scientists such as *Bertillon and *Galton.

criminalistics Derived from *kriminalistik*, a word used by Austrian Hans *Gross, an early pioneer of the field, to describe the application of natural sciences to matters of law and law enforcement. There is still a journal published in the field that has this name. Currently, the term is often associated with forensic disciplines such as trace evidence analysis and pattern evidence analysis. Its usage appears to be on the decline.

criminology A social science based on the study of criminals, crime, and the penal system. This term is often confused with *criminalistics, which involves the application of physical sciences (chemistry, geology, physics, and so on) and biological sciences to the analysis of physical evidence. The two terms are related but not interchangeable.

Crippen case A famous murder case from 1910 in which Dr Hawley Crippen was eventually convicted of and executed for the murder of his wife Cora while they resided in London. The case was sensational for many reasons including a dramatic transatlantic steamer chase in an era when wireless communications were just coming of age. Both Crippen and Cora were American by birth and moved to England in 1900. The last time Cora was alive was in February of 1910. For three years prior to the disappearance, Crippen was having an affair with his younger secretary, Ethyl Leneve. Driven by suspicions of Cora's friends, New Scotland Yard launched an investigation. Early into the process, Crippen fled with his secretary, she being dressed as a boy and being passed off as his son. Crippen boarded a ship and was recognized by the captain. The two were arrested as the ship entered Canadian waters. A thorough search of the Crippen's home revealed remains buried in the coal cellar that consisted of a woman's clothing, hair, *adipocere, heart, lungs, intestines, and stomach among other tissues.

DR CRIPPEN & ETHEL LENEVE ON TRIAL, LONDON

Crippen and Ethyl Le Neve on trial

Notably absent were reproductive organs that could have been used to establish the sex of the body. Also missing was a head, hands, feet, and limbs and these factors combined made a definitive identification impossible. There were two key forensic findings—the identification of the poison scopolamine (a barbiturate) in the remains and Dr Bernard *Spilsbury's identification of a scar on the remains that was crucial in linking them to Cora based on surgical scars she was known to have.

critical speed The critical speed of a car is the fastest speed it can travel around a curve without leaving a scuffmark. When the vehicle exceeds the critical speed, the tyres skid across the pavement sideways and can leave a critical speed scuffmark that can be used to estimate the speed of the car when the mark was made based on the curvature of the path.

cross-contamination The contamination of one piece of evidence by materials or compounds found on another piece. This can occur if items are improperly packaged at a crime scene. For example, if two swabs are collected from two different stain sources, cross-contamination could occur if both swabs were stored in the same container.

crossed-over electrophoresis An older method used to determine the species of origin of a bloodstain prior to the advent of *DNA typing. The method is based on gel *electrophoresis. An extract prepared from blood or body fluid stains containing antigens is placed in a gel well nearest the cathode while *antibodies for different species are placed in nearby wells closer to the anode. Each stain extract is tested against several species such as human, dog, cat, and whatever other species might have been the source of the stain. When power is applied, antigens and antibodies move rapidly towards each other. If the antibody reacts with the antigen (such as with human blood and anti-human antigen), a milky white precipitate will form in the gel.

crossed polars In *polarized light microscopy (PLM), the observational condition in which the sample is placed between two polarizing filters. The filters are oriented such that the light they emit is polarized in perpendicular directions. Thus, if any light reaches the eyepiece, it is a result of interaction with the sample.

cross-examination In a courtroom proceeding, the process of questioning a witness who was called by the opposing party. The party that called the witness questions them in direct questioning which is followed by the cross-examination. There can be several iterations of the process.

cross-projection sketch A type of crime scene sketch that is based on the *bird's eye view perspective. The difference is that in a cross-projection sketch, things such as walls or doors are drawn as if laid down rather than upright. For this reason, this type of sketch is also referred to as an exploded view.

cross-reactivity In an immunological reaction between an antigen and antibody, a reaction in which an antibody reacts with something other than the specific antigen. This can be a consideration in forensic toxicology where *immunoassay is used as a screening technique.

cross-section A commonly used criteria in fibre comparison. To observe a cross-section, a fibre is cut across its width and observed under a microscope. The shape of the cross-section can often be correlated to the function or type of fibre such as a carpet or in a garment.

Crowle's reagent A developing reagent used to visualize
*latent fingerprints. It is particularly useful for bloody prints.
The application of the method is also referred to as 'Cowles
double staining'. The reagent contains the dyes crocein scarlet 7B
and comassie brilliant blue R250.

cryptology In forensic computing contexts, the study of
codes and methods of encoding data so that they cannot be
viewed by any unauthorized person. An example is digital
signatures which are encrypted to prevent tampering or alteration.
See also CIPHERS.

crystal tests Also called microcrystal tests and microcrystalline tests; a
group of *presumptive tests used as part of seized drug analysis. There are
also crystal tests used to confirm the presence of blood through reactions
with haemoglobin as well as tests for explosives. Crystal tests are
performed by placing a small amount of the sample or sample extract on a
microscope slide and adding the appropriate reagent. The shape of the
crystals is examined using a microscope. *See also* TAKAYAMA TEST;
TEICHMANN TEST.

Example drug microcrystals made with cocaine and gold chloride

CSI effect A term used to describe increased public awareness of forensic science as a result of the American television show *CSI* and its spin-offs still airing in many parts of the world. The increased awareness may have had impacts on expectation of forensic science by law enforcement agencies and justice systems and probably played a role in the increasing number of students pursuing forensic science degrees in the early to mid-2000s.

Culliford, Brian (1929–97) A British forensic serologist best known for his book entitled *The Examination and Typing of Bloodstains in the Crime Laboratory*, which was published in 1971 while he was with the Metropolitan Police Laboratory in London. These methods were widely used to type blood and bloodstains before the widespread adaptation of *DNA typing.

cuticle The outermost part of a hair consisting of scale-like structures that cover the cortex. The scale pattern of the cuticle provides important information for classification of a hair.

cutting agents (diluents) Materials used to dilute drugs such as cocaine, methamphetamine, and heroin. Cutting agents, also known as diluents or adulterants, range from caffeine to flour, starch, and sugars such as table sugar (sucrose), dextrose, mannitol, inositol, and fructose. Diluents are pharmacologically inactive; cutting agents are usually defined as pharmacologically active (caffeine for example) although the terms are frequently used interchangeably.

cyanide (CN) A poison that can kill by ingestion, inhalation, or absorption through the skin. The most common forms of cyanide encountered in forensic science are the powders sodium cyanide (NaCN) and potassium cyanide (KCN) which can react in the presence of carbon dioxide or acids to form the acid HCN, also known as hydrogen cyanide, hydrocyanic acid, or prussic acid. Cyanide is also sometimes detected in the blood of those who have died in fires; cyanide can be released as a by-product of combustion of some synthetic materials.

cyanoacrylate The polymeric adhesive used to develop latent fingerprints using fuming techniques; also known as Super Glue. This method of latent fingerprint development originated in Japan in 1978 and is usually conducted in a cabinet or other enclosure. The cyanoacrylate forms a whitish film on fingerprint residues and is often combined with other developers.

cyberforensics *See* COMPUTER FORENSICS.

cystolithic hair A microscopic feature found on the upper surface of the leaves of *marijuana. Also known as 'bear claws' because of their distinctive shape, cystolithic hairs have a relatively broad oval base supporting the claw-like structure that encases an aggregation of calcium carbonate ($CaCO_3$, the cystolith). Since they are found on the leaves, cystolithic hairs are indicative of marijuana and *hashish, but since marijuana is not the only plant that has cystolithic hairs, it is not a conclusive test.

cytosine One of four *nucleotide bases that comprise DNA and RNA. Because of its molecular structure, cytosine will associate with guanine (G), and the two are referred to as complements of each other.

DAB *See* DNA ADVISORY BOARD.

dactylography (dactyloscopy) An older term describing the study of *fingerprints and *friction ridge patterns.

data mapping In forensic computing investigations, searching and exploration procedures that attempt to draw linkages and uncover connections between different data sets or sources.

date rape drugs (predator drugs) A class of drug used to facilitate sexual assault by rendering the victim unable to effectively resist the attack. Examples include gamma hydroxybutyrate (*GHB), alcohol, and *rohypnol (flunitrazepam). *See also* DRUG FACILITATED SEXUAL ASSAULT.

Daubert decision and Daubert trilogy Three critical United States Supreme Court cases that have contributed to the precedents regarding the admissibility of scientific evidence and testimony in that country. *Daubert v Merrell Dow Pharmaceuticals* (113 S Ct 2786 (1993)) involved a case in which parents claimed that the birth defects of their children were the result of a morning sickness medication. The court ruled that it was the role of the judge to determine if scientific evidence is relevant and reliable. This role assigned to the judge is often referred to as the 'gatekeeper'. The two other cases were *General Electric v Joiner* (522 US 136; 1997) and *Kumho Tire Co., Ltd. v Carmichael* (119 S Ct 1167; 1999). Both decisions contributed to the expansion of expert witnesses and the effect of *Kumho* was to apply Daubert standards to all expert testimony, not just strictly scientific expert testimony.

deadman switch A protective device that interrupts power to a machine or device if the person operating it ceases to be actively engaging it. The state of this switch is useful in forensic engineering investigations.

death investigation (medico-legal investigation of death) An investigation designed to determine the cause and manner of death. This investigation typically includes an autopsy, toxicological analysis of biological samples collected at autopsy, and an investigation of the events leading up to it. The cause is the event or process such as a disease or injury that led to the death. The mechanism of death is set in motion by the cause of death. The manner of death is the category that describes the circumstances that led to infliction of the cause of death. The common categories used are homicide (intentional killing by someone beside the victim), suicide (self-homicide), accidental, natural (disease), treatment induced (for example, death during surgery or drug interaction), and indeterminate. The acronym NASH is often used for possible manner of death: natural, accidental, suicidal, or homicidal. The category of 'indeterminate' is also seen. The system of death investigation varies among countries and even within countries. In the UK, variations of the *coroner system are used while in the USA, both coroners and *Medical Examiner systems exist.

decomposition The sequential process that begins after death and ends with skeletonization. Although the phases of decomposition are known, environmental factors, principally temperature, dramatically affect the progress in individual cases. As a result, the progress of decomposition is not alone sufficient or reliable for estimating the *post-mortem interval (PMI). The stages can be generally described as bloating (caused by gas production by native bacteria) and changes in the appearance of the skin, passing through stages of green before reaching black ('black putrefaction'). The characteristic foul odours of decomposition are associated with the putrefaction stage. Stages of advanced decomposition can be reached in 12–18 hours in warm and humid environments, but in cold or freezing areas the process slows dramatically, stretching into weeks, months, or even years depending on how cold it is. Dry decay or mummification follows putrefaction. Eventually, most or all tissue will be dried and will decay away, leaving only bones (skeletonization). *See also* ENTOMOLOGY, FORENSIC; TAPHONOMY.

deductive logic A form of reasoning in which conclusions are drawn based on evidence and facts that are already established; a deduction based on existing established facts. For example: all plants contain chlorophyll and thus have green coloration; therefore grass is a plant.

deflagration Strictly defined, a region of combustion or flame front that is moving at subsonic speeds, as opposed to *detonation, which proceeds at supersonic speeds. Informally, rapid burning is often referred to as deflagration.

dehydrogenases A class of enzymes that catalyse many reactions in the body. The best known in forensic science is perhaps alcohol dehydrogenase (ADH) which catalyses the conversion of ethanol to acetaldehyde (an oxidation).

delta A *friction ridge feature found in fingerprints; the name originates from comparison of ridge patterns to flowing streams or rivers. The delta is the ridge point that is closest to the point of divergence.

delusterant A particulate material, often titanium dioxide, that is used in paints, fibres, and other coatings to reduce the shininess (reflectiveness) of the surface. The particulates scatter light, causing the delustered appearance.

denaturization In proteins, the loss of three-dimensional shape and structure that occurs when hydrogen bonds are disrupted by factors such as changes in temperature or pH.

density gradient Glass or plastic tubes filled with liquids of known densities. These were at one time used to determine relative densities of particulate evidence such as glass and soil.

dental stone A plaster-like material used to create casts of three-dimensional impressions such as tyre and shoe prints. As it cures, the material gives off heat (an exothermic reaction) and thus is not useful on snow.

dentistry, forensic *See* ODONTOLOGY, FORENSIC.

deposition A sworn statement that is given under oath but not in a regular courtroom setting. The person documenting the deposition is an officer of the court and the statement is taken by a court reporter or other officer of the court.

depressants Drugs that depress the central nervous system (CNS) and cause drowsiness and slowed heart rate. Examples include *ethanol, *diazepam, and *barbiturates.

depth of field The depth or thickness of a sample that is in focus; also called depth of focus. The DOF is described by the equation:

$$DOF = \frac{n\lambda}{NA^2}$$

where NA is the *numerical aperture and n is the *refractive index of the media. In general, the higher the magnification, the smaller the depth of field.

derivatization The conversion of a compound that does not chromatograph well under typical *gas chromatography (GC) conditions into a more volatile compound. Compounds that are often derivatized include *methamphetamine and *GHB.

dermal nitrate test A *presumptive test for the presence of *gunshot residue (GSR), also called the paraffin test, that is no longer used. The dermal nitrate test was based on detecting the nitrate ion (NO_3^-), an ingredient in *propellants used in *ammunition. For the test, the hands of the suspect were painted with hot wax (paraffin) that was allowed to dry. The cast was then removed and tested using the reagent *diphenylamine combined with sulphuric acid (H_2SO_4). Locations on the cast that showed a blue colour indicated the possible presence of nitrate. In addition to gunshot residue, nitrates are common in many materials that could be found on the hands including tobacco, cosmetics, fertilizers, and urine. This large number of potential *false positives led to the test being abandoned since it was not sufficiently specific to GSR.

dermatoglyphics The scientific study of the markings and patterns on skin, such as the ridge patterns in fingerprints. The term was coined in the early 20th century and refers to a generalized study of markings on skin surfaces and is not a synonym for forensic fingerprint analysis.

dermis The inner layer of skin that constitutes the bulk of the mass of skin. The dermis is a dense layer of connective tissue that contains fibrous and elastic tissues and collagen. The dermis contains the majority of the sweat and oil glands.

Derome, Wilfrid (1877–1931) A Canadian forensic scientist who formed the first forensic laboratory in the Americas in Montreal in 1909. Derome had studied in Paris, obtained a degree in legal medicine, and visited *Locard's laboratory while there. He returned with an enthusiastic report and was able to convince the local Attorney General to fund a similar facility. The lab, called the Laboratoire de Recherches Médico-Légales opened in 1914. As Locard's lab had served as a model for Derome, his lab would later serve as a model to American J. Edgar Hoover. Derome's laboratory has become recently famous for its role in the fictional series of books by anthropologist Kathy Reichs who works in the lab, and her fictional character Tempe Brennan who also works there part time.

designer drugs Illegal drugs synthesized in clandestine labs that are closely related to controlled substances in structure and effect. The first designer drugs were derivatives of *methamphetamine and *amphetamine and appeared in the 1970s. MDMA, also known as *ecstasy, is 3,4-methylenedioxymethamphetamine while MDA is the amphetamine equivalent. Other examples of designer drugs include the *cannabinomimetics which have recently emerged.

destructive analysis Tests or analyses that destroy the sample tested. Most forensic analyses, such as drug testing or analysis of swabs for DNA, are destructive. However, in most cases enough of the original sample is not tested and thus not destroyed.

deterrent (deterrent coating) Chemical treatments of *propellants designed to control the rate of burning and performance of the ammunition. Different size weapons (calibres) and the necessary projectile velocities, along with other considerations, determine optimal burn rate. Fundamentally, the role of the propellant is to burn rapidly to produce large quantities of hot, expanding gas that propel the projectile down and out of the barrel of the weapon at optimal speed. Too fast a burn will stop producing gases too quickly while too long a burn will continue burning even after the projectile has exited the barrel. *See also* NEUTRAL BURNING POWDER; PROGRESSIVE BURNING POWDER.

detonation An extremely rapid combustion reaction that is initiated by compression and produces a shock wave of hot expanding gases. In an explosive, a detonation wave travels faster than the speed of sound, which differentiates it from a rapid burn.

detonator A device used to initiate a *detonation reaction in an explosive. A *blasting cap is an example of a detonator.

DFO (1,8-diazafluoren-9-one) A compound used as a developing reagent for *latent fingerprints. It serves as a substitute for *ninhydrin. Like this compound, DFO reacts with amino acids in the skin to create a coloured product that also fluoresces when exposed to green light.

diastereoisomers Molecules that have the same molecular formula, but different arrangements of the atoms in space. Stereoisomers have the same formulas and same geometries. Diastereoisomers are a special class of stereoisomers in which the mirror image of one cannot be superimposed on top of the other. Diastereoisomers have different physical and chemical properties and are sometime an issue in the case of *cocaine. Cocaine has two *enantiomers, d-cocaine and l-cocaine, and they are mirror images of each other. There are three other such pairs of cocaine enantiomers, d- and l-pseudococaine, d- and l-allococaine, and d- and l-pseudoallococaine. These pairs are all diastereoisomers of cocaine. *See also* EPHEDRINE AND PSEUDOEPHEDRINE.

diatoms A form of algae that exist in fresh and salt water that have been exploited in drowning cases. If the heart is still beating when a person enters or is forced into the water, the circulatory system can deliver the diatoms to remote parts of the body such as the liver, kidney, or bone marrow. Finding diatoms in tissues far removed from the lungs can be interpreted to mean that the person was alive when they entered the water. Diatoms are characterized by a hard outer shell made of silicates.

diazepam (Valium) A *benzodiazepine that was one of the first completely synthetic drugs created. Introduced in the early 1960s, it remains one of the most widely prescribed drugs in the world and one frequently abused.

diazo coupling A chemical reaction type exploited in several colour-forming *presumptive tests and in the creation of dyes. In this type of reaction, an N=N bond is formed.

dichroism A property of materials such as fibres in which the colours that are absorbed (and thus the colour that the material appears to have) is a function of direction. In a dichroic material, the absorption pattern varies depending on the direction or orientation of the material or on the orientation of *polarized light that illuminates it. Although often associated with colours and thus visible light, infrared absorption patterns can also be dichroic. To observe dichroism in a material, it is mounted on a microscope slide and examined using *polarized light microscopy (PLM). As the stage is rotated, the colour of the material will change since the pattern of absorbance is changing.

differential scanning calorimetry (DSC) A thermoanalytical technique used to characterize explosives, drugs, and polymeric materials. In DSC, the sample and a reference are maintained at the same temperature throughout a temperature ramping programme. Any differences in the heat flow can be related to the characteristics of the sample, which can change over time. For example, a change in phase such as melting will change heat flow characteristics. The typical output of a simple DSC experiment is heat flow versus time. DSC is frequently used to characterize materials such as explosives and occasionally drugs and pharmaceuticals.

diffraction colours and gratings A grating, also referred to as a reflection grating, is a device used in many types of spectrophotometers to disperse electromagnetic radiation into component wavelengths. Gratings work by setting up patterns of constructive and destructive interference of light that separate individual wavelengths and disperse them to different physical locations. Diffraction colours are produced by similar patterns of interference; for example, the colours seen on an oil sheen.

diffusion The natural process of movement of materials from areas of high concentration to areas of lower concentration of that same material. For example, if a drop of food colouring is dropped into a glass of still water, it will diffuse naturally until it is evenly distributed throughout the glass. Concentration gradients are frequently seen as the driving force of diffusion.

digestion A process used during sample preparations to break chemical bonds and to free the target *analyte or analytes from a complex matrix. A digestion attacks the matrix in contrast to an *extraction in which target analytes are removed from the matrix by solvent extraction or related techniques.

digital forensics *See* COMPUTER FORENSICS.

Dille–Koppanyi test A presumptive test used in drug analysis, specifically to identify barbiturates. The test consists of two separate reagents added in two stages. It starts with the addition of a solution of cobalt acetate (dissolved in methanol) to the unknown sample (powdered), followed by a methanolic solution of isopropylamine. A reddish violet colour is indicative of barbiturates, but not definitive. It is a modification of an older test called the Zwikker test.

dilute and shoot A simple sample preparation method in which a portion of a sample is diluted in solvent prior to introduction into an instrument.

diphenylamine (DPA) A compound found as a stabilizer in propellants. The compound is also the basis of an older presumptive colour test for the detection of nitrates that are part of *gunshot residue (GSR).

directionality A descriptive term that describes the direction of travel of an object such as a bullet or a fluid such as blood that is or was at one time in motion. In *bloodstain pattern analysis, the shape of a blood drop will often indicate the directionality of the blood or how it was moving when it struck the surface.

disarticulated joint Limbs or joints that have become separated from a body. As soft tissues such as ligaments and tendons decay or are torn, the joints come apart and the bones can become scattered, either by natural processes or by animals (scavengers). A corpse may also be purposely disarticulated to hide or otherwise dispose of the body.

discrimination index (discrimination power) The ability of a given forensic analysis to distinguish, classify, or identify evidence. For example, in *DNA typing, the discrimination index is the probability that any two people selected at random in a given population will have a *different* DNA type. In forensic chemistry, simple colour tests have a lower discrimination power than an instrumental method based on *mass spectrometry. Often, a forensic analysis will include a series of linked tests in which the combined discrimination index is significantly higher than any one test would be taken alone.

discwipe (diskwipe) A type of computer program or utility that is designed to completely remove all traces of a data that was stored on media such as a hard drive, CD, or external storage device.

disguised writing Handwriting that is purposely altered to make it difficult to identify the writer. This is differentiated from forgery, where the writer is attempting to copy the handwriting of another. An example would be a right-handed person writing with their left hand.

disk imaging The process of copying all contents of a storage device such as a hard drive to another by copying every bit, whether it is being used to represent data or not. *See also* DISK MIRRORING.

disk mirroring A computing protocol in which the contents of one hard drive are routinely copied to a separate location, such as another hard drive, to create a mirror image of the first location at the second location. This is often ongoing so that the disk copies are always in agreement. The practice is used to protect and back up critical data.

dissociative anaesthetics Psychoactive substances that produce a strong analgesic effect along with a sense of separation or dissociation from the body. *Ketamine and *PCP are dissociative anaesthetics.

distance determination An experimental estimate of the distance between a firearm and a target when the weapon was discharged; a recreation of a shooting incident. The examiners attempt to recreate the event as closely as possible, including environmental conditions, weapon, and ammunition. *Sodium rhodizonate is often used to visualize propellant residues as part of the distance determination.

distribution coefficient A coefficient (K_d) that quantitatively describes the distribution of a compound or *analyte between two different phases such as liquid and gas or between two immiscible liquids.

DNA (deoxyribonucleic acid) DNA is composed of complementary strands of *nucleotides in which the base pairs organize themselves opposite to their partner via hydrogen bonding interactions. The interactions of the A-T and C-G pairs cause the two strands to twist around each other in a helical coil. The double helix shape of DNA was first proposed in 1953 by Francis Crick (from England) and James Watson (an American), although their work was the culmination of much research in the field. DNA can be replicated by first 'unzipping' the separate strands, a process that requires enzymes. Once separated, new complementary strands can be synthesized from nucleotides that will arrange themselves in the same opposite pairings as in the original strand, creating two copies of the original or parent DNA molecule. In this way, each parent strand acts as a template for a new one. Polymorphisms in the order of base pairs and the length of specific base pair sequences are the basis of modern *DNA typing methods.

DNA Advisory Board (DAB) A group formed in the United States as a result of the passage of the DNA Identification Act of 1994. This group established *QA/QC guidelines for forensic *DNA typing. The information and current guidelines are kept by the National Institutes of Science and Technology (NIST).

DNA typing (DNA analysis) A group of related procedures that has replaced traditional blood typing (forensic *serology) in forensic labs. DNA typing techniques were pioneered by molecular biologists and entered into the forensic arena in the late 1980s and early 1990s. Since then, they have grown quickly into the tool of choice for the analysis of blood and body fluids. Rapid advances in the field continue, so DNA typing applications and techniques continue to change and evolve. Smaller and smaller samples can be analysed (currently as little as a billionth of a gram of DNA is needed), while the discriminating power (the ability of a typing test or tests to link a sample to an individual) is increasing. In addition to blood and body fluid stains, DNA typing can be used on a variety of different samples including hair, skin scrapings, and even dandruff. The first methods used were based on *restricted fragment length polymorphism (RFLP), which have largely been replaced by methods based on *short tandem repeats (STR) at several loci in the genome. The DNA typed in forensic practice is usually that found in the nucleus of cells (nuclear DNA) although methods for typing *mitochondrial DNA are also used. *See also* CODIS; JEFFREYS, SIR ALEC; MULLIS, KARY; PCR.

documentation, crime scene A group of procedures and protocols used to document and record a crime scene in as much detail as is needed and feasible. Documentation is critical for noting what type of evidence was found, in what exact location, and in what exact orientation. The documentation is essential for crime scene reconstructions and for interpreting the value and meaning of evidence. There are several forms of crime scene documentation including hand-drawn and computer sketching, photography, and videography. Typically, multiple forms of documentation are used and several people may participate in the documentation process.

d-orbital splitting A phenomenon that is responsible for colour changes in some colour-based *presumptive tests. In transition metals such as cobalt and molybdenum, complexes can appear coloured as a result of splitting of the normally degenerate d-orbitals. The cobalt thiocyanate presumptive test for cocaine (and other drugs) is an example of a test that relies on d-orbital splitting.

dot matrix printer A type of computer printer. The printer has a ribbon similar to that found in typewriters and letters are created by selective activation of pins that impact the ribbon and impart an image to the page. This design of printer was common in the late 1980s and is still used in some applications such as automated printing of cheques.

double-base powder A type of *smokeless powder (*propellant for *ammunition) that consists of *nitrocellulose (NC) and *nitroglycerin (NG). Other ingredients include stabilizers such as *diphenylamine (DPA) and *deterrents. *See also* NEUTRAL BURNING POWDER; PROGRESSIVE BURNING POWDER.

Doyle, Sir Arthur Conan (1859–1930) A British author famous for creating the Sherlock Holmes character, who has become a widely recognized symbol of scientific detective work. Many forensic scientists were inspired to their careers by his adventures, published between 1887 and 1927 in the form of short stories and novellas. Doyle, a physician, described many tests and techniques in his stories that would not become common tools of forensic science until years later. Early pioneers in the field, particularly Edmond *Locard and Hans *Gross praised Doyle's works and cited them as personal inspiration.

DQ-alpha (DQ-α) A locus on DNA that was the first to utilize *PCR methods and the first to be targeted in forensic *DNA typing using a commercial kit. The locus contains 242 base pairs in sequence and this sequence is polymorphic meaning that the sequence of base pairs is different for people who have different types. This contrasts with current *STR methods in which the sequence of base pairs is the same and the number of repeats of the sequence is what differentiates types.

Dragendorff reagent A reagent used as a colour-based *presumptive test for drugs. The reagent consists of the transition metal molybdenum, and it is used for colour testing as well as a developer for *thin layer chromatography (TLC).

drawback effect Blood (or another liquid substance) that was present on the barrel of the firearm and that has been withdrawn deeper into the barrel as a result of, or during, the process of firing.

drip pattern A *bloodstain pattern created by blood dropping from a height to a surface such as a floor. A drip pattern can be used to determine if the source was stationary or moving, and often the direction and speed of movement. *See also* PASSIVE BLOODSTAIN.

drug A single substance that, when ingested, produces a physiological effect, pharmacological effect, or change. This contrasts with a medicine or formulation that may contain one or more active ingredients.

drug classification Methods used to categorize drugs. There are several methods including those based on the drug's use, effects, or legal classification. A common method is classification by physiological effect. In this scheme, drugs are classified as:

- Narcotics: substances that relieve pain (analgesics) and promote sleep.
- Depressants: substances that depress the Central Nervous System (CNS) and can produce effects including loss of coordination, impairment of judgement, and sleep.
- Stimulants: substances that stimulate the CNS, producing a feeling of wakefulness, decreased fatigue, decreased appetite, and general well-being. In higher doses, many stimulants can also act as hallucinogens.
- Hallucinogens: substances that alter visual and auditory stimuli and produce hallucinations.

drug facilitated sexual assault (DFSA) A sexual assault that is facilitated by administration of a drug such as a *dissociative anaesthetic. Examples of drugs frequently used in this manner are *GHB and *rohypnol. Drugs used in this manner are referred to as predator drugs or *date rape drugs. Both men and women can be the victim of this crime.

DRUGFIRE An automated computer system for the identification of markings on firearms evidence in the United States. It has been phased out in favour of the older National Integrated Ballistics Network or NIBN system.

druggist's fold (pharmacist's fold) A folding pattern used on paper that encloses small amounts of physical evidence such as a powder, hairs, or fibres. The name originates from the way druggists at one time dispensed small amounts of powders.

drug interaction The interaction of drugs and metabolites that produces physiological effects that differ from those produced by the individual drugs alone. These effects may be *synergistic or antagonistic. The increasing use and abuse of prescription medications has led to increasing occurrences of drug interaction toxicity and death. *See also* POLYDRUG.

drug profiling The chemical and isotopic analysis of drugs that is used to compare seizures and to assess similarity and differences among seizures and exhibits. *See also* ISOTOPE RATIO MASS SPECTROMETRY.

drug recognition expert (DRE) In the United States, a law enforcement officer trained to evaluate drug impairment and to determine what drug or drugs a person has taken to become intoxicated.

drying oil An oil used as an ingredient in a paint or other colourant coating that polymerizes over time and thus appears to dry. However, the process is not simply solvent evaporation. Linseed oil is an example of a drying oil.

dry origin impression An impression, such as a *latent fingerprint or *shoe print, that is found or created in a dry material such as dust or powder.

duplicates Two or more samples collected from the same parent or bulk sample at the same time and under the same conditions. This contrasts with *replicates which are usually created in the laboratory by the analyst.

Duquenois–Levine test A colour-based *presumptive test for *marijuana and related seized drugs. Also called the Duquenois test or the modified Duquenois–Levine test, it consists of three reagents that react with the active substance in marijuana, Δ^9tetrahydrocannabinol (THC). The reagents are a 2 per cent solution of vanillin and 1 per cent acetaldehyde in ethanol, concentrated hydrochloric acid (HCl), and chloroform. Dried plant matter, seeds, or seed extracts, or other material to be tested is placed in a test tube and the reagents added in order. The sample is shaken and a positive result is indicated by a purple colour in the lower chloroform layer.

dye A compound that is used as a colourant. A dye is soluble in the solvent *vehicle while a pigment is suspended rather than dissolved. Many of the colour-based *presumptive tests work via production of dyes.

dynamite A high explosive developed by Alfred Nobel in 1886 that consisted of nitroglycerin (NG) adsorbed onto an inert solid such as diatomaceous earth (DE) or a clay material. As a result, the usually unstable NG was rendered much more stable and safer to handle. Modern formulations often include sodium or ammonium nitrate as oxidizers ($NaNO_3$ or NH_4NO_3), nitrocellulose (NC), sulphur (S), ethylene glycol dinitrate (EGDN), and other filler materials.

eccrine sweat The aqueous fluid excreted by the sweat (eccrine) glands in the skin. These pores are found on all skin surfaces, while sebaceous glands (oil glands) are found in more limited areas. Sweat is a complex mixture of inorganic and organic materials dissolved or suspended in water, which makes up about 98 per cent by volume.

ecstasy (MDMA, 3,4-methylenedioxymethamphetamine) A *designer drug that is an analogue of methamphetamine. MDMA had a brief history of legitimate use before its popularity as an illegal drug. Ecstasy use is increasing among adolescents and young adults. Ecstasy produces a sense of euphoria and heightened empathy, and can lead to hallucinations.

Ehrlich, Paul (1854–1915) A German chemist and Nobel Prize winner (The Nobel Prize in Physiology or Medicine 1908, shared) who worked in the area of dye chemistry and developed, among many other procedures, the Ehrlich test. His work was also crucial in development of the gram staining procedure still used to distinguish bacterial types as gram positive versus gram negative. He was considered to be a bit eccentric and was known for carrying around a box of cigars, of which he smoked 25 a day.

(((()))) SEE WEB LINKS

• A summary of his life and work as well as information regarding the Prize. The Nobel site has lots of information on all of the prize winners. Last accessed May 2011.

Ehrlich test A presumptive test used to detect LSD and related *ergot alkaloids as well as other basic drug compounds. The reagent contains p-dimethylaminobenzaldehye (p-DMAB) in a solution of sulphuric and hydrochloric acids and is often referred to as the p-DMAB test or by the older term Van Urk test.

ejector marks and extractor marks Markings created on *cartridge cases by the metal-to-metal contact between the cartridge case and the extractor and ejector mechanisms in the weapon. The extractor mechanism removes a cartridge from the chamber, while the ejector

throws the cartridge away once it is extracted. Revolvers do not have
ejectors, but automatic and semi-automatic weapons (pistols and rifles)
do, and as a result the cartridge cases used in such weapons are designed
differently from ammunition used in revolvers. Ejector marks can be
studied using a comparison microscope and may be useful in
individualizing cartridge cases.

Two examples of ejector marks, both the lower right of the cartridge case. The
primer is the circular region just visible.

electrochemical etching A chemical technique that is used to
chemically etch metal such as when creating rifling or when attempting to
restore an obliterated serial number. Reagents are placed in contact with
the metal surface causing an *oxidation/reduction reaction that dissolves
the metal in a controlled fashion.

electromagnetic radiation (EMR) Energy, including visible light, is
composed of both electrical and magnetic energy and can be described as
both a wave and a particle. When describing it as a wave, two terms are
important: the wavelength (λ) and the frequency (υ). The idea can be
visualized by imagining dropping a rock into a still pond. Energy ripples
away from where the rock was dropped in waves that can be described by
their wavelength (distance from crest to crest) and by their frequency (how
many waves per second pass a fixed point). Electromagnetic radiation that
is high energy has short wavelengths and high frequency; low energy EMR
has long wavelengths and low frequencies. When EMR is thought of as a
particle, the source of the energy can be thought of as a gun that 'fires'
discrete packets of energy, which are referred to as photons. The energy of a

photon is described by the relationship $E = h\upsilon$, where h is constant (Planck's constant) and υ is the frequency. Thus, the wave model and particle model are related through the frequency. *Spectroscopy describes a family of analytical techniques based on the interaction of EMR and matter. Most common in forensic applications are IR, UV/VIS, and *Raman spectroscopy.

electroosmotic flow (EOF) A fluid flow that arises in *capillary electrophoresis and related techniques that is generated by interactions along the wall of the capillary tube. The capillary surface (if untreated) will develop a net negative charge which attracts positive ions in the solution within the capillary. This layer of positive charge will naturally be drawn towards the *cathode, generating a flow within the capillary that is independent of the analytes present. Thus, even a neutral molecule will move, carried along by the EOF.

electropherogram The output (printed or electronically displayed) of a *capillary electrophoresis instrument.

electrophoresis Generally, a technique of separating large charged molecules such as proteins based on their mobilities in an applied electrical field. In forensic science, slab gel electrophoresis was extensively used up until the mid-1990s for the typing of *isoenzymes in blood. Electrophoresis can be conducted in a gel media (or similar material such as polyacrylamide), or in capillary tubes containing gels or *buffers. In gel or slab gel electrophoresis, the analyst dissolves the substrate in hot water and pours it into a rectangular mould. As the solution cools, it forms a stable gel a few millimetres thick. Sample is introduced by cutting a thin slit near the end of the gel for sample introduction. One way to accomplish this is to cut a piece of thread that is a few millimetres long, soaking the thread in the sample, and then inserting the sample into the gel.

To begin the analysis, the gel is placed atop a cooling bath. At each end of the gel rectangle, an absorbent material is draped from the end of the gel and into a buffer solution. Because the gel is mostly water and the buffer contains ions, an electrical field can be set up across the gel by placing electrical leads at both ends, one positive (the *anode) and one negative (the *cathode). Once the field is applied, the charged molecules in the sample such as proteins will migrate in the electrical field until they reach their *isoelectric point in the gel.

The basis of separation in electrophoresis is differences in size-to-charge ratios. For example assume molecule A and molecule B are both charged and move in a gel. The speed of this movement is dictated by the charge on the molecule as just described. Additionally, the gel impedes movement of molecules and in general, the larger the molecule, the greater the slowing effect of the gel.

Capillary methods are similar in that there is an anode and a cathode but there are many variants of the technique. Generally, instead of a large rectangular slab, the charged materials migrate through a capillary tube filled with a gel, buffer, or similar material. *DNA typing is carried out using *capillary electrophoresis.

electrospray ionization (ESI) a technique used to ionize molecules at atmospheric pressure prior to analysis using *mass spectrometry, *ion mobility spectrometry, or related techniques. Solvent and analyte enter the ionization source where an electrode imparts surface charge to solvent droplets. The droplets are then dried, bringing the surface charges closer to each other as the droplets shrink. When the droplet gets so small that the charges are too close, the repulsion of the like charges will cause the droplet to burst into a fine mist; this is also referred to as a 'Coulombic explosion'. As a result, most of the solvent is driven off before the material enters the mass spectrometer. ESI is classified as a soft ionization technique, meaning that there is limited fragmentation of chemical bonds in the source. ESI is used as an ionization source for high performance liquid chromatography coupled to mass spectrometry (LC-MS) and for *ion mobility spectrometry (IMS).

electrostatic deposition apparatus (ESDA) A device used to visualize *indented writing or patterns left in dry powdery material. An example would be a shoe print left on a dusty floor. A sheet of thin plastic is placed over the paper that has the suspected indented writing, and both are placed in a vacuum chamber. A charge of static electricity is imparted to the plastic and then toner powder is applied to the surface of the plastic. An image of the indented writing or pattern will be created on the plastic and can be visualized by application of toner materials similar to that used in laser printers.

electrostatic lift The process of using static electricity to lift or transfer a dry impression to a black background, such as a shoe print in dust. A high voltage source is used to create the charge in the dust particles which are then drawn to a substrate where further development can take place. *See also* ELECTROSTATIC DEPOSITION APPARATUS.

elimination prints *Fingerprints or palm prints collected at a crime scene from all personnel who were in and at the scene and who might have inadvertently touched physical evidence.

eluent (eluant) In *chromatography, the eluate is the solvent, fluid, or gas that emerges from the end of the analytical column. The eluent is the mobile phase that is introduced into the column and used to move the sample molecules through the column.

embalming The process used to help preserve a body and slow post-mortem decay. The body is drained of fluids and blood, which are replenished with a fluid that impedes the growth of bacteria that drive decomposition. Examples of compounds found in embalming fluid are ethanol and formaldehyde.

Emde method One of several synthetic routes than can be used to produce *methamphetamine and related compounds. In the Emde synthesis, ephedrine or pseudoephedrine are typically reacted with thionylchloride to produce chloroephedrine. This compound is then subjected to catalytic hydrogenation to yield the desired product.

emission spectroscopy A form of spectrophotometric analysis principally used for elemental analysis. In emission spectroscopy, an input of excitation energy is used to place atoms into excited states that produce characteristic emissions of *electromagnetic radiation upon relaxation. Thus, the wavelengths detected and the intensity of the emission are used to obtain qualitative and quantitative data. Early forms of emission spectrometry used flames or sparks to initiate the emission processes, with *inductively coupled plasmas (ICP) now being the most common ionization sources. ICP-atomic emission spectroscopy (ICP-AES) is the most common type of emission spectroscopy although forensically, *ICP-MS methods are more frequently utilized for elemental analysis.

enantiomers Molecules that have the same arrangement of atoms in terms of bonding but that are non-superimposable mirror images of each other. *See also* DIASTEREOISOMERS.

encapsulation A process used to cover *nanoparticles, such as those made with gold or cadmium sulphide (CdS) with a material that allows the nanoparticles to be used to visualize *latent fingerprints.

encryption The process of hiding or encoding data on computers or related devices to prevent unauthorized persons from viewing or accessing the data in question. The process typically requires an encryption and reverse encryption program and a key. *See also* CIPHER.

endogenous A compound that is normally found in the body. For example, calcium is endogenous. This contrasts with *exogenous materials, which are not typically found. *See also* XENOBIOTIC.

energy of activation (E$_a$) The energy required to initiate a chemical reaction.

engineering, forensic The application of engineering knowledge and techniques to legal matters. Forensic engineering includes traffic accident reconstruction, failure analysis (as when buildings collapse), investigation of industrial accidents, product liability issues, and the investigation of transportation disasters such as airline crashes.

entomology, forensic The application of the study of arthropods such as flies and beetles to legal proceedings and legal investigation. Arthropods are animals with jointed legs and include insects, arachnids (spiders), centipedes, millipedes, and crustaceans. Forensic entomology, principally related to insects, has become a common tool in death investigation and for assigning *post-mortem interval (PMI). The state of *succession of insects on a body can be used to estimate how long it has been in a certain location. For example, flies arrive soon after death and lay eggs that hatch into maggots. Beetles then arrive to feed on the maggots even as the maggots progress through their life cycle. *See also* ENTOMOTOXICOLOGY.

entomotoxicology The chemical analysis of insects found at a death scene to determine what substances they ingested while feeding on a body. Preparation of insects for chemical analysis uses techniques similar to those developed for the analysis of hair and fingernails, since the chemical composition of insect shells is similar to these materials. Entomotoxicology can be valuable in cases when a body is discovered so long after death that the blood and tissues needed for standard toxicological analyses have disappeared.

enzyme kinetics Evaluation of the speed of chemical and biochemical reactions that are catalysed by *enzymes. *See also* FIRST ORDER REACTION; SECOND ORDER REACTION; PHARMACOKINETICS.

enzyme-linked immunoassay (ELISA) An immunoassay technique used in toxicology to detect drugs and metabolites. Immunoassay relies on an antigen-antibody reaction between the drug being tested and an antibody specific for it. The antibody is attached to a solid surface such as the bottom of a plastic or glass well. A complex that consists of the drug and a label is added and the reaction occurs. As a result, the labelled drug is bound to the antibody. A sample that may contain the drug, such as urine, is added to the plastic well. If there is no drug or very little drug present, the labelled drug-antibody complex will remain undisturbed. However, if there is a large concentration of the drug, this will displace the labelled drug from the antibodies, releasing the labelled drug into solution. The higher the drug concentration in the sample, the more will be displaced. The amount of the displaced labelled drug is then measured. In ELISA, a chemical substrate is added to the solution in the well. The label is an enzyme that catalyses a reaction in which the substrate is changed, forming a coloured solution. The deeper the colour, the greater the concentration of the enzyme label present, which in turn implies a greater concentration of the drug.

enzymes A biochemical that speeds up a chemical reaction that would otherwise take place very slowly. Enzymes are protein molecules that are used in many biochemical procedures in forensic science and the naming conventions used describe how an enzyme functions. For example, a dehydrogenase enzyme such as alcohol dehydrogenase (ADH) catalyses the removal of hydrogen from molecules such as ethanol, which is an oxidation reaction.

ephedrine and pseudoephedrine Compounds that are used in clandestine laboratories as the starting point for the synthesis of methamphetamine. Ephedrine has two *chiral centres, two pairs of *enantiomers (*d*-ephedrine and *l*-ephedrine) consisting of four *diastereoisomers. These are (1R, 2S)-(–) ephedrine, (1S, 2R)-(+) ephedrine, (1S, 2S)-(+) pseudoephedrine, and (1R, 2R)-(–) pseudoephedrine. Ephedrine and pseudoephedrine occur naturally in plants in the *Ephedra* family. Ephedrine is a central nervous system (CNS) stimulant.

epidermis The outer portion of the skin that is made up of several distinct cell layers beginning with the basal cell layer and progressing to the outer layer, where all epidermal cells are eventually sloughed off.

equivocal death A death in which the manner (natural, accidental, suicidal, or homicidal) cannot be definitely determined.

erasure The purposeful removal of letters, numbers, words, phrases, or other notations from a document. The erasure can be abrasive (such as from rubbing with an eraser or wetting and rubbing); chemical (such as bleaching); or cut-outs (using a razor or other sharp knife). This is in contrast to *obliterations in which existing writing is overwritten or hidden but not removed.

ergot alkaloid A class of *psychoactive substances derived from a fungus (*Claviceps purpurea*) that lives on grains such as rye. Approximately 30 drugs have been derived from this fungus including ergotamine (used to treat headaches) and lysergic acid which can be easily converted to *lysergic acid diethylamide (LSD).

ergotism Also known as St Anthony's Fire, a type of poisoning that can result after ingestion of *ergot alkaloids. Symptoms include convulsions and hallucinations.

error Generally, an expression of the difference between an experimentally obtained measurement and an accepted true value. Error can be expressed generally as a combination of the *systematic and random error components associated with a given analysis. Error can be expressed in several ways such as absolute error (the difference between the experimental value and the true value) or the per cent relative error, defined as this difference divided by the true value multiplied by 100.

erythrocyte acid phosphatase (EAP) A polymorphic *isoenzyme system with six common *phenotypes present in blood. Prior to the widespread adoption of *DNA typing, this and other isoenzyme systems were typed in bloodstains using gel *electrophoresis.

ESDA (electrostatic deposition apparatus) A device used to visualize indented writing and to lift patterns off dry powdery surfaces. Prior to application of ESDA, the paper may be placed in a controlled humidity environment. Once equilibrated, the paper is placed in the device and a thin sheet of Mylar is placed over the surface and a vacuum applied to ensure uniform and tight contact. Typically, a handheld wand is passed repeatedly over the surface to impart a residual static charge to the paper. Toner, similar to that used in photocopiers, is then applied to the surface and adheres to the Mylar as a function of charge. The effect is to develop a pattern corresponding to the indented writing. This pattern is photographed and can be preserved by placing a second sheet of adhesive plastic over the Mylar surface. Note the underlying evidence, the paper with the indented writing, is unaffected. *See also* ELECTROSTATIC DEPOSITION APPARATUS.

establishing photo At a crime scene, an establishing photo is intended to show the evidence of interest in more detail than shown in the *overall photo, which shows a larger picture of the evidence in context. The establishing photo focuses on the item of evidence and should include markers and measurement devices for scaling.

esterase D (ESD) A polymorphic *isoenzyme system with five common *phenotypes. Prior to widespread adoption of *DNA typing, this and other isoenzyme systems were typed in bloodstains using gel *electrophoresis.

ethanol A two-carbon alcohol that is the psychoactive substance in alcoholic beverages. Secondarily, ethanol can be used in forensic contexts as a solvent, cleaner, and preservative. *See also* BLOOD ALCOHOL; BREATH ALCOHOL.

eumelanin A type of *melanin (colouring pigment) found in the skin and hair; dark brown to black in colour.

Eurachem A professional group formed in 1989 that focuses on applications of *metrology to analytical chemistry. Although based in Europe, the group's documents and guidelines are used internationally.

(SEE WEB LINKS)

- An excellent resource on analytical chemistry and measurement. Last accessed May 2011.

evaporative staining A process used to develop latent fingerprints on surfaces by volatilization of the reagent. The gas-phase material condenses on the surface and makes the print visible.

evidence, physical Any type of material that can be analysed, studied, or tested to yield information regarding an event that has legal consequence. This contrasts with testimonial evidence, which is information relayed to a trier of fact via written or verbal means.

evidence, testimonial Evidence provided to a trier of fact verbally, in writing, or occasionally through videoconferencing or other electronic means.

Examination and Typing of Bloodstains in the Crime Laboratory A handbook published in 1971 and authored by Brian *Culliford of the United Kingdom. This book was a standard manual for the analysis of such evidence until the advent of *DNA typing. The book describes methods of typing blood and body fluids and associated stains for *blood groups and *isoenzyme systems.

excipient In a drug formulation, a compound or compounds that are physiologically inactive; a filler.

excitation The stimulation of matter by *electromagnetic energy (EMR) that results in atoms or molecules being placed in excited (unstable) states. When the atoms or molecules return to the ground state, energy is released and the type and characteristics of this energy can be exploited for analytical or visualization purposes. An example is *fluorescence, widely used in forensic applications.

exemplar An example; a sample collected under controlled conditions or from historical examples. A signature on an old credit card slip or cheque would be an example of an exemplar in a *questioned document examination. The term is also used occasionally to refer broadly to standards used in any comparative analysis.

exhibit An item that has been accepted by a trier of fact as evidence in a legal proceeding.

exogenous A material, substance, or compound that is not synthesized or found naturally within the human body; the opposite of *endogenous. *See also* XENOBIOTIC.

exon A sequence of *base pairs in DNA that code for the amino acid sequence for a protein.

exonuclease An enzyme used in *DNA typing procedures. Specifically, exonucleases cleave *nucleotides one at a time from a strand of DNA.

expirated blood Blood that is contained in exhaled breath and that can create characteristic *bloodstain patterns. *See also* PROJECTED BLOODSTAIN PATTERN.

explainable difference An incongruity or inconsistency that arises during a comparative analysis (such as fingerprints) that can be satisfactorily explained based on the data and information available.

exploded view *See* CROSS PROJECTION SKETCH.

explosion A rapid expansion of hot gases that generates a destructive pressure wave. Strictly defined, the pressure wave in an explosion moves supersonically, as does the detonation wave. This is in contrast to rapid burning or deflagration which may be incorrectly described as an explosion. *See also* DETONATION; EXPLOSIVES; EXPLOSIVE TRAIN.

explosive power index (relative explosive power) A comparative numerical value used to rank the relative power of an explosive based on the heat and volume of gases produced by detonation of 1.0 gram of the explosive. The value is reported relative to that of *picric acid:

$$PI = \frac{QV_{explosive}}{QV_{picric\ acid}}$$

Where Q is the heat released by the detonation of one gram and V is the volume of gas produced. Another method used is a measure relative to the mass:

$$relative\ explosive\ power = \frac{explosive\ power}{unit\ mass} = \frac{QV}{m^2}$$

Where m is the mass of the explosive.

explosives Chemical compounds or mixtures that decompose rapidly to produce heat and gas in the form of an explosion. The reaction is called a *detonation and it is distinctly different from typical burning or decomposition in that compressive force drives the reaction and the reaction front propagates at speeds that exceed the speed of sound. There

are several methods of classification of explosives such as *low explosives
and *high explosives. Low explosives decompose very quickly and must be
kept in a confined space to explode. Examples include *propellants used in
ammunition. High explosives are further divided into primary and
secondary explosives. Primary high explosives are shock and/or heat
sensitive and are often used as *primers that ignite secondary high
explosives. Secondary high explosives are more stable and are usually
detonated by the shock generated from a primary explosive. High
explosives decompose at a much faster rate than low explosives and
detonations generate shattering power, produce smaller, sharper
fragments, and generally leave minimal residue.

explosive train A series of combustible or explosive materials
arranged from most sensitive to least and designed to result in a
detonation of the primary explosive in the device.

exsanguination Bleeding to death.

extenders Compounds used in various formulations as fillers or
diluents. Forensically relevant examples include extenders in *paint and
*propellants.

external ballistics The characteristics and behaviour of a bullet for
the period after it leaves the muzzle and before it reaches the target. An
understanding of external ballistics is needed for trajectory analysis and
for reconstruction of crime scenes that involve discharge of firearms.

external standard A method of *calibration of instrumentation such
as *GC-MS in which a calibration curve is created using standards that are
made in media that does not contain any of the sample itself. For example,
if a toxicologist uses an external standard calibration to determine the
amount of a drug in a blood sample, the calibration curve would be made
using that drug in a different media such as an organic solvent rather than
in blood. *See also* INTERNAL STANDARD; STANDARD ADDITION.

extinction angle In *polarizing light microscopy (PLM), that angle at
which the *polarizer must be rotated to make a *birefringent sample
appear dark against a dark background.

extraction A type sample preparation; the process of preparing the
sample such that the compounds or compounds of interest are separated
from any materials that may complicate or interfere with the analysis of
those samples. DNA has to be extracted from stains prior to analysis for
example. *See also* DIGESTION.

extractor In automatic and semi-automatic firearms, a metal piece that
extracts a spent cartridge from the chamber of the weapon.

extractor marks *See* EJECTOR MARKS AND EXTRACTOR MARKS

extrinsic data Information that is associated with an electronic file, but that is not part of the contents. Examples of extrinsic data include the name of the file creator, date created, dates modified, size, storage path, etc.

extruded powder A type of *smokeless powder made by forcing a soft solid of the formulation through a mould (extruded) and cut to size. The extruders are often cylindrical.

eyepoint When using a microscope, the optimal location (height above the eyepiece) for viewing.

fabric impressions A type of impression evidence that can result when fabric comes in contact with a surface capable of retaining the pattern. A fabric impression can be studied for class characteristics such as weave and whether the fabric has unique features such as tears, wrinkles, creases, or wear patterns. Fabric impressions can also be left by contact of the cloth with a dusty or bloody surface.

facial reconstruction A group of techniques used to assist in the identification of badly decomposed or skeletal remains. A two-dimensional reconstruction is simply a drawing (or computer-generated drawing) of the face of the deceased, while a three-dimensional reconstruction is a sculpted likeness built upon a skull or portions of it. Forensic sculptors are forensic artists that specialize in three-dimensional reconstructions.

failure analysis A technique used in forensic *engineering as part of the investigation of building collapses, airplane crashes, or other events that involved the failure of some kind such as mechanical, electrical, or material. For example, if a bridge collapses, various components used in construction such as bolts and cables would be subject to failure analysis as part of the investigation.

false acceptance rate (FAR) The fraction of comparisons of two items (typically fingerprints) that are falsely accepted as a match or as coming from the same common source. In terms of *hypothesis testing, a false acceptance is a *type II error.

false classification rate (FCR) In automated processing and classification of fingerprints, a term that expresses the fraction of fingerprints that upon initial classification are assigned to the incorrect class.

false exclusion An incorrect elimination of an item from the class it belongs to. For example, consider two bullets that were fired from the same gun and subsequently examined. If one bullet had been damaged after firing and some of the characteristic marks obliterated or altered, the firearms examiner might incorrectly conclude that the two bullets were not fired from the same weapon, a false exclusion.

false inclusion When examining class characteristics of an item or items, an inclusion of one in a class to which it does not belong. A false inclusion also occurs when an item is incorrectly included when attempting to find a common source.

false negative A type of error that occurs when a test or analysis produces incomplete or negative results when it should have been positive and/or definitive.

false positive A type of error that occurs when a test or analysis produces a positive result or incorrect result when it should not have.

false rejection rate (FRR) The fraction of comparisons (typically of fingerprints) that are falsely rejected as a match. In terms of a *hypothesis test, a false rejection is a *type I error.

falsifiability One of the hallmarks of scientific theories and the scientific method. A scientific theory, explanation, or result in a forensic report is purposely designed and stated so there is a way to test it and thus to prove it false. Scientific theories are stated this way either by using a specific mathematical formula or by wording the theory in such a way that it can be verified by experimentation or observation.

Faulds, Henry (1843–1930) A Scottish physician who, while working in Japan, became interested in fingerprints. He authored a famous letter, published in the respected periodical *Nature* in October 1880, that made the first known mention of the value of *fingerprints found at a crime scene. He was a contemporary of William *Herschel, another key figure in the early development of fingerprint comparison.

fentanyl A synthetic opiate that is approximately 100 times as potent as *morphine. It is frequently used in time-released skin patch formulations.

fibres Tendrils of material that can be natural or synthetic; animal, vegetable, or mineral in origin. Fibres can be first classified as natural or artificial fibres. Natural fibres include those of mineral origin such as glass wool or asbestos; vegetable origin (cotton and linen) and animal origin (wool). *Hair is a specialized fibre of animal origin. Human hair is included in this category. Cotton is the most common vegetable fibre and is composed of cellulose, as are all plant fibres. The artificial or synthetic fibres encompass those that are derived from natural fibres and those that are completely synthetic. The principal forensic tool in fibre analysis is *polarizing light microscopy.

Nylon fibres viewed under crossed polars in a polarizing light microscope

figures of merit Terms that are used to describe the performance of analytical methods and the data that are produced by these methods. These terms are typically defined by international standards organizations such as *Eurachem, the American Society of Testing and Materials (ASTM), and the International Union of Pure and Applied Chemistry (IUPAC). Example figures of merit are *accuracy, *precision, *repeatability, *limit of detection (LOD), *limit of quantitation (LOQ), and sensitivity.

film-forming agent A compound added to materials such as *paint and *ink that is designed to form a protective film over the deposit. Most such agents form polymers.

fingerprint developers Materials, chemicals, or reagents used to visualize latent fingerprints so that they can be clearly imaged

for searching and comparison. Developers are selected based on
the substrate characteristics such as colour and porosity.
Examples include *fingerprint powders, chemical developers such
as *DFO and *ninhydrin, chemical fuming agents such as
*cyanoacrylate (Super Glue) and *nanoparticles such as cadmium
sulphide (CdS).

fingerprint powders Powders that are dusted onto *latent
fingerprints to improve visualization. The powders adhere to the
oily components found in the fingerprint residue. Powders are
selected based on colour to maximize contrast with the background.
If a print were on a white surface such as a countertop, a grey
or black powder would be selected. Additionally, powders may
be magnetic and applied with a magnetic brush. Powders
are also available that have other desirable properties such
as *fluorescence.

fingerprint region The region in an *infrared spectrum (IR) that
spans the wavenumber region (cm^{-1} region) between ~1,500 cm^{-1} and
700 cm^{-1}. This region of the spectrum shows a complex pattern of
radiation absorbance that is considered to be sufficient in
almost every case to definitively identify a chemical compound.
For such identification, the sample that is analysed must
be pure or nearly so.

fingerprints An impression, either two or three dimensional,
produced by contact of a finger with a substrate. A two-dimensional
fingerprint would be one deposited on a flat surface
while a three-dimensional print, or plastic print, would be found
in material such as putty. *Latent fingerprints such as those
on a surface such as glass or paper consist of the residues
produced by *eccrine sweat glands along with oils, fats, ions, and
amino acids.
    Fingerprints are defined by the patterns of *friction ridges on the fingers.
As a mark of individuality, fingerprints have a long history. Ancient
cultures such as the Babylonians and Chinese used them as a signature
although it is not known if the ancients recognized that fingerprints were
unique to each individual. Modern interest in fingerprints as an aid to law
enforcement (also called dactyloscopy) traces back to the middle of
the 19th century. Pioneers in the field include William *Herschel,
Henry *Faulds, Francis *Galton, Edward Richard *Henry, and Juan
*Vucetich.
    Fingerprints have both *class characteristics used to divide fingerprint
patterns into categories. The patterns of fingerprints can be divided into

four basic types: whorls, tents, arches, and loops, each of which can be further subdivided. Systems of fingerprint classification are based on the presence or absence of these features and are used to categorize similar patterns into smaller groups that can then be searched and compared for the *minutiae used to make identifications. Fingerprints are formed *in utero* and do not change throughout the lifespan except for expansion due to growth. They are also unique—even identical twins do not have the same fingerprints.

firearms Weapons that exploit expanding gases created by a *propellant to expel a projectile from the barrel of the weapon at high speed. Modern firearms include pistols or handguns, rifles, shotguns, automatic and semi-automatic weapons, homemade firearms, and hobby guns. Pistols are smaller guns designed to be fired with one hand and include the revolver and semi-automatic pistols, often erroneously called automatics. True automatics fire continuously as long as the trigger is pulled. Semi-automatic guns exploit gas pressure and springs to eject the spent cartridge, load a new one, and cock the weapon for the next shot, but a separate trigger pull is required to fire the next cartridge. Homemade weapons are usually small handguns that carry few or one shot and have been referred to as 'zip guns' and 'Saturday Night Specials'. Hobbyists typically own smooth bore guns with round projectiles (ball shot) and *black powder.

Firearms analysis focuses on *class characteristics and individualized patterns of markings on *bullets and *cartridge cases. Modern guns all have rifled barrels, meaning that a series of grooves (*see* LANDS AND GROOVES) are machined into the barrel in a spiralling pattern. When the bullet is forced over these lands and grooves, spin is imparted to the bullet, which stabilizes the trajectory and greatly increases accuracy over smooth bore weapons. This contact creates distinctive *striation patterns on the bullet that can later be matched to the weapon. The striations are usually unique to one gun based on the way the gun is manufactured and used. The primary tool of firearms examination is the *comparison microscope. *See also* GODDARD, CALVIN.

fire load The amount of flammable material that is available in a given place such as a structure or an aircraft. Fire load is typically reported in units of BTU/ft^2.

firing pin impression Small marks created in the *primer by the impact of the firing pin. The action of pulling the trigger of a firearm causes the firing pin to strike the primer,

The interior of the barrel of a modern firearm. Here a semi-automatic pistol is rifled to impart spin to the bullet.

which consists of a tiny amount of a shock sensitive explosive. Ignition of the primer in turn ignites the *propellant causing a rapid build-up of gases behind the bullet. The pressure drives the bullet down the barrel and out toward the target. The surface of the primer struck by the firing pin is relatively soft metal, which can pick up the pattern on the surface of the firing pin. Either as a result of the original machining or through use and wear, the markings on the surface of the firing pin will become unique.

first order reaction A process or chemical reaction in which the rate of the reaction depends only on one reactant. Many metabolic reactions are first order. The generic equation governing first order reactions is:

$$\ln C_t = -kt + \ln C_0$$

Where C_0 is the initial concentration of a compound or analyte; C_t is the concentration at a time (t) that has elapsed since the initial condition, and k is the rate constant associated with the reaction or process.

Firing pin impressions as viewed through a comparison microscope

first pass metabolism Metabolism of a drug or other ingested
substance that occurs in the liver after oral ingestion. Losses due to first
pass metabolism play a significant role in determining the *bioavailability
of drugs that are swallowed.

first responder The first person or persons to arrive at a crime scene
in an official capacity. This could be a police officer, fireman, or medical
personnel. The first responders typically are the ones that would call for
law enforcement and crime scene personnel once it is recognized that a
criminal act may be involved.

flashover A phenomenon that may occur if a fire is contained within
a room or other area and becomes hot enough to bring all materials in
that room to ignition temperature at nearly the same time. Flashover
results as these materials catch fire, causing rapid spread.

flash point The temperature at which a liquid will give off enough
vapour to form an ignitable mixture. For gasoline, the flash point is –50
°F/–46 °C. The National Fire Protection Association (NFPA) defines a
flammable liquid as one with a flash point of less than 140 °F/60 °C.

float glass Glass that is made by pouring molten glass over liquid tin (Sn), where it is allowed to cool and solidify, producing a flat glass. The infusion of small amounts of tin into the glass can be useful in identifying a sample as float glass since the residual tin will fluoresce when exposed to ultraviolet light.

flow cell In an instrument such as an *HPLC or *capillary electrophoresis, a small cell in which liquid is directed for analysis using a form of *spectroscopy. The flow cell is designed to allow for sufficient sample to be interrogated while the flow continues.

fluorescein A reagent used as a *presumptive test for blood that works similarly to *luminol. It is used most commonly to visualize stains not visible to the eye, such as when a scene has been cleaned. Fluorescein is used in conjunction with an *alternative light source (ALS) that produces fluorescence.

fluorescence Emission of *electromagnetic energy at a lower energy than that which was absorbed. When atoms or molecules absorb electromagnetic energy of the appropriate wavelength, the energy that is absorbed can be used to promote the electrons into what is called an excited state. When the electrons decay back to their original ground state, energy is emitted. In the case of fluorescence, the energy is emitted in the form of electromagnetic energy that is the same wavelength or longer (lower energy) than the excitation energy. This emission of energy is called fluorescence, and it ceases as soon as the excitation energy source is turned off. If the emission continues after the source is turned off, the phenomenon is called phosphorescence, familiar to many in the form of glow-in-the-dark watches. Fluorescence can be used to classify and identify many materials of interest to the forensic scientist and can be performed using techniques called spectrofluorimetry or using fluorescence microscopes.

fluorescence microscopy A form of microscopy in which an excitation source such as a UV lamp is situated in a standard light microscope. Specimens such as currency and fibres will often *fluoresce under these conditions.

fluorescent polarization immunoassay (FPIA) A type of *immunoassay in which degree of polarization of plane *polarized light passing through the media is altered as a result of binding of a labelled drug molecule. A common method is based on the fluorescent dye *fluorescein, which can bind to many drug molecules. The dye absorbs light at 485 nm and emits it in the range of ~535–50 nm. If the bound pair of the fluorescein and the drug are immobilized, the emitted light will be proportionally more polarized (less random) because the individual emissions from bound materials can only come from one orientation. If the labelled drug is not bound into a fixed position, the molecules will be in free motion within the solution and will be emitting light in random directions. As a result, the emitted light will be proportionally less polarized with more unbound material.

focal length The distance between the principal focus point and the lens as measured from the geometric centre of the lens.

follicle The small cavity in the skin in which a hair is anchored. The hair grows out of the hair follicle.

footwear impression *See* SHOE IMPRESSIONS.

forensically clean A term used in *computer forensics investigations to indicate that digital media (such as a hard drive or CD) have been erased and that all residual data and traces have been removed, including viruses and other malicious software.

forensic copy In forensic computing investigations, an exact, bit-for-bit copy of media such as a hard disk drive or CD. Because all bits are copied, even those not used for current data storage, this copy represents an exact replica of the evidentiary media. *See also* DISK MIRRORING.

Forensic Science Services (FSS) Until recently, the main provider of forensic services in the United Kingdom (England, Ireland, Wales, and Scotland). The FSS, part of the Home Office of the UK government, was established in 1991 and consolidated several forensic laboratories throughout England and Wales under the umbrella of a private company. The Metropolitan Police Laboratory (city of London) was merged into the FSS in 1996.

Fourier transform A mathematical series that is used to express a curve as a sum of sine and cosine terms. The Fourier transform, coupled to a device called a *Michelson interferometer, is the base of **Fourier transform infrared spectroscopy** (FTIR). Mirror movements create a series of waves that undergo periodic constructive interference and destructive interference before reaching the sample. Although computationally intensive and complex, application of the Fourier transform allows the resulting signal curve to be decomposed into signals at individual wavelengths and an infrared spectrum. FTIR offers many advantages over traditional instruments including speed and greater sensitivity. FTIR is the predominant type of infrared spectroscopy used in forensic science.

free base In drug molecules with one or more basic *ionizable centres, the unprotonated form B versus the protonated form BH$^+$.

frequency **1.** The rate of occurrence in a population of a genetically controlled trait or characteristic. For example, the frequency of the A blood group is approximately 43 per cent of the population. The other common usage of frequency in forensic science is related to *DNA typing.

2. The frequency of electromagnetic energy is defined as the number of waves that pass a given point in space per second. The higher the frequency, the greater the energy. Frequency is related to wavelength and the speed of light in a vacuum by the equation $c = \lambda \upsilon$ where c = the speed of light, λ is the wavelength, and υ is frequency. The units of frequency are Hz (sec^{-1}).

3. Data such as infrared spectrum can be expressed in the frequency domain rather than the time domain by using the Fourier transform algorithm.

friction ridge Skin surfaces that have ridges that provide friction to increase gripping power. In humans, these surfaces are the soles of feet, palms of the hands, and fingers. These form patterns such as whorls etc. for classification.

Froehde reagent A *presumptive test in drug analysis that is most often used to detect the presence of LSD. It consists of a solution of molybdic acid and sulphuric acid, and it will turn an olive greenish to blue-green colour in the presence of LSD. Froehde's reagent can also be used to indicate the presence of heroin (purple to olive green colours), mescaline (yellow to greenish colour), and psilocybin.

Frye decision A court ruling handed down in 1923 by the United States Supreme Court that has greatly influenced how scientific evidence and expert witness testimony is admitted and used in that country. This ruling led to criteria referred to as 'general acceptance' that governed the admissibility of scientific evidence in many jurisdictions. General acceptance is referred to as the Frye standard.

fuel/air ratio The ratio between a fuel such as natural gas (CH_4) and air, typically reported as a weight per cent value. The fuel/air ratio must be in the proper range to support combustion. If there is insufficient fuel, the mixture is lean and if the mixture has too much fuel, it is considered rich. A **fuel-air explosion** can result when an ignition source is introduced into an environment in which the fuel/air ratio can support combustion.

function testing The process of testing a firearm to determine if it is in working condition and if there are any problems or malfunctions present.

Gabor filters

Gabor filters A mathematical algorithm used to enhance digital images of latent fingerprints. These filters treat the patterns of ridges and valleys in localized areas of a fingerprint image as a wave pattern (a sine wave) that can be treated with filters designed for signal processing. Information regarding the number of features and directionality can be recovered. These filters are typically one step in a multistage analysis of the latent print image.

Galton, Francis (1822–1911) An English researcher in heredity and a pioneer of early fingerprint studies. He was also the cousin of

Taille 1ᵐ		Long⁻	Pied g.		N⁰ de cl.	Âge de
Voûte	dr. Tête.	Larg⁻	Médius g.	l'Iris g.	Auriᵗ	né le
Enverg 1ᵐ	Oreille	Long⁻	Auricᵗ g.	de	Périᵗ	a
Buste 0,		Larg⁻	Coudée g.	Coul⁻	Partᵗ	dept
						Âge appᵗ

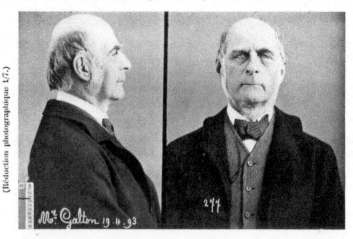

(Réduction photographique 1/7.)

Mᵉ Galton 19.4.93

277

Front.	Inclin⁻	Sex.	Racine (cavité)	Oreille droite.	Bord o. s. p. f.	Barbe	Coul⁻ (pigᵗ
	Haut⁻		Dos Base		Lob. c. a. m. d.	Cheveux	'sang⁻
	Larg⁻		Haut⁻ Saillie. Larg⁻		A. trg. i. p. r. d.	Car Teint.	
	Partᵗ		l l		Pli. f. s. b. E	Autres traits caractéristiques :	
			Partᵗ		Part.	Sigᵗ dressé par M.	

Francis Galton. The card was produced by *Bertillon, who was a contemporary of Galton's.

Charles Darwin. He is credited with developing the first classification system for fingerprints, which was adopted by the British government as an adjunct to the *Bertillon system of body measurements and photographs that was then the primary method of identification of criminals. In 1892, he published the influential book *Finger Prints*, which helped bring fingerprinting to the forefront of criminal identification. It is still considered to be one of the primary references in the field. The book was notable for stating the fundamental principles that fingerprints are unique and unchanging. Galton was also the first proponent of classification using the basic patterns of the loop, arch, and whorl.

Galton model The first attempt to address statistically the rates of occurrence of different fingerprint (friction ridge) patterns and, in particular, *minutiae. The model was proposed by Francis *Galton in 1892 and, although never widely adopted, was the first step in a continuing discussion concerning the probabilities associated with a given fingerprint. In his approach, he divided the print into regions which were then analysed individually and independently of the other regions.

gas chromatography (GC) One of the key instrumental systems used in forensic toxicology, seized drug analysis, and the analysis of fire debris evidence. GC is a separation technique that is used as a sample inlet to a detector; the types of detectors commonly used in forensic science include *mass spectrometers (MS), flame ionization (FID) and *nitrogen-phosphorous (NPD). The combination of GC with a detector is an example of a *hyphenated technique and would be written as GC-MS for example. In GC, a heated inert carrier gas such as helium, hydrogen, or nitrogen flows over a solid phase that compounds within the gas flow will interact with to various degrees. The more a compound interacts with the stationary phase, the longer it will stay in the column. This is an example of selective partitioning, which is the basis of all chromatographic separations. There are dozens of commercially available solid phase columns, and the selection of a column for a particular analysis depends primarily on the polarity of the analytes. In general, the separation of polar analytes such as alcohols or ketones requires a more polar column while separation of non-polar analytes such as hydrocarbons seen in *arson cases requires a more non-polar stationary phase.

In older GC systems, the stationary phase was coated on tiny beads and packed into glass columns with diameters of approximately 5-10 millimetres and lengths of between 2 and 4 metres, wound into a coil. The heated gas flowed over the beads, allowing contact between sample molecules in the gaseous mobile phase and the stationary phase. Called 'packed column chromatographs', these instruments were widely used for drug, toxicology, and arson analysis. In the 1980s, packed column chromatography began to give way to capillary column GC, in which the liquid phase is coated onto the inner walls of thin capillary tube usually on the order of 0.32mm in diameter and anywhere from 15 to 100 metres long, also wound into a coil. Capillary column chromatography represented a significant advance in the field and greatly improved the ability of columns to separate the multiple components found in complex drug and arson samples.

GC-FID systems are used in forensic science for *blood alcohol analysis and for the analysis of fire debris for accelerants such as petrol (gasoline). GC-NPD is used occasionally for the screening of drug and toxicological samples for the detection of basic drugs or metabolites which contain an amine group. The most common GC system in forensic laboratories are GC-MS instruments which are used for drug analysis, toxicology, and trace evidence analysis. The primary limitation of GC is that the analytes must be volatile at instrumental temperatures (typically –40 to 400ºC) and stable under high temperature conditions. These criteria eliminate many compounds from consideration, including explosives such as TNT and drugs such as psilocybin. For these compounds, *high performance liquid chromatography (HPLC) is used.

gauge A method used to identify the size of a *shotgun barrel. Gauge originally referred to the number of lead pellets having the same diameter of the barrel that would be required to obtain one pound of lead. Thus, the larger the diameter of the barrel, the larger the pellets, and the fewer would be needed to make a pound. Thus, a 12-gauge shotgun has a larger barrel diameter (0.730 inches) than a 16-gauge (0.670 inches). There is one exception, the 0.410 gauge shotgun in which the barrel diameter is 0.410 inches. This convention is similar to the calibre naming convention used in handguns and rifles.

Gaussian error A term sometimes used to refer to *random error due to the typical Gaussian distribution followed by such errors.

GC-MS (GCMS, GC/MS, GCMSD) Abbreviations used for instruments coupling a gas chromatograph (GC) with a *mass spectrometer. GC-MS systems are fundamental in many toxicology and forensic chemical analyses. The gas chromatograph serves to separate a complex mixture into individual components (in most cases) and the mass spectrometer can often provide definitive identification and quantitation of these components. In GC-MS, identification is based on two factors—the retention time of the compound and the mass spectrum—and in forensic practice, definitive identification usually requires analysis of a trustworthy independent standard as confirmation.

gel A supporting media for electrophoresis. Gels can be made of agarose, a derivative of seaweed, or polyacrylamide. Gels are structured materials that can absorb large amounts of water and thus electrolytes and ions that are dissolved in the water. The presence of water and electrolytes allows the gel to conduct electricity.

general acceptance A term used to describe one method of determining the admissibility of scientific evidence and expert testimony. In the United States, general acceptance usually refers to the *Frye decision (1923) in which the court ruled that if a technique is generally accepted by the relevant scientific community, it is admissible.

General Electric v Joiner A court case in the United States that relates to the admissibility of scientific evidence and expert witness testimony. The case, decided in 1997, was a civil case in which an employee of General Electric contended that he contracted cancer as a result of his work. The ruling solidified the concept of the judge as the 'gatekeeper' who is ultimately responsible for determining the admissibility of scientific evidence and testimony. Furthermore, the decision emphasized that the evidence presented must be relevant to the matter in hand as well as reliable.

genetic markers and genetic marker systems Prior to the ascendancy of DNA in forensic biology, the typing of genetic marker systems was one of the foundational techniques used in forensic *serology. To be of use in forensic applications, a genetic marker system must exhibit *polymorphism, i.e. there exist variants within the population that have known frequencies and that can be typed using techniques such as gel *electrophoresis. The *ABO blood group system is an example of a genetic marker system, but many more were applied in forensic serology. To be useful in forensic work, a genetic marker system should have several variants that subdivide the population into several smaller groups, the more the better. Furthermore, the system must be robust and must resist degradation long enough to be typed in bloodstains that may be old and/or in very poor condition. This last requirement limited the widespread typing and use of many genetic marker systems. Although fairly easy to type in fresh whole blood, many of the systems are fragile and could not be routinely and reliably typed in stains.

Blood can be subdivided into different fractions, all of which contain genetic marker systems. After centrifuging, blood separates into serum and the cellular components. Serum, a yellowish liquid, contains serum blood group systems such as haptoglobin (Hp) and group-specific components (Gc) that are polymorphic. Within the cellular component, white blood cells (leucocytes) contain the human leucocyte antigen system (HLA) that contains many different factors and types. Both the serum blood group systems and HLA system were difficult to type in stains and were not routinely used in forensic casework.

Unlike red blood cells, the white blood cells have a nucleus, which is the source of DNA used in *DNA typing. The thirteen loci that are usually typed in current practice can also be classified as genetic markers since they are inherited and polymorphic. Red blood cells are the richest source of non-DNA genetic marker systems that were once widely used in forensic serology. These cells (erythrocytes) have on their surface the antigens that make up blood group systems such as ABO and Rh. Within the cell are found the isoenzyme systems such as phosphoglucomutase (PGM) and esterase D (ESD) as well as variations of the haemoglobin molecule. The ABO blood group and isoenzymes were the most used in casework.

genetics The study of heredity, the fundamental unit of which is the gene. Genes are encoded in DNA, and the place in which a particular gene is found is called its locus. Multiple sites are called loci. Different forms of the same gene are called alleles. Human genes are found on 46 chromosomes organized into 23 pairs. Within those pairs, one chromosome originated from the mother, the other from the father. Many of the genetic characteristics of interest in forensic science are co-dominant, meaning that the allele from both the mother and the father is expressed. For example, the ABO blood group system is a genetic marker system with the types A, B, AB, and O. The A type is a result of AA alleles. The observable, measurable way in which any gene is expressed is called the phenotype, and so the phenotype of AA is A in this example (disregarding sub-types). When such variations occur at a given locus, it is referred to as a polymorphism ('many forms') since variants exist within the population. Population genetics, the study of the relative frequencies of different types or variations within a given population (such as Caucasian, African-American, and so on) is of critical importance in interpreting the result of forensic DNA analysis.

genetics, forensic The application of genetics to forensic science. Most often this term refers to population genetics, *frequency estimates, and issues related to *DNA typing.

genotype The actual alleles found at a gene locus, as compared to the phenotype, which is how the trait is expressed. For example, the *ABO blood group system is a *genetic marker system with the types A, B, AB, and O. The A type is a result of AA alleles and the genotype is AA. The observable, measurable way in which any gene is expressed is called the phenotype, and so the phenotype of this person with the AA genotype is A, since he or she will have A antigens on the surface of the red blood cells and will have Type A blood (disregarding sub-types). Similarly, a person whose genotype is AO will have a phenotype of A. The concept of genotype and phenotype is not directly applicable to DNA typing results since the variants do not code for any traits (as currently understood).

geology, forensic The application of the geological sciences and primarily the study of soils in the forensic context. Soil is one of the most common forms of transfer evidence and was recognized early on as a potentially valuable source of information. Hans *Gross and Edmund *Locard, pioneers of early forensic science, were among the first to exploit soil evidence in linking an individual to a particular place. Early work and explorations of forensic geology were reported in the middle of the 19th century, but the first documented cases are generally credited to Georg Popp of Frankfurt, Germany. In the early 1900s, Popp used soil analysis, and particularly evidence found in layers of soil, to link suspects to crime scenes. This is still one of the primary roles of the forensic geologist. The analysis of soil is similar to the analysis of glass in that it relies heavily on the measurement of physical and optical properties. Perhaps the most important tool for the forensic geologist is microscopy using stereomicroscopes, polarizing light microscopes (PLM), and scanning electron microscopy/energy dispersive X-ray instruments (SEM/EDX).

Gettler, Alexander O. (1883–1968) A key figure in the development of forensic toxicology in the United States. Gettler was hired by the Medical Examiner Dr Charles Norris and he proceeded to establish an analytical laboratory for the office. He made significant advances in areas such as the detection of poisons, identification of drowning as a cause of death, and alcohol poisoning.

GHB (GBL) (Gamma hydroxybutyrate) A substance classified as a predator drug or *date rape drug. It was at one time used as a body-building supplement but was pulled off health food store shelves in 1990. Easily synthesized, it has been abused in much the same way as *rohypnol. Low doses relieve tension and promote relaxation, but higher doses produce sleep (sometimes suddenly) and nausea, with alcohol enhancing these effects. The drug can exist as an open chain (GHB) or as a closed ring (the lactone form, GBL), depending on pH. GHB can be difficult to detect because it clears rapidly from the system and is found naturally in the body at parts-per-million levels.

Gamma hydroxybutryate GHB

Gamma butrylactone GBL

The two forms of GHB

glass analysis Glass is an amorphous solid lacking the rigid, ordered crystal structure of materials such as table salt. In the strictest sense, glass is considered a viscous solid or a super-cooled liquid rather than a true solid. Because of this lack of order and pattern at the molecular level, glass breaks in random patterns and has other unique properties that make it such a valuable and widely used material. The most common ingredient in most glass is quartz sand, SiO_2. Soda lime glass, of which windows are usually made, has additives of Na_2O, CaO, MgO, and Al_2O_3, all metal oxides. Different additives are used to impart different physical characteristics to the glass. Coloured glasses are made by adding oxides from the transition metal family. Red glass is made by adding cadmium or selenium, while adding cobalt compounds can create blue glass. Leaded glass used in fine crystal contains high concentrations of lead oxide (PbO). Tempered or safety glass is created by subjecting the glass to thermal cycling during the manufacturing process, resulting in a glass that breaks into small squares rather than into sharp shards. Windshields are yet another type of specialty glass made by sandwiching glass on both sides of a plastic sheeting material. Most glass made today is called float glass because of the way it is manufactured. Earlier processes used blowers or rollers to mould molten glass into flat sheets. Float glass is made by pouring the molten material onto a bath of melted tin, resulting in a very smooth surface that needs little or no additional polishing.

Broken glass is frequently encountered as evidence in burglaries or violent crimes. The process of breaking glass creates a shower of particles both in the forward and reverse direction, which may be transferred to the person breaking the glass if they are standing close enough. In many (but not all) cases, it is possible to determine from what direction the glass was broken. An impact in glass produces two kinds of fractures, radial (radiating out from the point of impact) and concentric (forming a circle around the impact). The patterns found in the cross-sections of these fractures can indicate from which direction the force was applied. The lines created in the glass, called ridges, conchoidal lines, or Wallner lines, show distinctive patterns depending on whether the fractures from which they are collected are concentric or radial. If there are multiple impacts in the same pane of glass, the sequence of events can be deduced from the fracture patterns. Existing fractures from the first impact act as barriers to fractures created by the second impact and these abrupt terminations are easily identifiable. Shattering of glass by heat creates a distinctive and different fracture pattern characterized by wavy smooth cracks.

Currently, the only way to unequivocally link two fragments of glass to a common source is by the process of physical matching. Since glass breaks randomly, each breakage is considered to be a unique event. As a result, if a fragment of glass such as a piece of a broken window or headlight can be fitted back into the original like a puzzle piece, that fit individualizes the glass and proves that it could only come from that source. The two most common physical parameters used to characterize glass samples are measurements of the *refractive index (RI) and density.

To determine the RI, two methods are used. The first is to place the glass in a series of oils of known refractive index and to observe the fragment microscopically. When the RI of the oil matches that of the glass, the edges of the glass will seem to disappear from the field of view. The other method is an automated variation of this procedure in which the glass is placed in an oil and heated as the image is captured or viewed. Because refractive index is a function of density and thus temperature, the RI of the glass can be calculated from the temperature at which it was no longer visible. These instruments are referred to as GRIM units for glass refractive index measurement. The other approach to the chemical analysis of glass is based on elemental analysis using X-ray spectroscopy and, more commonly, *inductively coupled plasma (ICP) techniques such as *ICP-MS.

glass transition temperature (T$_g$) The temperature at which the amorphous regions of a semi-crystalline material such as a synthetic polymer fibre change to a more fluid, amorphous state. Molecules that were previously held in place acquire some mobility and the material becomes softer and more rubbery.

GLO *See* GLYOXALASE I.

glucoronidation The process linking a xenobiotic substance to glucoronic acid to form (typically) a more water soluble substance. Many drugs form **glucoronides** and are excreted in this form. The process of glucoronidation occurs principally in the liver and is mediated by enzymes. The reaction is a type of biotransformation and is considered to be Phase II *metabolism.

glue lifts An informal term describing the development and recovery of *latent fingerprints using cyanoacrylate (Super Glue).

glyoxalase I (GLO) An *isoenzyme system with three common types, 1, 2-1, and 2.

Goddard, Calvin (1891–1955) An American physician and gun enthusiast credited with early achievements in forensic firearm examinations using microscopy. Goddard was a retired army physician and professed gun enthusiast who had risen to the directorship of the Johns Hopkins Hospital in Baltimore, Maryland. In 1925, he joined the Bureau of Forensic Ballistics, which owed its existence to the famed *Stielow case, which had played out a decade earlier. Goddard worked briefly with Charles *Waite at the Bureau before Waite's premature death. Goddard's next famous case arose in the late 1920s, the *Sacco and Vanzetti case in which his testimony was critical in obtaining a conviction. Because of his growing reputation, Goddard was called to examine evidence of the infamous St Valentine's Day Massacre in Chicago in 1929. During the coroner's grand jury inquest, he was able to show that two Thompson submachine guns had killed all the murdered men. Some of the jurors in that case later raised money to establish a forensic laboratory at Northwestern University in Evanston, Illinois, called the Scientific Crime Detection Laboratory. It was not the first forensic laboratory formed but one of the most influential. Goddard served as the first director and stayed until 1932. The laboratory moved to Chicago and became the Chicago Police Department laboratory in 1938. Goddard also assisted the FBI in establishing a firearms analysis capability at their new lab, inaugurated in 1932.

good laboratory practice (GLP) A series of guidelines for laboratory analysis designed to ensure the goodness and reliability of the results produced. Originally designed for use in environmental, food, and pharmaceutical analyses, the concept of GLP has expanded to cover any type of laboratory analysis. Although specific GLP guidelines vary among disciplines and laboratories, they generally cover aspects such as personnel training and testing, laboratory procedures and protocols, documentation, facilities and equipment, calibration and standardization, and quality assurance/quality control (QA/QC).

Gradwhol, Rutherford B. (1877–1959) A physician and founding member of the American Academy of Forensic Sciences who worked in St Louis, Missouri. He served as the director of the St Louis Police Laboratory and was an important figure in the professionalization of forensic science in the United States. The AAFS's highest award is named for Gradwohl.

gram negative/gram positive A method of classifying bacteria based on its response to a specific staining technique. Gram-negative bacteria will not hold a stain of crystal violet when rinsed with alcohol or acetone while a gram-positive bacterium does. The test was named after Danish physician that developed it.

Gravelle, Philip O. (1891–1955) An American and contemporary of Dr Calvin *Goddard who worked with firearms evidence. He played an important role in extending the use of the *comparison microscope to firearms examination. He, along with Goddard, worked with Charles *Waite in the Bureau of Forensic Ballistics in New York.

Green River Killer A prolific serial killer, Gary Ridgeway, who was convicted of 48 murders in the Seattle, Washington, area from the 1980s to 1998. He targeted prostitutes and other high risk women. The case spanned the time in which *DNA typing was developed and ultimately DNA evidence was critical in the arrest, conviction, and linking of the crimes. Ridgeway was interviewed by police in 1984, early in the spree, and took and passed a polygraph test. It was not until 2001 that DNA testing was applied to evidence, including a sample Ridgeway had provided.

grid search One of several methods that can be used to search a relatively large area of a crime scene. To execute a grid search, a rectangle of known dimensions is laid out with gradations along the x and y axes. The length and orientation of each axis is recorded and documented. This creates an xy (*rectangular) coordinate system that can be used to establish the exact location of any evidence found using *triangulation. On some occasions, a triangular grid is used.

Griess, Johann Peter (1829–88) A German chemist who described a type of reaction called diazotization in which an amine compound (one containing an $-NH_2$ group) reacts with nitrite ion (NO_2^-) under acidic conditions to yield diazonium salts that are often highly coloured. The reaction can continue on to coupling reactions that produce highly coloured products. This reaction is the basis of the *Griess test used for the detection of nitrates and nitrites.

Griess test A presumptive test used to detect the residuals of gunpowder or explosives. The test detects the nitrite ion (NO_2^-) and can be modified to also detect the nitrate ion (NO_3^-). Reagents used in the test are napthylamine in methanol, sulphanilic acid in acetic acid, and zinc metal. Nitrates and nitrites are produced whenever a gun is fired, and nitrate is a breakdown product of nitroglycerin, an ingredient found in many explosives and in smokeless powder used as a propellant in ammunition. Thus, this test was at one time widely used in an attempt to determine if a suspect had recently fired a gun or had handled explosives containing nitroglycerin.

grooves **1.** In firearms, a feature (along with *lands) machined into the barrel of a rifle or pistol that imparts spin to the bullet. The pattern of striations produced on the bullet by the lands and grooves are characteristic of that weapon.

2. In a tyre, grooves are part of the tread design.

Gross, Hans (1847–1915) An Austrian lawyer and self-taught forensic generalist. He coined the label 'criminalistics' for comparative analytical science as he applied it. He was an investigator for the legal system in Graz, Austria. Gross viewed forensic science holistically and believed that experts from diverse fields would contribute to the analysis of physical evidence and solving crimes. He understood the value of biological evidence, soil, dust, and many other types of transfer and trace evidence. One of his most important contributions was to the literature of forensic science. He first penned a compilation of scientific methods and techniques translated as *Handbook for Examining Magistrates* to share what he had learned with other investigators. It was significant in that it was the first forensic book to include many topics—geology, chemistry, blood, pathology, toxicology, and others—in one volume. In 1893, he published the first textbook in forensic science, which was translated into English under the title of *Criminal Investigation*, and he started a journal called *Kriminologie*, which is still published.

group-specific antigens and group-specific component (Gc) A *genetic marker system found in the serum of blood. Gc is

produced by the liver and shows variations in the populations with the primary types of 1, 2-1, and 2. Type 1 is the most common, with about 51 per cent of the population showing it. Type 2-1 is found in about 41 per cent, with the remainder being type 2. Typing can be accomplished using *electrophoresis and *isoelectric focusing.

guaiacum test   One of the first presumptive tests for blood developed. It relied on guaiacum (a resin isolated from trees) in combination with hydrogen peroxide. If a stain turned blue when treated with these reagents, it was considered a positive result indicative of blood.

guanine (G)   One of four *nucleotide bases that comprise DNA and RNA. Because of its molecular structure, guanine will associate with cytosine (C), and the two are referred to as complements of each other.

Guide to the Uncertainty of Measurement (GUM)   A document published by the Bureau International des Poids et Mésures (BIPM) and created by an international working group, the Joint Committee for Guides in Metrology. The purpose of the *GUM* is to recommend methods to estimate the uncertainty of quantitative measurements. The guide is generic, but is increasingly being applied in quantitative forensic measurements.

(⊕) SEE WEB LINKS

• An internationally accepted publication that describes how uncertainty can be estimated for a variety of measurements and tests.

guncotton (nitrocellulose (NC))   A highly flammable material created by treating cotton with nitric and sulphuric acids, resulting in nitration of hydroxyl groups on the glucose units in the cellulose. NC is typically 12.5 per cent or more nitrogen by weight. It is an ingredient in modern *propellants.

gunpowder   A generic term used to describe the *propellants used in ammunition. There are two kinds of powder available, both classified as a *low explosive, and the term gunpowder has been applied to both. Black powder, the original gunpowder, consists of 75 per cent potassium nitrate (KNO_3 or saltpetre), 10 per cent charcoal, and 15 per cent sulphur. Because of the smoke produced, use in firearms ended in the 1800s, but black powder is still available for hobby guns and is used in applications such as fuses. Smokeless powder is used in modern firearms and consists of nitrated cotton or nitrocellulose (single base) or nitroglycerin combined with nitrocellulose (double base). 'Gunpowder' usually refers to smokeless powder because it is the modern standard, but the term can and often is used to describe black powder, particularly in a historical context.

gunshot residue (GSR)   The residue that escapes from a gun when it is fired. GSR is considered a type of transfer evidence and can be detected using chemical tests and instrumental analyses. The residue comes mostly from the primer, which is part of the cartridge containing the bullet and propellant in modern ammunition. Particles of unburned powder are also part of the residue. The most common elements found in GSR are lead (Pb), antimony (Sb), and barium (Ba), and this combination of elements is telling. When a particle is found to contain these three elements, it is almost certainly gunshot residue. Other elements that can be found include copper (Cu), aluminium (Al), iron (Fe), and zinc (Zn). Chemicals in the propellant (usually smokeless powder) that can be found in GSR are nitrate ions (NO_3^-), nitrite ions (NO_2^-), nitrocellulose, and nitroglycerin. During the firing process, other compounds can form between metal elements and atoms such as carbon, nitrogen, oxygen, and hydrogen, which are produced as a result of the combustion. Thus, GSR is chemically complex, particularly at the trace level. The size of the GSR particles and their chemical make-up will vary depending on the type of weapon, powder, primers, and projectiles used. The particles themselves as well as the individual elements and the chemical compounds in GSR can be detected using chemical, microscopic, and instrumental methods of analysis. Presumptive tests for GSR that have been and are used include the Griess test, the diphenylamine test, dermal nitrate test, Walker test, and sodium rhodizonate.

haem The non-protein part of the haemoglobin molecule, the part that carries the oxygen molecule. Each haem group can complex one O_2 molecule, for a total of four O_2 per haemoglobin. The haem group can act as a catalyst for oxidation/reduction (redox) reactions and this is the basis of presumptive tests for blood.

haematin test *See* TEICHMANN TEST.

haematoma A pooling or collection of blood that has leaked out of a blood vessel. It can be manifested externally as a bruise and can cause significant swelling. A subdural haematoma and the accompanying swelling are frequently seen as a cause of death involving blows to the head.

haemochromogen test *See* TAKAYAMA TEST.

haemoglobin (Hb) The predominant protein in red blood cells that is used to transport oxygen from the lungs to the tissues. The haemoglobin molecule is made up of four protein subunits (the globin portion), two alphas (α) and two betas (β), and for this reason, haemoglobin is classified as a tetramer. Each of the four subunits possesses a haem unit with an iron ion (Fe^{2+}) at the centre, and it is the haem units that bind to the oxygen, four per haemoglobin molecule. Presumptive tests and microcrystalline confirmatory tests for blood used in forensic science rely on reactions with the haemoglobin molecule. There are also variants of haemoglobin that can be typed using electrophoresis and isoelectric focusing techniques.

hair An animal fibre characterized by a scaly cuticle that is easily recognizable when viewed under a microscope. The primary method (and often the sole method) of hair analysis is visual examination. Hair is produced below the surface of the skin in the follicle, and the base of the hair comprises living tissue. As the hair grows and reaches the surface, the cells die and become keratinized. Keratin is a strong protein that is found in high concentrations in the fingernails and imparts to the hair durability and resistance to degradation and chemical attack. Inside the follicle is the root where the living portions are found, along with the bulb and sheath tissue. The follicle is associated with an oil gland called the sebaceous gland.

Hair possesses scales that protrude from the outer cuticle, with the unattached 'flap' of the scale pointing toward the tip of the hair. On the surface, the scales form an irregular pattern most often compared to shingles on a roof. The shine of hair is related to the position of the cuticles and how loose they are on the cuticle. Inside the cuticle (the cortex), hair consists of fibrils of protein arranged in a stacked arrangement of an individual protein strand enclosed in a protofibril, which in turn is encased in a microfibril and then a macrofibril. A tubular structure called the medulla runs down the middle of the hair, and it may be thick, thin, continuous, or discontinuous. Pigment granules are responsible for colour and are scattered throughout the cortex. Except for true blondes and redheads, there are only three colours of pigments found in human hair: yellow, black, and brown. The cortical fusi are void spaces within the cortex that are concentrated nearer the root end.

Individual hair growth occurs in three stages (*anagen, *catagen, and *telogen) independent of neighbouring follicles. The structure and appearance of the root (its morphology) can be used to determine at what phase a hair was lost. Likewise, if a hair is forcibly removed, which is often the case in violent crimes, portions of the follicular tissue will adhere to it and can be identified microscopically. Hair differs in appearance depending on what part of the body it is from, an important consideration since hair comparisons must be made based on hairs that come from the same area.

half-life ($t_{\frac{1}{2}}$) The amount of time required for one-half of the original amount of material to decay or otherwise change form. The term is used to describe radioactive decay and in relationship to metabolic reactions.

hallucinogen A drug or other psychoactive substance that produces hallucinogenic effects such as seeing things that are not present or hearing sounds that do not exist.*Marijuana is a hallucinogen as is *mescaline. At high doses, many stimulants become hallucinogenic.

hanging Death by means of asphyxia (loss of oxygen to the brain) caused by a noose or other ligature tightened by the body weight of the victim. The pressure of the noose quickly cuts off the blood flow to the brain, leading to the rapid onset of unconsciousness. The airway also closes, leading to death in a few minutes. This effect can be achieved without complete suspension, so people can die of hanging while kneeling or otherwise still in partial contact with the ground.

haploid cell A cell such as a sperm or an egg cell that contains only half of the organism's genetic material or one set of chromosomes.

haptoglobin (Hp) A serum blood group system and *genetic marker system. Prior to the ascendance of *DNA typing, this was one of the systems that could be typed in bloodstains using electrophoresis. There are three types of haptoglobin with 2-1 being the most common, found in approximately 40–50 per cent of the population depending on race. Type 1 is shown by about 20–30 per cent and type 2 by 20–35 per cent.

Hardy–Weinberg law A relationship used to estimate the frequencies of alleles (variants of a gene) and the resulting distribution of types within a population. It provides a statistical method to test frequencies and to provide estimates of the discriminating power of a given type. A coin flip provides a simple example.

Two consecutive flips of a coin mimic the combination of two genes (one from a mother and one from a father) to create a variant at the site of the gene (its locus). For any one toss, the probability of obtaining a heads (H) is 0.50, meaning that 50 per cent of the time, heads should appear. This is assigned to a variable labelled p. The variable q, the frequency of tails (T), is also 0.50 and p + q must always equal one. In terms of the Hardy–Weinberg law, this is expressed as $(p + q)^2$, and then by using a technique called a binomial expansion, the expression $p^2 + 2pq + q^2$ is obtained. This is the equation that can be used to estimate frequencies. If a coin is tossed twice, there are three possible outcomes: two heads (HH), one of each (HT), and two tails (TT). The equation can be used to estimate how often each combination is expected to occur. HH would correspond to p^2 or $0.50 \times 0.50 = 0.25$ or 25 per cent. This means that 25 per cent of the time, when a coin is flipped twice, a combination of HH should occur, and the same for TT. For one of each, the predicted frequency is $2 \times 0.50 \times 0.50$ (2pq) or 0.50, meaning that half the time, two flips will result in one of each. These are the frequencies expected assuming the coin tosses are completely random and the coin is not altered to favour heads or tails. This simple example can be extended to genetic marker systems and *DNA typing, except that population data is available for the actual frequency of types. A test called the chi-squared test is used to determine if this difference is significant.

hash A number that identifies a document. A hash mark is considered to be unique to one file and can thus be used for comparison and to detect alterations. The hash mark is generated by computer code called a hash function

hashish (hash oil) A potent derivative of *marijuana (*Cannibis sativa* L) that has a high concentration of the psychoactive ingredient, Δ^9 tetrahydrocannibinol (*THC). Hashish is a tarry substance that varies in colour from dark green to almost black. It is the resin of the marijuana plant that is often prepared by extracting the flowering tops with an alcohol. Like marijuana, hashish is classified as a hallucinogen.

headspace and headspace analysis Headspace is the void or empty space above a solid or liquid held in a sealed container. In a sealed container, the headspace will contain components that have evaporated out of the liquid in concentrations that correlate with the vapour pressure and *Henry's Law constant of the substance that is evaporating. Analysis of headspace can be utilized in cases where the analytes of interest are found in significant concentrations in the air about the liquid phase. The two predominant forensic applications of headspace analysis are for *blood alcohol (BAC) and the analysis of *accelerants in fire debris.

Both applications work on the same principles. The sealed sample container is heated gently and allowed to come to equilibrium. A needle is inserted through a septum and enters the headspace and a sample of the gas is withdrawn and introduced into an instrument, typically a *gas chromatograph (GC). This is an example of static headspace analysis; dynamic headspace methods are also used. In DHS, the gas above the liquid is swept out of the container and directed over a material that can trap the components contained in it. This technique is also known as purge-and-trap. In the analysis of fire debris, several variations of headspace sampling have been or are used including cold headspace, heated headspace with collection on a charcoal trap, collection of headspace vapours on a charcoal strip, and dynamic headspace with a charcoal trap.

hearsay Testimonial evidence from a witness that relates to events that the witness does not have personal knowledge of. Rather, the witness is testifying about something he or she heard another person say while that other person was not under oath. In a courtroom, if a witness is on the stand and asked a question such as 'What did Mr Jones say about that?' or 'What did you hear Mr Jones say about that?' the response the witness gives would be hearsay evidence. Hearsay evidence is usually inadmissible, but there are numerous exceptions to the hearsay rule including instances of expert witness testimony.

heat of combustion The heat that is released by an exothermic combustion reaction. The theoretical heat of combustion can be calculated from table values for bond energies or standard heats of formation; the quantity can also be measured experimentally. The actual heat released varies based on many factors including the balance of fuel to air.

heat of explosion The heat released during an explosion. This value can be estimated using models or measured experimentally. The actual heat of explosion depends on many factors including products created, their heat capacities, and the ratio of reactants.

heavy metals In forensic science, this term usually refers to metals that are also *poisons. In this context, the metals of interest include arsenic (As), lead (Pb), mercury (Hg), cadmium (Cd), bismuth (Bi), antimony (Sb), and thallium (Tl). Of these, arsenic is the best known as a poison—accidental, suicidal, and homicidal. Strictly speaking, it is classified as a metalloid or semi-metal in terms of chemical properties and behaviour. Antimony is also found in gunshot residue, and thallium is used in the electronics industry.

Heinrich, Edward Oscar (1881–1953) An American nicknamed the 'wizard of Berkeley'. He was noted for his contributions to crime scene investigation and forensic microscopy. He considered crime scene interpretation from a logical, cause-and-effect perspective. Heinrich was a physicist by profession but consulted widely in the area of forensic crime scene analysis and is generally credited with formulating the scientific underpinnings of crime scene analysis.

Helpern, Milton (1902–77) An American forensic pathologist who was the third person to hold the job of Chief Medical Examiner in the city of New York from 1954 to 1973. He was co-author of a textbook entitled *Legal Medicine and Toxicology*, published in 1937, considered to be one of the most important in the field published in the United States during the 20th century.

Henderson–Hasselbach equation An equation that is used to describe the concentrations of species in situations involving weak acids or weak bases. It can be used to design *buffer systems or to estimate the range at which a pH indicator will change colour. In forensic science, the most common use of the equation is in the area of *seized drug analysis and *toxicology. Here, the equation is used to select pH values at which drugs with *ionizable centres will be completely ionized or completely un-ionized. The equation generically is expressed as:

$$HA \rightleftharpoons H^+ + A^-$$
$$pH = pK_a + \log\frac{[A^-]}{[HA]}$$
$$pH = pK_a \pm 2.0$$

The top equation is a generic expression of an acid dissociating in water while the middle reaction is derived from the K_a expression. The bottom equation shows how it is frequently used. For example, assume an acidic drug has a *pKa value of 5.2; at a pH of 3.2, the drug will be predominantly in the HA form while at a pH of 7.2 and above, it will be in the ionized form. The factor of 2 arises from the log term and the assumption that if the concentration of one form is 100 times that of the other, that is sufficient for extraction and other purposes. The log of (1/100) is –2 and the log of (100/1) is 2, leading to the ± 2 term.

Henry, Sir Edward Richard (1851–1931) An English police officer who, like *Galton and *Vucetich, was a key figure in the early use of fingerprints in criminal investigations. He first employed them for identification purposes while he was the Inspector-General of Police in Bengal, India. Later, he became Commissioner of the Metropolitan Police in London (Scotland Yard) and in 1901 his fingerprint classification system was adopted. Modifications of the Henry system are still used throughout Europe and in the United States.

Henry's law An expression that describes the relationship between the solubility of a gas in a liquid as a function of pressure. The equation is written as:

$$K_H = \frac{[A]}{P_A}$$

in which K_H is called the Henry's law constant; [A] represents the concentration of gas A dissolved in a liquid and P_A represents the pressure of that gas over the liquid in question. At a set temperature, the value of K must remain the same, which means that if the pressure of a gas increases over a liquid (P_A increases), then the concentration of that gas dissolved in the liquid ([A]) must also increase. *See also* HEADSPACE AND HEADSPACE ANALYSIS.

Henry system A fingerprint classification system developed by Sir Edward *Henry. Based on a bin system, it classified sets of all ten fingerprints into smaller categories that made it easier to store and catalogue large numbers of fingerprints. A modified Henry system is still used in the United States and Europe, although searching is now done by computers such as those that are components of the *AFIS system.

heroin An *opiate and derivative of morphine that is highly addictive and widely abused. In the United States the word 'heroin' is used to refer to both the street drug and its active ingredient diamorphine, also called diacetylmorphine, or acetomorphine. In the United Kingdom the active ingredient is always referred to as diamorphine and the word 'heroin' refers only to the drug as it is sold on the street. Diamorphine is easily synthesized from morphine by the addition of acetyl chloride or acetic anhydride. It is most commonly found in the form of a hydrochloride salt with a white or off-white colour; however, a brownish black resinous form known as 'black tar' is also seen.

Herschel, Sir William (1833–1917) An Englishman who, along with Henry *Faulds, is credited with advancing the use of fingerprints as a means of criminal identification. Herschel was stationed in India in 1853 and used fingerprints as a form of signature in contracts with natives; he also studied *ridge patterns and noted that they were unchanging. Herschel developed a classification system but it was never widely adopted.

hesitation wounds (hesitation marks) Wounds found on the body of suicide victims that indicate earlier unsuccessful attempts. For example, a person that commits suicide by slitting their wrists may have multiple shallow cuts or slices on the wrist from their first tentative cuts.

heterogeneous assay A type of *immunoassay in which the labelled antigen-antibody complex must be separated from the bulk solution before a reading is obtained. This is typically required when the bound and unbound form give the same type of response. For example, when the label is radioactive (*radioimmunoassay or RIA), the signal detected by the radioactive decay is the same whether the labelled substrate is attached to the antigen or not. Therefore, the unbound form must be removed before a reading is taken. *See also* HOMOGENEOUS ASSAY.

hexamethylene triperoxide diamine (HMTD) An organic peroxide explosive. Classified as a primary *high explosive, it is a white crystalline solid which is extremely sensitive to initiation by impact, friction, or electrical discharge. HMTD has been used as a *primer in several terrorist plots.

hidden data A file stored on a computer or related device in a location that is not immediately or obviously visible.

high explosive Explosives that are relatively sensitive and easily detonated or ignited using heat or mechanical force. High explosives are often divided into two categories, primary and secondary explosives. Primary high explosives are shock and/or heat sensitive and are often used as *primers that ignite secondary high explosives. An example of this is the *primer used to ignite the *propellant used in modern ammunition. Many types of blasting caps also use primary high explosives. Secondary high explosives are more stable and are usually detonated by the shock generated from a primary explosive. In some cases, an explosive train is used to detonate a secondary high explosive; the train starts with the most sensitive material and ends the least, each component set off by ignition or detonation of the component preceding it. High explosives decompose at a much faster rate than low explosives and detonations generate shattering power, produce smaller, sharper fragments, and generally leave minimal residue. High explosives include the famous nitroglycerin (NG) ('nitro'), which was invented in 1847, trinitrotoluene (*TNT), *HMX, *RDX, tetryl, and *PETN. *See also* HIGH ORDER EXPLOSION.

high order explosion An explosion in which the blast wave is the primary destructive force and moves at supersonic speeds. Objects in the immediate vicinity tend to be shattered. This is opposed to a low order explosion in which the blast wave causes more pushing and stretching compared to the high order event.

high performance liquid chromatography (HPLC) An instrumental system based on chromatography that is widely used in forensic science. The 'HP' portion of the acronym is sometimes assigned to the words *h*igh *p*ressure (versus *h*igh *p*erformance), but it refers to the same analytical system. Like all chromatography, HPLC is based on selective partitioning of the molecules of interest between two different phases. Here, the mobile phase is a solvent or solvent mix that flows under high pressure over beads coated with the solid stationary phase. While travelling through the column, molecules in the sample partition selectively between the mobile phase and the stationary phase. Those that interact more with the stationary phase will lag behind those molecules that partition preferentially with the mobile phase. As a result, the sample introduced at the front of the column will emerge in separate bands (called peaks), with the bands emerging first being the components that interacted least with the stationary phase, and as a result moved quicker through the column. The components that emerge last will be the ones that interacted most with the stationary phase and thus moved the slowest through the column. A detector is placed at the end of the column to identify the components that elute. Occasionally, the eluting solvent is collected at specific times correlating to specific components. This provides a pure or nearly pure sample of the component of interest. This technique is sometimes referred to as preparative chromatography.

Many detectors are available for HPLC. The simplest and least expensive is the refractive index (RI) detector. Although this detector is a universal detector, meaning it will respond to any compound that elutes, it does not respond well to very low concentrations and as a result is not widely used. On the other hand, detectors based on the absorption of light in the ultraviolet and visible ranges (UV/VIS detectors and UV/VIS spectrophotometers) are the most commonly used, responding to a wide variety of compounds of forensic interest with good to excellent sensitivity. The photodiode array detector (PDA) is especially useful since it can produce not only a peak-based output (a chromatogram) but also a UV/VIS scan of every component. Recently, HPLC has been coupled with *tandem mass spectrometer detector systems greatly increasing their utility in forensic science, particularly in toxicology. A recent advance in HPLC methods is the introduction of systems that operate under extremely high pressures (in the range of 10,000 psi) and utilize smaller particle sizes than traditional HPLC. This technique is referred to as UPLC for ultra-high pressure liquid chromatography.

high velocity impact spatter A *bloodstain pattern created by a high velocity impact on a person's body. High velocity spatter patterns are created by gunshot wounds and by some striking wounds where great speed and force are used. High velocity spatter patterns are characterized by fine tiny droplets that may approach a mist.

HLA-DQA1 See DNA TYPING.

HMTD See HEXAMETHYLENE TRIPEROXIDE DIAMINE.

HMX A high explosive that is formed as a by-product during the synthesis of another high explosive, *RDX. The chemical name for HMX is cyclotetramethylenetetranitramine, and the meaning of the acronym HMX is unclear; 'his Majesty's explosive' and 'high melting point explosive' have been offered as possibilities.

Hoffman, Albert (1906–2008) A Swiss chemist best known for the synthesis, use, and advocacy of the hallucinogenic drug *LSD. He discovered the drug while working on *ergot alkaloids for the pharmaceutical company Sandoz. He was able to synthesize LSD from lysergic acid in 1938 but several years passed before the importance of the compound was understood when he ingested it himself in 1943.

hollow viscose A type of semi-synthetic *rayon fibre. Rayon is derived from cellulose and the individual fibres can be made hollow through a chemical process that results in the generation of carbon dioxide gas.

Holmes, Sherlock See DOYLE, SIR ARTHUR CONAN.

Holzer, Franz Joseph (1903–74) A forensic pathologist who studied under Karl *Landsteiner. He developed many forensic tests targeting the ABO blood group system including the absorption-elution test in 1931. He was instrumental in developing tests for determining if a person is a *secretor. See also LATTES, LEON.

homemade explosives Explosives that are synthesized or mixed from easily obtainable materials. Examples include the peroxide-based explosives, sugar-perchlorates, and explosives based on fertilizer compounds such as ammonium nitrate.

homogeneous assay A form of *immunoassay in which the response of the labelled antigen is different when bound to the antibody than when it is unbound. If this is the case, then there is no need to separate the bound from unbound forms before a reading is taken. *See also* HETEROGENEOUS ASSAY.

hot shock The breakage or damage of a filament used in lamps. The typical forensic application is in the investigation of automobile accidents where the question arises as to whether the headlamps were on or off at the time of impact. If the headlamp is filament based, the filament is hot when light is being produced. If the glass or plastic enclosing the filament is broken during impact, the shock of the impact and exposure to air can cause distinctive damage.

hot stage An accessory used with a microscope for the analysis of fibres and glass. In glass analysis, a piece of glass is immersed in oil with a known refractive index (RI). The hot stage gradually heats the oil, changing the refractive index while the analyst observes a feature known as the *Becke line. The Becke line is a halo of light that surrounds the particle but vanishes when the refractive index of the liquid matches that of the glass. This method allows the examiner to determine the refractive index of the glass. For the analysis of fibres, the hot stage heats the fibre while the analyst observes the behaviour and records observations such as fibre swelling, curling, contraction or burning. The melting point of the fibre (if there is one that can be reached with the hot stage) is also useful in identifying the type of fibre, as is a study of changes in the optical properties of the fibre as heat is applied. Hot stages can control temperature very accurately and can increase it by tenths of a degree per minute. Hot stage analyses can also be automated to some extent, simplifying tasks such as determining the refractive index of many glass fragments.

HPLC/HPLC-MS and variants *See* HIGH PERFORMANCE LIQUID CHROMATOGRAPHY.

hue One of three descriptors of colour, along with chroma and lightness. The hue of a colour is the degree to which it differs from red, green, blue, or yellow. For example, two objects may be blue, but one may be described as 'navy blue' and the other as 'light baby blue'. The adjectives reflect the hue description.

human growth hormone (HGH) A compound used medically and abused by athletes and thus a concern for *human performance toxicology. It is banned by the World Anti-Doping Agency (WADA).

human leucocyte antigens (HLA) Antigens that are found on the
surface of the white blood cells rather than the red blood cells where the
ABO blood group antigens reside. There was interest in developing
systems to type these antigens and some research in that direction, but
*DNA typing methods have eliminated the need for such typing.

human performance toxicology 1. A division of forensic toxicology
dealing with substances that are typically taken to improve athletic
performance. This is also referred to as doping. This type of toxicology
differs from other types of toxicology in that many of the substances are not
illegal but rather banned by national and international sports governing
agencies such as the World Anti-Doping Agency (WADA).
   2. Toxicology as it relates to human impairment such as occurs with
alcohol intoxication. An older term used is behavioural toxicology and a
primary goal is to relate dose to degree of impairment.

(⊕) SEE WEB LINKS
- This resource is published by the United States National Highway Traffic
  Transportation Safety Administration and discusses impaired driving and
  drugs that are commonly seen in these cases. Last accessed May 2011.
- A compilation of information and lists related to sports doping. Last accessed
  May 2011.

hybridization In *DNA typing, the process of 'unzipping' the double
helix of the DNA molecule into two separate strands (templates) and
allowing the exposed bases to bind with their complement to create two
new strands. The terms annealing and reannealing are sometimes used
interchangeably with hybridization; however fundamentally all refer to
complementary base pairs bonding with DNA fragments.

hydrolysis A chemical reaction in which water is added to a compound
or chemical group or in which addition of water results in a breakdown
of the molecule. The process of making soap from fats and a strong base
(saponification) is an example of a hydrolysis reaction; many drugs,
metabolites, and conjugates also undergo hydrolysis.

hydrophilic Literally, 'water loving'; a compound that is water soluble
as opposed to fat (lipid) soluble (lipophilic). Hydrophilic compounds are
lipophobic.

hydrophobic Literally, 'water fearing'; a compound that is fat
(lipid) soluble as opposed to water soluble (hydrophilic). Hydrophobic
compounds are lipophilic.

hypergeometric sampling An approach for qualitative sampling
(rather than sampling with the goal of quantifying the samples)

that can be used to select a subset sample size from a large parent population. The hypergeometric sampling method is based on the sample-without-replacement approach, meaning that once a sample is taken, it will not be put back in the population. As a result, the probabilities associated with subsequent selections are altered. A common example is a deck of playing cards—the probability of selecting at random the ace of spades is 1/52. If a card is selected and it is not the ace of spades, in the hypergeometric protocol, it is not put back in the deck and now the probability is 1/51. Knowing these probabilities, it is possible to select a subset for testing and, based on the results for the subset, to make probability-based inferences regarding the original large seizure.

hypervariable regions A genetic location (locus) that has many different alleles throughout the population. As a consequence, such loci are valuable in forensic science and can greatly aid in attempts to individualize a sample. Locations called hypervariable regions 1 and 2 are used in typing of mitochondrial DNA (mtDNA).

hyphenated technique An instrument that has two components, most often a separation module and a detector module. One of the most widely used instruments in forensic science, a gas chromatograph coupled to a mass spectrometer, is a 'hyphenated technique' since it is usually referred to by the acronym GC-MS or simply GCMS. In this case, the GC separates the mixture into individual components that are introduced into the mass spectrometer one at a time for identification.

hypophosphorous route (Hypo route) A method of manufacture of *methamphetamine. Hydroiodic acid is made in situ by adding hypophosphorous acid and iodine. This method does not require any red phosphorus in the reaction because hypophosphorous acid itself acts as the reducing agent and can be used as an alternative to red phosphorus. The reaction can be conducted as a single step reduction of ephedrine/ *pseudo*ephedrine using iodine to generate hydroiodic acid 'in situ' in the manufacture of methamphetamine. This method is also referred to as the *red cook method.

hypothesis test (statistical hypothesis test) A test that compares two hypotheses using a statistical test, distributions and desired levels of certainty, and table values to assess which is most likely to be correct. One of these hypotheses is the null hypothesis and the other is the alternative. The test that is used depends on the question being asked. An example frequently used in forensic science is a test of means. For example, assume that on a Monday, a forensic laboratory receives a case containing ten small plastic bags of a white powder. Each is found to contain cocaine, the average purity is found to be 18.5 per cent. Another similar seizure is received on Wednesday and the analysis again shows ten plastic bags, all containing cocaine, this time with a mean purity of 19.1 per cent. A reasonable question would be 'are these from the same batch?' and the data available for testing are the mean purities. The null hypothesis would be that there is no statistically significant difference in the per cent purity values. The alternative hypothesis is that there is a significant difference. A reasonable test would be the t-test of means with a desired confidence of 95 per cent. The prescribed calculation results in a value that is compared to a table value and if the calculated value is less than that of the table, the null hypothesis is accepted. If the calculated value is greater than the table value, the null hypothesis is rejected and the alternative is accepted.

IAFIS *See* AFIS

ICP *See* INDUCTIVELY COUPLED PLASMA TECHNIQUES.

ICP-MS An instrumental method of analysis that links *inductively coupled plasma and *mass spectrometry. ICP-MS is used for elemental analysis. There are two methods of introducing sample into an ICP-MS. In the first, the solid material (such as glass or soil) is dissolved using acids and heat and then aspirated into the plasma where solvents evaporate, compounds break down, and ions are formed. The cations then enter the mass spectrometer where they are identified. The second method involves the use of a laser to ablate a tiny portion of the surface for introduction into the instrument. This is called laser ablation ICP-MS or LA-ICP-MS.

IDENT1 The national database of *fingerprints and related biometric patterns in the United Kingdom. It is maintained by the National Policing Improvement Agency (NPIA). Anyone who is arrested has their fingerprints and palm prints collected and these are entered into the database which is searched using automatic fingerprint identification (*AFIS) computer technology.

(⊕) SEE WEB LINKS

• Information regarding the United Kingdom's fingerprint database. Last accessed May 2011.

identification A term that has unique and sometimes disputed meaning in forensic science. In disciplines such as toxicology or *seized drug analysis, chemical compounds are routinely identified, i.e. a sample is found to contain cocaine; the cocaine was identified. However, a statement such as 'the blood was identified,' meaning that it was shown to come from one specific person, is technically incorrect in the forensic context. What is typically meant by this type of statement is that the blood was linked to an individual as the common source.

IED *See* IMPROVISED EXPLOSIVE DEVICE.

ignition energy The minimum amount of energy that must be input into a fuel/air system to initiate combustion.

ignition point **1.** The *ignition temperature or minimum ignition temperature required for thermal initiation of a fuel/oxidant mixture. **2.** The physical location at which a fire was ignited and began to burn.

ignition source In *arson and fire investigation, the source of the initial spark or other combustion inducing event. The source of ignition may be electrical (such as a heated wire), a flame (such as a match), a spark, or an incendiary device.

ignition temperature The temperature at which a flammable material will ignite. For petrol (gasoline), the most common accelerant used in arson, the ignition temperature is in the range of approximately 260 to 450 °C (500 to 800 °F), depending on type and grade.

immediate cause (**immediate cause of death**) The medical/physiological cause of death. In criminal matters, a medical cause of death is not necessarily the legal cause. Cause of death is also distinct from the circumstances of death, which comprise the situation and conditions that led up to the fatal encounter. For example, assume a man is found with a gunshot wound to the chest and is taken to hospital, where he dies a week later of an infection that arose from surgery performed to save his life. The immediate cause of death is the infection, but the legal cause would be the gunshot wound. The circumstances of death would be whether it was accidental (the gun went off while he was cleaning it), homicide, or suicide.

immunoassay A group of techniques used in forensic toxicology for the detection of drugs in urine, blood, and other body fluids. The term 'immunosorbent assay' is also used, and these techniques yield both quantitative and qualitative information. Immunoassay relies on an antigen-*antibody reaction between the drug being tested and an antibody specific for it. The antibody is attached to a solid surface such as the bottom of a plastic or glass well. A complex that consists of the drug and a label is added and the reaction occurs. As a result, the labelled drug is bound to the antibody. A sample that may contain the drug, such as urine, is added to the plastic well. If there is no drug or very little drug present, the labelled drug-antibody complex will remain undisturbed. However, if there is a large concentration of the drug, this will displace the labelled drug from the antibodies, releasing the labelled drug into solution. The higher the drug concentration in the sample, the more will be displaced. The amount of the displaced labelled drug is then measured. Types of immunoassay include ELISA (enzyme linked immunoassay), EMIT (enzyme multiplied immunoassay technique), RIA (radioimmunoassay), and FPIA (fluorescent polarization immunoassay).

immunodiffusion Immunological techniques that were once widely used in forensic serology to determine the species of a blood sample. Crossed-over electrophoresis is also used in this role. Immunodiffusion is a precipitin test, meaning that a positive result is evidenced by the formation of a precipitate or solid (also called an immunoprecipitate) that is easily visualized. In this case, the solid forms as a result of an immunological reaction between antigens found in the blood sample and *antibodies found in purified antisera applied in the test. Immunodiffusion tests rely on the process of diffusion, the natural spreading of a concentrated material or reagent into the surroundings. Types of immunodiffusion include single and double with the name referring to how and in how many dimensions the antigens and antibodies move through the gel.

immunological techniques Tests and analysis that are based on reactions between antigens and *antibodies. Once a staple of forensic serology, *DNA typing methodologies have largely supplanted immunological analytical methods. Immunological reactions are the basis of the immune response, in which an organism synthesizes antibodies to react with and neutralize foreign substances. If a person contracts a cold, the immune response includes synthesis of antibodies that attack the invading cold virus and eventually overcome it. Examples of forensic uses of immunological techniques include ABO blood group typing, immunodiffusion and precipitin tests to determine the species of bloodstains, and immunoassay techniques used in forensic toxicology.

impact printing A type of computerized or mechanical printing that is based on the impact of a surface against paper or against a ribbon that strikes paper (or other substrate). Examples include typewriters and dot matrix printers.

impact spatter A blood spatter pattern created when blood (or a surface that it is on) is subject to an impact that causes that blood to spatter. The spatter then strikes another surface such as a wall or floor, creating the impact spatter.

implied consent A legal doctrine in which a person's consent (or agreement) is inferred from their actions rather than by a direct statement. This concept arises often in cases of arrests for driving while intoxicated and the breath and alcohol testing associated with it.

impression evidence Physical evidence that results from the contact between two objects or surfaces. Impression evidence is also referred to as imprint evidence or markings and as a group represents one of the largest classes of forensic evidence. Examples of impression evidence include markings made on cartridge cases and bullets; bite marks; toolmarks; fabric impressions; shoe prints; tyre prints; and in many cases, fingerprints. Impression evidence can be divided into groups depending on how they were made. Scraping produces impressions called *striations, examples of which include bullet markings and many toolmarks. The other way impressions can be made is by compression of one surface under the weight of another such as when shoe impressions are made in mud or a fabric impression is transferred to a bullet passing through clothing. In general, an imprint is considered to be a flat impression (thin, as a fingerprint on glass), while an indentation also has depth such as the muddy shoe print. In other words, imprints are two dimensional while indentations are three dimensional.

improvised explosive device (IED) A makeshift explosive device made from common, easily obtainable materials, or easily synthesized materials. Examples include the peroxide-based explosives used in the *London bombing in 2005 and the 'shoe bomb' Richard Reid attempted to use in late 2001 while travelling on a cross-Atlantic American Airlines flight. He was restrained by passengers and crew while attempting to light a fuse and was convicted in 2003.

incendiary device Devices that are used to ignite an accelerant in an arson fire. They can range from simple to sophisticated and include items such as road flares, fireworks, cigarettes, matches, black or smokeless powders, or homemade mixtures such as sugar and chlorates. Mechanical or electrical components may also be incorporated, with items such as flashbulbs used to ignite an accelerant. The incendiary device is typically found at the point of origin and thus it or the portions of it that remain are critical components of the physical evidence associated with arson.

incendiary fire A fire that is caused by purposeful human action. All arsons are incendiary fires but the reverse is not always true.

incidental accelerant A material that is present in a fire but not purposely used as an accelerant. If a fire occurred in a garage where petrol (gasoline) for a lawnmower was stored, that petrol would be an incidental accelerant.

incised wound A wound created by cutting using an object such as a knife or scissors as opposed to a tearing injury from blunt trauma or a puncture wound.

inclusionary evidence Evidence, including the results of a forensic analysis, that does not exclude a given possibility or disprove a given hypothesis. Inclusionary evidence is the opposite of exclusionary evidence.

inconclusive result A result that is not useful or fails to answer pertinent questions. Inconclusive results can occur in many situations such as when there is too small a sample (a tiny spot of blood so small that it cannot be reliably typed), fragmentary evidence (a fragment of a bullet), or because of the limitations of procedures or instrumentation. Such problems can lead to incomplete, contradictory, or inconsistent results that are impossible to interpret with any confidence. Another instance that can lead to an inconclusive result is when two analysts examine the same evidence and come to different conclusions. If the two interpretations cannot be resolved, the result is considered to be inconclusive.

inculpatory evidence Evidence that suggests or supports the idea that a person or persons were involved in the crime or action in question. Finding a suspect's fingerprint at a crime scene would be inculpatory evidence; however, taken alone it is not conclusive.

indented writing Writing that is transferred by the pressure of the writing instrument (pen, pencil, and so on) to the paper or other material that is beneath it. Indented writing is often undetectable to the naked eye and as such can be overlooked by a criminal. Accordingly, indented writing is a common form of *questioned document evidence. *See also* ESDA.

indirect transfer A transfer of physical evidence that is not directly from the source. For example, a person could carry fibres from the carpet in their home on their clothing and these could in turn be transferred to a car seat and then to another person. These are all indirect transfers as opposed to a direct person-to-person transfer.

individualization The process of linking physical evidence to a common source. Individualization starts with identification, progresses through classification, and leads, if possible, to assigning a unique source for a given piece of physical evidence. The term individualization is often used (incorrectly in the forensic context) as a synonym for *identification. Fingerprints are an example of evidence that may be individualized, as can pattern evidence such as toolmarks and firearms. Less obvious but extremely important in forensic analysis is individualization by way of a physical match. It is not that the evidence itself is unique but rather the way in which it was separated and pieced back together that allows for linkage to a common source.

inductively coupled plasma techniques Instrumental techniques used for inorganic and elemental analysis. ICP stands for *i*nductively *c*oupled *p*lasma and refers to the method used to convert a sample to its constituent atoms or ions. In an ICP torch, gaseous argon

(Ar) is ionized by a Tesla coil to form Ar^+ and free electrons. These ions are accelerated and confined in a stable magnetic field. The resulting high energy collisions generate heat in the range of 10,300 °C (~18,500 °F). Under these conditions, most chemical compounds are broken apart forming free atoms and ions in the plasma which consists of free electrons (electrons not associated with a specific atom), atoms, and ions and is characterized by an intense glow reminiscent of a flame. Plasmas are also found in the sun.

There are two ICP instrumental techniques used in forensic science. ICP-AES is a form of emission spectroscopy (*a*tomic *e*mission *s*pectroscopy) in which the heat of the plasma is not only sufficient to atomize the sample but also to place many of the atoms into the excited state. In such a state, an atom emits characteristic wavelengths of light in the visible and ultraviolet ranges that can be used to identify specific elements in the sample and also to determine their concentrations. The second forensic application of ICP is in *mass spectrometry (ICP-MS) in which the plasma is the source of elemental ions. Samples can be introduced into the instrument via acid digestion or by a laser ablation accessory (LAB-ICP-MS). ICP-MS has also been coupled to high pressure liquid chromatography (HPLC) to allow for *speciation of metals.

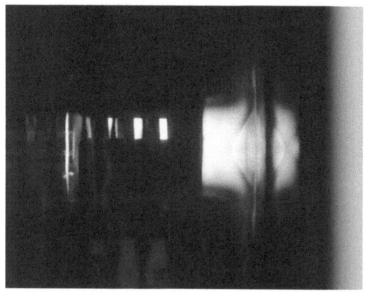

The torch of an ICP-MS instrument. The cone-shaped orifice that leads to the mass spectrometer is to the left.

inductive reasoning (inferential reasoning) A mode or process of thinking that is part of the scientific method and complements deductive reasoning and logic. Inductive reasoning starts with a large body of evidence or data obtained by experiment or observation and extrapolates it to new situations. By the process of induction or *inference, predictions about new situations are inferred or induced from the existing body of knowledge. In other words, an inference is a generalization, but one that is made in a logical and scientifically defensible manner. A forensic example is fingerprints. Every person's fingerprints are unique, but this is an inference based on existing knowledge since the only way to prove it would be to take and study the fingerprints of every human being ever born.

inference (inferential reasoning) The process of drawing a conclusion based on the existence of other facts. For example, if a person leaves a fingerprint at a scene, it can be inferred that the person was at one time present at the scene.

infrared microscopy *See* INFRARED SPECTROSCOPY.

infrared spectroscopy A form of absorption spectroscopy in which electromagnetic radiation in the infrared range is absorbed by molecules, resulting in vibrational mode changes. This range of the electromagnetic energy spectrum is usually characterized by reciprocal wavelengths or wavenumbers, in units of cm^{-1}. There are three infrared (IR) ranges in the electromagnetic spectrum: the near infrared; the mid-infrared, and the far infrared. Forensic applications and instruments typically utilize the mid-IR range. The pattern of absorption across this range is unique for each different molecule and as a result, an IR spectrum usually provides specific identification for compounds. The region of the IR spectra from 1,500 to 500 cm^{-1} is called the fingerprint region and is usually distinctive enough to identify specific compounds. However, definitive identification of a single compound is only possible if the sample being studied is pure. IR is also used to characterize materials such as paints and inks that are mixtures as opposed to pure compounds. In these applications, the IR spectrum is used for *pattern matching purposes and not for identification per se. IR methods are most widely used for the analysis of organic compounds such as drugs, synthetic fibres, and plastics but the technique can also be used for many inorganic materials such as might be found in soil or paints. *Raman spectroscopy is another form of vibrational mode spectroscopy. Most IR spectrophotometers sold since 1990 use a device called a *Michelson interferometer that is coupled to a mathematical operation called a *Fourier transform to obtain spectra. In this approach, all wavelengths of light are presented to the sample simultaneously rather than sequentially (a scanning instrument design). The resulting interference pattern is then mathematically analysed to yield the spectrum. This type of instrument and technique is referred to as FTIR. This instrumental design allows for many variations of IR applicable in forensic science and forensic chemistry. These include attenuated total reflectance (ATR), diffuse reflectance (drifts), internal reflectance, and microspectrophotometry (micro-FTIR) in which the instrument is coupled to a microscope.

ingestion To take something into the body. *Modes of ingestion include swallowing, inhalation, and injection and are important considerations in forensic toxicology. For example, drugs that are ingested by smoking produce almost instantaneous and maximized pharmacological effect while drugs that are ingested via swallowing take much longer to produce effects.

inhalants A class of psychoactive components ingested by inhalation. Also called 'glue sniffing' or 'huffing', ingestion of inhalants became significant in the 1960s and remains most popular among teenagers and young adults. Inhalants are volatile (evaporate easily) and most are gases at normal room temperatures and pressures. Abusers typically fill a plastic bag or soak a rag with the substance to dose themselves. Unlike drugs of abuse, inhalants are components of common products such as paint or cleaning solvents and are typically not regulated. Many are propellants used in spray cans containing paint or other similar materials. Inhalants are considered to be central nervous system depressants with effects similar to alcohol, although achieved much faster. Abuse of inhalants carries high risks, particularly of kidney, liver, and brain damage.

inherent luminescence Emission of light by excitation with an alternative light source (ALS) that is caused by a compound naturally present in the sample. For example, some fingerprints fluoresce naturally when exposed to UV light even without treatment. Similarly, drugs such as LSD (lysergic acid diethylamide) will fluoresce without any chemical alteration or treatment.

inkjet printing A type of computer-controlled printing in which *inks are sprayed onto the paper (or other) substrate. Inkjet printers utilize a liquid ink in contrast to laser printers that utilize *toners and heat to create the image and letters on a substrate.

inkless fingerprinting Fingerprints collected digitally using a scanning device rather than by older inking and rolling techniques.

inks and ink analysis The composition of inks is much like paints—a solvent base (also called the *vehicle) which may contain one or more solvents such as water or organics, colouring materials (pigments or *dyes, natural and synthetic), and other additives such as resins and components that control thickness and final appearance. The oldest ink, called India ink but originally used in China, consists of carbon black (ground charcoal) suspended in water and containing adhesive gums and varnishing components. Solvents that have been used include mineral oil, glycols, and more recently phenoxyethanol and phenoxyethoxyethanol. Iron gallotannate inks contain inorganic colourants along with tannic acid and are used in fountain pens. Inks used in ballpoint pens contain synthetic dyes dissolved in organic solvents such as phenyoxyethanols along with additives to maintain a thick consistency and to insure proper flow characteristics. Gel pens contain synthetic dyes impregnated into gel.

The analysis of inks usually focuses on the analysis of the colourants using *thin layer chromatography (TLC). Historical methods included solubility testing with a variety of solvents and solutions. *Video spectral analysis is a powerful and non-destructive method widely used to compare inks, microspectrophotometry is increasingly being used, principally UV/VIS, IR, and Raman methods. Ageing and dating of inks is addressed through solvent drying characteristics (in the early stages) and then by weathering and degradation studies.

intaglio printing A printing process frequently used to produce currency. The method creates distinctive textures that make counterfeiting more difficult. In this method, an engraved plate (with channels engraved into it creating the image) is coated with a thick layer of ink. The substrate paper is then pressed against the coated plate, imparting a thick printed layer that is elevated off the substrate rather than simply absorbed into it.

interference colours Colours that are created as a result of constructive and destructive interference of visible light. *Polarizing light microscopy relies on the creation of interference colours as a means to probe the underlying structure of a material. Interference colours are not true colours but rather an artefact created by the constructive and destructive interference of visible light rays. Another example of interference colours are the colours that appear visible when an oily sheen lies atop a water surface or a CD is moved under a light source.

interferences (interferents) Substances that can affect or alter the results of an analysis or chemical test. Presumptive tests such as those for blood have a number of interferences that may lead to *false positive or *false negative results.

interior ballistics *See* INTERNAL BALLISTICS.

interlaboratory variation A term used to describe the small variations in quantitative results that can occur when different laboratories (forensic or other) analyse the same sample. Some analyses should not produce any differences such as *DNA typing or fingerprint analysis. However, areas such as quantitative drug analysis may. For example, if a single sample is submitted to 50 different laboratories to determine its purity, a range of values could result. One lab may find a value of 50.0 per cent while another might find 50.5 per cent and yet another 49.8 per cent. A determination of interlaboratory variation in such cases helps to set a baseline of what variation is normal and natural, the result of small random discrepancies. Measurement of variation is an important part of *quality assurance/quality control (QA/QC). *See also* ROUND ROBIN.

interleave A method of storing data on a hard disk drive or other magnetic storage media in which the data is not physically stored in one contiguous block. This is usually done to decrease access time.

internal ballistics The ballistic characteristics of a bullet's travel and movement from the moment the primer ignites until the bullet exits the muzzle. This involves the propellant ignition and burn, the generation of hot expanding gases and the build-up of pressure, and the movement of the bullet once it is free of the *cartridge.

internal standard calibration A method or compound used in a chemical quantitation. Internal standard quantitation is highly accurate and provides a method for correction of problems associated with loss or suppression of an analyte during sample preparation and analysis. The most common forensic application is in chemistry (drug analysis and toxicology). An internal standard is a compound or element that is different from the analyte of interest, but still closely related to it. For example, lidocaine or procaine would be good choices as internal standards for the analysis and quantitation of cocaine, as long as neither compound is found in the sample itself.

International Organization for Standardization (ISO) A cooperative international organization comprising national and regional groups that work toward international standardization of processes and practices. The organization began to generate documents called 'standards' in 1947. Forensically, ISO plays a key role in forensic laboratory *accreditation as well as in establishing standard definitions of key terms and measurement units.

(⊕) SEE WEB LINKS

- This site lists standards as well as history, members, and role of ISO. Last accessed May 2011.

interpupillary distance The distance between the centres of the pupils of the eyes. This distance plays a role in *microscopy and microscope design.

intravenous injection A *mode of ingestion relevant to forensic toxicology. In this mode, a *xenobiotic, drug, or poison is injected directly into a vein and is rapidly distributed throughout the bloodstream without undergoing *first pass metabolism.

invasive sampling A means of obtaining a biological sample that requires penetration of the body in some way. Drawing blood is an example of invasive sampling; pulling hair is not invasive, and collection of saliva is considered to be minimally invasive. There are often legal considerations regarding situations in which invasive versus non-invasive sampling can be used.

in vivo A process or study that takes place within an organism or tissue.

in vitro A process or study that takes place outside of an organism or tissue, in a place other than it would naturally occur. For example, metabolic processes can be studied *in vitro* using enzymes or human liver cells.

iodine fuming A process used to visualize *latent fingerprints and one of the oldest in use. Crystals of iodine (I_2) are placed in an enclosed cabinet (fuming cabinet) and gently warmed, causing the iodine to vaporize without going through a liquid phase, a process called sublimation. Although the mechanism of reaction is not completely understood, it appears that I_2 is physically absorbed, imparting an orange colour to the prints.

iodoplatinate A transition metal complexing agent used as a visualization reagent for nitrogenous bases such as cocaine separated by *thin layer chromatography (TLC). It is a 1:1 combination of H_2PtCl_6 with KI.

ion exchange The process of replacing one ion in solution with another while maintaining charge balance. Commercial ion exchangers are used to soften water, e.g. to remove calcium and magnesium ions. To perform an ion exchange, the sample is forced through a column bed that contains an exchange resin. In a water softener, the goal of ion exchange is to remedy hard water problems by removing Ca^{2+}, Mg^{2+}. To do this, the water supply is directed over a bed charged with sodium ions (Na^+). In the column, the calcium and magnesium will displace the sodium at a 1:2 ratio to maintain charge balance. For every magnesium or calcium ion that is removed by the resin, two Na^+ cations will be released into solution.

Water hardness is removed by trapping calcium and magnesium in the bed, but as a result, soft water has a higher concentration of sodium, which can present problems to people with high blood pressure. Thus, ion exchange does not remove ions from solution, only replaces one ion with others of the same overall charge. Ion exchange mechanisms are also used extensively in *solid phase extraction (SPE) methods used for drugs and metabolites.

ionizable centre A functional group site on a molecule that can become charged based on protonation or deprotonation. Basic drugs such as *methamphetamine and *cocaine have one amine group that is the ionizable centre, generically RNH_3^+ which deprotonates to RNH_2 as a function of the pH. Acidic drugs have ionizable centres typically based on carboxylic or phenolic groups that also protonate and deprotonate as a function of charge ($HA \rightarrow A^-$) Some drugs such as morphine are amphoteric, meaning there is one acidic site and one basic site. *See also* ISOELECTRIC POINT.

ion mobility spectrometry (IMS) A portable instrument used in forensic science to detect drugs, explosives, tear gas, and chemical warfare agents. Originally called plasma chromatography, IMS works similarly to *electrophoresis, except the charged species are separated in the gaseous state rather than in a gel. IMS works at atmospheric pressure, making it ideally suited for use as a portable monitoring system, and the military in several nations use IMS routinely for battlefield detection of chemical weapons. Most IMS instruments are based on a drift tube, which is a small cylindrical structure that is a few centimetres in length. An air sample is drawn into the instrument and directed through an ionization region, where the radiation emitted by radioactive ^{63}Ni causes an initial ionization of the nitrogen and oxygen in air. A complex series of linked reactions lead to the formation of ion/molecule clusters such as $H(H_2O)_3^+$. An electronic pulse of a wire shutter (which looks very much like a screen door) admits clusters into the drift tube where they move against a flow of a drift gas such as air or nitrogen. The clusters are separated based on the ratio of their size to their charge, much as separation is accomplished in gel electrophoresis, with the smaller clusters moving ahead of the larger ones. The clusters arrive at the detector and the pulses are recorded as peaks, the height of which is proportional to concentration. IMS has been used to detect drugs in closed shipping containers and is also being explored for a wider role in explosives detection at airports.

ion pair A pair of oppositely charged ions associated by electrostatic attraction. Usually the term is applied to relatively complex polyatomic ions and molecules with an *ionizable centre that can become charged depending on the pH.

ion trap A type of *mass spectrometer (MS) in which ions are temporarily trapped in a confined space where they can build up to some extent. For detection, the electronics are such that different ions are allowed to exit at different times, producing the mass spectrum. The most common design involves ion introduction in pulses into a circular ring. There, they move in an orbital path that is determined by their mass, charge, and the electrical fields created in the ring. At certain settings, only one mass-to-charge ratio will achieve a stable trajectory. Thus, specific ions can be trapped in the ring before being introduced into the detector. There are also linear ion traps that are not circular but based on quadrupoles or similar designs. Ion trap techniques are useful for biomolecules such as proteins and in *tandem (dual) mass spectrometers.

IP address (internet protocol address) A series of numbers that specifies the address of a computer on the internet. The IP address consists of a string of four numbers such as 192.xxx.x.x.

isoelectric focusing (IEF) A technique used in forensic serology to type isoenzyme systems. In isoelectric focusing, a pH gradient is created in a gel (much as used in *electrophoresis), meaning that the pH changes with gel position. Protein molecules are charged, but at a given pH, they become neutral and will cease to move. This point is called the *isoelectric point, and proteins with different structures can be distinguished based on where they stop moving in the gel. IEF proved to have a higher resolving power than traditional gel electrophoresis and thus could distinguish more types within some of the isoenzyme systems; however, the reagents are more expensive and prevented the routine use of IEF in forensic serology and with developments in DNA technology, isoenzyme typing itself is rarely performed now.

isoelectric point (IEP) The pH at which a molecule, typically a protein or a drug, has no net charge. Proteins contain acidic groups such as OH and NH_3^+ that can ionize to O^- and NH_2. At low pH values (high concentrations of H^+), protonation of O^- to OH is favoured, but so is protonation of NH_2 to make NH_3^+, a charged species. Conversely, high pHs (low H^+ concentration) favour O^- and NH_2. Depending on the structure of the protein, there will be some pH at which all acidic groups are protonated, and at that point, the protein molecule has no net charge. This property is exploited in *isoelectric focusing (IEP).

isoenzymes and isoenzyme systems Prior to the widespread acceptance of *DNA typing, isoenzymes were used in conjunction with

ABO blood group typing to individualize blood and body fluid evidence to the extent this was possible. These isoenzymes are found on the surface of red blood cells and are thus sometimes called red cell isoenzymes. Enzymes are biological catalysts necessary to speed up reactions that would otherwise be far too slow in an organism. The term isoenzyme refers to the group of red blood cell enzymes that are polymorphic, meaning that they exist in multiple different forms and that what form a person has is determined genetically. Since heredity (genes) determines the form, the isoenzymes are considered to be genetic marker systems. The analysis and typing of isoenzymes was accomplished using gel *electrophoresis or closely related techniques. The six common systems typed were: phosphoglucomutase (PGM); adenylate kinase (AK); acid phosphatase (ACP or EAP); glyoxalase I (GLO I); esterase D (ESD), and adenosine deaminase (ADA). The advent of DNA typing has all but eliminated the routine use of isoenzymes in forensic biology.

isotope An isotope of an element is an atom that has the same number of protons in the nucleus but a different number of neutrons and thus a different mass. Isotopes may be natural or synthetic, and contrary to a popular misconception, not all isotopes are radioactive. For example, hydrogen atoms have one proton in the nucleus, and the predominant form of hydrogen has no neutrons. Deuterium is a non-radioactive isotope of hydrogen containing one proton and one neutron in the nucleus while tritium is a radioactive isotope containing one proton and two neutrons. Both isotopes are chemically identical to hydrogen.

isotope dilution A technique used in *mass spectrometry (MS) to obtain extremely accurate quantitative analysis of samples. The technique can be used for inorganic or organic analysis. Since the natural isotopic abundances are known, the addition of a known amount of a given isotope to a sample containing that element allows for ratios of isotopes to be related to concentration of the isotope in question. For example, to determine the amount of benzene (C_6H_6) in a sample, deuterated benzene (benzene-d6, C_6D_6) can be added to the sample. Since the deuterium isotope of hydrogen is chemically identical to hydrogen, it will behave exactly as benzene would during the course of the analysis; however, since its mass is different, the mass spectrometer can determine the concentrations of each type of benzene separately. Using this data and knowledge of the natural abundance of deuterium, it is possible to determine the concentration of benzene with a high degree of accuracy.

isotope ratio mass spectrometry (IRMS) A specialized form of *mass spectrometry used forensically in *drug profiling studies. There are many variants of instrumental design, the most common of which in forensic applications is a *gas chromatograph linked to a series of post-column reaction chambers and finally a magnetic sector mass spectrometer. This type of instrument targets organic compounds such as found in plant-based drugs (cocaine for example). The isotopes of interest are the naturally occurring stable isotopes such as carbon-13 (^{13}C), ^{14}N, and ^{16}O.

As the organic compounds exit the GC column, they enter a combustion chamber where the compound decomposes completely (ideally) to CO_2 and H_2O. This is accomplished by heat and catalysis. Nitrogen in the sample is converted to oxygenated species. The combustion products then enter a reduction chamber to convert the nitrous oxides to N_2. After removal of water using a cooling loop, the gases enter the mass spectrometer. In a magnetic sector design, separation of the ions is based on mass-dependent differences in ion trajectory in a magnetic field.

In the case of ^{13}C studies, only three ions are usually monitored, all corresponding to CO_2, but different isotopic combinations. At mass/charge 44, the compound is $^{12}C^{16}O^{16}O$; mass/charge 45, $^{13}C^{16}O^{16}O$ and $^{12}C^{17}O^{16}O$; and for mass/charge 46, $^{12}C^{16}O^{18}O$. Information obtained can be used to measure the relative amounts of the carbon and oxygen isotopes present in the compound that was combusted. In turn, this information can be used to compare plant-based materials and to generate information regarding possible geographic origin. GC-IRMS can also be used to study drug synthesis methods as a means to elucidate specific mechanisms.

isotropic Literally, the same. The term is most often used in conjunction with microscopy and *polarizing light microscopy specifically. Isotropic materials are those which have only one refractive index such as glass. *Anisotropic materials, such as quartz, have more than one refractive index. *See also* BIREFRINGENCE.

jacketed bullets Lead bullets that are encased in copper or a similar alloy. Jacketing of a bullet allows it to feed smoothly in automatic and semi-automatic weapons. Jacketing may be partial or complete (full metal jacket).

Jeffreys, Sir Alec (1950–) An English researcher who was the first to apply *DNA typing to forensic science. Dr Jeffreys, who works at the University of Leicester, is not a forensic scientist but rather a molecular biologist working on regions of DNA that are variable from person to person, which is a logical jumping-off point to human DNA typing. Jeffreys zeroed in on regions of DNA referred to as *short tandem repeats or STRs, and, at the time the first case arose, was working on a project concerning grey seals through the British Antarctic Survey office located in Cambridge. Jeffreys was seeking the structure of the gene that encodes for the protein myoglobin, which carries oxygen in muscle tissues. Since grey seals produce more myoglobin than humans do, they provided an easier place to begin the hunt. Jeffreys retrieved seal meat from the Survey office, went about finding the seal gene, and then moved on to the human counterpart. In the human gene, he found a repetitive segment.

   The serendipitous discovery led to the realization that portions of the repeating section were similar to sections found in other *minisatellite regions that had been found, which at that time were very few. This hinted at some underlying similarity shared by some of the minisatellite regions in human DNA. Jeffreys created a molecular probe to search DNA for this characteristic core sequence to ferret out other minisatellite regions encompassing similar cores. To investigate if these varied between people, he applied the probe not to one person's DNA but to that taken from several people. He published the results of that work in *Nature* in 1985.

   The cases that pushed Jeffreys into the spotlight involved the rape and murder of two 15-year-old girls who died within miles of Jeffreys's lab at Leicester. The killings were three years apart but similar enough that investigators believed that both died at the hands of the same man. They had a suspect, a young man named George Howard of limited mental capacity, who eventually confessed to accidentally killing one victim. The physical and serological evidence was unconvincing, and they had no link to the other killing.

Investigators asked Jeffreys to test blood from Howard as well as semen found on the clothing of the two victims. Prophetically, the first forensic DNA test exonerated an innocent man and debunked a false confession. Police released Howard in 1986 and the investigation stalled. At the time, the number of human DNA profiles in population databases was zero. Having clear results from the case samples was of little investigative use without such data. Thus, Jeffreys had data without context, and investigators had nothing they could use to further the investigation.

The solution, collection of samples from all men in the area, proved prophetic as well. It was the first *biological dragnet. Police began collecting blood samples and eventually had 4,000-plus non-matching samples. No one was particularly surprised; it was hard to imagine the killer happily turning over blood that would prove his guilt. This realization led indirectly to his capture. A group of people sitting in a pub overheard a conversation in which one man said that he had given his blood in place of another. The man skipping the test was Colin Pitchfork. Police found Pitchfork and obtained a sample for Jeffreys to complete the analysis that was eventually used to convict Pitchfork and sentence him to two life terms. He was made a CH in 2017.

jump drive *See* KEY DRIVE.

junk DNA Segments of DNA that do not appear to code for proteins and that consist of repeated sequences of *nucleotides. The term is a bit of a misnomer in that many such sequences have been found to have biological functionality, even if not for creating proteins directly. The STR loci typed in modern DNA methods could be classified as junk DNA.

junk science Practices and procedures that are labelled by some as science but that have no basis in science and do not adhere to the principles of the *scientific method. As an example, astronomy is a science, astrology is junk science. Courts and other triers of fact develop tests and guidelines to distinguish the two and to ensure that junk science is not admitted as scientific or forensic evidence.

Kastle–Meyer colour test A *presumptive test used to identify blood and bloodstains. The chemical substance used is a phenolphthalein solution, which is made by boiling powdered phenolphthalein in an alkaline solution containing potassium hydroxide (KOH). The test is also referred to as the K-M or KM test. Until recently, phenolphthalein was used as the active ingredient in some laxative products and is still commonly used in chemical analyses (titrations) of acids and bases. Despite some concerns about possible carcinogenic properties, the KM reagent is considered to be relatively safe. Phenolphthalein reacts with the haemoglobin in blood in the presence of hydrogen peroxide (H_2O_2) to cause a pink colour to form. Like any presumptive tests, the KM test is not specific for blood and can produce *false positives with substances such as horseradish.

keratin A tough fibrous protein found in hair and skin. The interlinking of keratin proteins is what provides the strength and makes it insoluble in water and resistant to chemical and biological attack.

ketamine A hallucinogenic drug, also considered a club drug, that is abused among juveniles and young adults taking part in parties or 'raves'. Ketamine is used as an animal anaesthetic, and the only illicit source of the drug is through theft, mostly from veterinary clinics. As a veterinary drug, it is supplied as a liquid or a soluble powder that can be injected, sprinkled on other material and smoked, added to drinks, or snorted.

key drive A generic term for an external storage device for computers and related equipment such as cameras, phones, etc. The drive interfaces with devices through a USB port. Other terms used for this include jump drive and thumb drive.

Kind, Stuart (1925–2003) A British forensic biologist whose career spanned some of the most significant advances in forensic science. Kind also founded the Forensic Science Society in the United Kingdom in 1959. He served in the Royal Air Force during the Second World War after which he was a professor before joining the Home Office forensic laboratory in Yorkshire. He is perhaps best known for his work on the Yorkshire Ripper case in the 1970s, and was instrumental in developing geographical methods and profiling as a forensic tool. He also founded (in 1958) a professional organization that would become the Forensic Science Society (FSS). In 1969, he assumed the directorship of the forensic laboratory in Newcastle and in 1978 he was appointed as the director of the Home Office Research Establishment at Aldermaston.

kinetic energy The energy of motion. It is defined by the equation $KE = \frac{1}{2} mv^2$ where m is the mass of the moving object and v is its velocity.

Kingston model A mathematical model for the classification and identification of *latent fingerprints proposed in 1964. This probability-based system is divided into three separate probability calculations, the first based on finding a given number of *minutiae in a given area. The next probability was based on the position of these features. The final probability was based on the likelihood that the observed minutiae would be found in the observed positions.

Kirk, Paul Leland (1902–70) Considered to be the father of modern American *criminalistics, both education and practice, and head of the first criminalistics programme in that country. Kirk became involved in criminalistics as a result of collaboration between the Berkeley Police Department and the University of California at Berkeley encouraged by August Vollmer, the Chief of that police department. Kirk established the criminalistics programme in 1937 and by 1948 it was a department under the university's School of Criminology. Kirk was active in research in many areas of evidence including *trace evidence and *bloodstain patterns as well as in teaching and casework. He authored a pioneering textbook, *Crime Investigation*, in 1953 and the second edition in 1974. Kirk's philosophy of criminalistics was generalist in the sense that he believed forensic scientists should have a broad scientific education and knowledge of many aspects of physical evidence. He considered the primary skill and distinction of forensic science as that of *individualization through successive comparisons.

Paul Kirk in his laboratory

knit fabric A textile that is formed by intertwining of continuous loops of the yarns or fibres.

known (K) 1. A sample or exhibit that is collected from a verifiable and reliable source. For example, in a forensic fibre comparison, fibres recovered from the body of a victim (the questioned fibres (Q)) can be compared to fibres collected by police from a suspect's vehicle (the known fibres).
    2. In chemical analysis, a generic term for a sample with a known and accepted composition.

Kohler illumination (Köhler illumination) An illumination scheme used in microscopy that is designed to obtain consistent and sufficiently bright light across the specimen. To obtain Kohler illumination, the microscopist conducts a series of alignments and adjustments within the optical train of the microscope while viewing a test specimen. Kohler illumination is particularly important when digital images of the sample are to be collected.

Koppanyi test *See* DILLE-KOPPANYI TEST.

Kriminologie A forensic journal launched by Hans *Gross, an Austrian lawyer and legal investigator. The journal is still published.

Kuhmo decision (*Kumho Tire Company, Ltd. v Carmichael* 526 US 137 1999) A decision by the United States Supreme Court that extended the 'gatekeeper' role of trial judges in determining if the testimony of an expert should be admissible. In the *Daubert decision of 1993, the Court assigned to judges the responsibility for deciding if the testimony of a scientific expert was admissible in the case in question. The Kumho decision extended the gatekeeper role to include the testimony of any expert in any field, not just in a scientific or technical discipline.

k

laceration A slice or cut that is created by the impact of blunt force rather than from actual cutting or stabbing by a sharp instrument. The edges or margins of the wound tend to be irregular and strands of connected tissue (bridging) may be seen spanning the wound.

LaFarge, Marie (1816–52) A French woman who was at the centre of one of the earliest trials in which modern scientific toxicological evidence was used. She was convicted of poisoning her husband by arsenic after a lengthy trial in 1840. She was 24 years old at the time. While on travel in December of 1839, her husband Charles complained of stomach distress after eating a cake sent by Marie. He returned home, and she attended to him, notably preparing food and drinks for his convalescence. His condition deteriorated, and he died in early January. Suspicion focused on Marie given her behaviour during the illness, her purchase of arsenic, and her handling of the food in question. She was arrested and charged with murder. Subsequent chemical tests on the food showed the presence of arsenic. Marie was defended by a man named Maître Palliet, who was also the personal lawyer to a man named Mathieu Joseph Bonaventure *Orfila (1787–1853), a toxicologist working in Italy at the time. This coincidence became pivotal in the case.

The case arose a few years after the *Marsh test for arsenic was developed and it was utilized in the case. The defence was able to cast doubt on the initial positive results because the doctors doing the test did not convince the court of their expertise in using it. Charles's body was exhumed for further testing and the results showed no arsenic even as tests on the food in question did. Orfila was invited in as a recognized and respected expert. He conducted thorough testing of the evidence using the Marsh test (in which he was skilled) and reported finding arsenic in the dead man's tissues and further ruled out the soil in which he was buried as the source. Marie was convicted and initially sentenced to death, but that was commuted to a life sentence.

Mᵐᵉ LAFARGE.

Dessinée d'après nature à la première séance.

Marie LaFarge

laminar flame A combustion in which there is a smoothly flowing flame front; a flame with distinct regions delineated by colour and temperature.

LAMPA (lysergic acid, n-(methylpropyl) amide) An *ergot alkaloid related to *LSD.

lands and grooves Structures that are cut into the barrel of a firearm. The lands and grooves are cut in a twisting pattern and as a result, the bullet emerges from the barrel spinning. A barrel that has lands and grooves is said to be rifled. A spinning bullet does not tumble or wobble and as a result is much more accurate than a projectile fired from a smooth bore weapon such as a musket.

The lands and grooves are visible in the barrel

Landsteiner, Karl (1868–1943) An Austrian physician and Nobel prize winning researcher in the field of immunology. Landsteiner discovered the ABO blood group system in 1900–1901. Typing of this group would be the mainstay of forensic *serology until the advent of *DNA typing techniques. In the late 1800s the first attempts at blood transfusions had led to many deaths when the blood of the donor caused the red blood cells of the recipient to clump together (agglutinate). Landsteiner noted that this reaction was not universal in that the blood of some individuals was compatible while others were not. These observations coupled with his research led to the identification of the ABO system, which was the first blood group system identified. Landsteiner also recognized that a person's blood group was inherited and thus would be useful in paternity cases.

Because the ABO system is inherited, it also served as a genetic marker system in forensic analysis of blood and body fluids for nearly a century. Landsteiner's discovery led to systematic typing for blood transfusions and saved untold thousands of lives. As a result, he was awarded the Nobel Prize in Medicine in 1930. Landsteiner eventually moved to New York and continued to work in the field of immunology, participating in the discovery of several more blood group systems including the Rh system.

laser (light amplification by stimulated emission of radiation) Light sources that emit very intense radiation at a specific wavelength (coherent light). This emission can be stimulated in a number of ways, and relies on a population inversion in which the majority of molecules of the lasing material are in the excited state. The process of promoting these molecules to the excited state is called 'pumping'. Lasers can be used to induce fluorescence, exploited in many forensic applications. Fluorescent detectors are among the most sensitive available for analytical instruments. Lasers can also be components of alternative light sources (ALS) used to visualize latent fingerprints. Finally, lasers can be used to vaporize a surface for introduction into instruments such as *mass spectrometers. This technique, called laser ablation, is suited for the examination of paint layers and any other samples in which a characterization of the surface is needed.

laser printer A computer or fax printing device that works by imparting an electrical charge to paper as directed by software in the computer. Initially, a drum surface is charged electrostatically in a fine grid pattern. A laser selectively scans the grid, discharging any grid that it strikes to create the pattern contained on the document to be printed. Toner is applied to the drum and adheres wherever the charge remains, and paper is then fed through using a roller or similar system. Toner adheres to the paper and is set in place using heat.

latent data *See* AMBIENT DATA.

latent fingerprint Strictly defined, fingerprints that are barely visible or not visible. However, the term 'latent prints' is often used to refer to any type of fingerprint regardless of visibility. Latent prints can be visualized with powders, chemical developers, physical developers, and many other techniques. Once developed, images are taken of the prints for submission to automated fingerprint identification systems (AFIS) that search databases and seek potential matches. *See also* AFIS; IDENT1; MAYFIELD CASE.

latex The milky exudate of the seed pod of the opium poppy. The latex is a rich source of opiate alkaloids such as *morphine and *codeine.

latex particle A particle that is suspended in a solvent (vehicle) of a substance such as a latex paint. The particle is engineered to remain dispersed in the paint until it is applied to a surface and the water evaporates.

Lattes, Leon (1887–1954) A professor at the Institute of Forensic Medicine in Turin, Italy, who was instrumental in applying Karl *Landsteiner's discovery of the ABO blood group system to forensic casework. In 1915, he developed a test that came to be known as the 'Lattes procedure' or the 'Lattes crust test' in which red blood cells were added to dried bloodstains to determine the ABO blood type of the stain. For example, if the stain came from a person with type A blood, the stain will contain anti-B antibodies. When type A cells are added to the stain, nothing happens, but when type B cells are added, they clump together (agglutinate). Although novel at the time, the Lattes procedure did not work well with old stains and interpretation of results was difficult. However it laid the groundwork for later more sensitive and robust testing methods such as absorption-elution that were widely used until *DNA typing supplanted blood group typing.

Lausanne University *See* UNIVERSITY OF LAUSANNE.

LC-MS (liquid chromatography mass spectrometry) An instrumental analysis technique used for identification of drugs (particularly in toxicology) and other large molecular species. The instrument consists of a high pressure liquid chromatograph (HPLC) coupled to a mass spectrometer (MS). The most common interface between the liquid chromatograph and the mass spectrometer detector is based on the electrospray technique. *See also* MASS SPECTROMETRY.

LD$_{50}$ *See* LETHAL DOSE.

lead azide A widely used inorganic primary explosive. The lead from this and other primer compounds contributes to *gunshot residue (GSR) in the form of condensed particles. The structure is shown in the next entry.

lead styphnate A shock sensitive compound used in the *primers of ammunition. The shape of the crystal affects the sensitivity. The lead from this and other primer compounds contributes to *gunshot residue (GSR) in the form of condensed particles.

lead(II) azide

Lead styphnate
Lead(II) 2,4,6-trinitrobenzene-1,3-bis(olate)

Two lead-containing initiator compounds. Lead azide is an inorganic compound and lead styphnate is organic.

lean mixture A mixture of fuel and air (or other oxygen source) that has an excess of oxygen present relative to what would be present at stoichiometric equivalence. This equivalence is the ratio of oxygen and fuel in a balanced chemical equation. For example, the combustion of methane is described by the following balanced equation:

$$CH_4 + 2O_2 \rightarrow CO_2 + 2H_2O$$

If these exact amounts of fuel and oxygen are present, the system is at stoichiometric equivalence. A lean mixture has excess oxygen (a deficit of fuel) relative to the equivalence amount.

Leeuwenhoek, Anton Von (1632–1732) A Dutch scientist pivotal to the development of early microscopes and microscopy. He built a number of simple single lens devices, some of which were capable of magnification factors of 300.

lens A device used to focus light and which can be designed to create a magnified image. A simple convex lens (wider at the centre than at the edges) serves to converge light to a single point, where an image is created. The *principal focus is the point at which an image will be formed from an object placed at an infinite distance away from the opposite side of the lens. In the case of a simple lens, the distance of X from the lens is also the focal length (f). A lens can be characterized by the "thin lens" equation:

$$\frac{1}{f} = \frac{1}{p} + \frac{1}{q}$$

Any pair of values of p and q that satisfy this equation are referred to as conjugate foci. Additionally, the magnification (m) is equal to q/p.

lethal dose The amount of a substance such as a poison or toxin that is necessary to cause death. Factors that influence the size of a lethal dose include health of the person, age, family history and genetics, and weight. For example, two extra strength aspirin tablets are a normal dose for an adult, but that same dose could be fatal to an infant. To account for this size dependence, dosages of drugs are normally defined in units of milligrams of the substance per kilogram body weight (mg/kg). Toxicologists often refer to a value such as the LD_{50}, or 'lethal dose 50', a value most often derived from animal studies. In such studies, a large population of experimental animals such as mice or rats is given increasing doses of the substance being tested. The dosage that is fatal for half the population is the LD_{50}. Although a useful estimate, an LD_{50} is specific only to the animal of interest and is not always directly transferable to human beings. Some LD_{50} values exist for humans, but this data is normally derived from studies of accidental or unintentional exposures.

Leuckart method A method used to manufacture *methamphetamine in clandestine laboratories. The starting material is phenyl-2-propanone (P2P) and a *reductive amination reaction results with the addition of a reagent such as methyl amine (CH_3NH_2).

leuco form The reduced form of an organic dye that is colourless. The intended colour of the dye is generated by some form of oxidation. Indigo is an example of a dye that has a colourless leuco form that turns blue when subject to oxidizing conditions.

leucomalachite green A *presumptive test for blood that is not as frequently used as the *Kastle–Meyer (KM) or *luminol tests. It is prepared by combining leucomalachite green and sodium perborate ($NaBO_3$) in water and acetic acid.

levels I, II, and III Terms that can be used to describe features in fingerprints. Level I consists of the pattern such as a loop; level II consists of ridge patterns such as deltas or bifurcations (minutiae); and level III consists of patterns and features of the pores.

Liebermann, Carl (1842–1914) A German chemist who did pioneering work in dye chemistry. He studied and worked with such notable chemists as Robert Wilhelm Bunsen and Adolf von Baeyer. He is best known for his synthesis of the dye alizarin. He also developed colour-based presumptive tests that resulted in dye formation. The *Liebermann test is still used in seized drug analysis to detect the presence of phenolic groups such as those present in aspirin.

Liebermann test (Liebermann reagent) A *presumptive test used in *seized drug analysis. The reagent is prepared by dissolving potassium nitrite (KNO_2) in concentrated sulphuric acid and it is used to test for cocaine (a yellowish colour indicates the possible presence of the drug) and morphine (a black test is positive).

lifting The process of recovering a *latent fingerprint from a surface. This may be done at a crime scene or in the laboratory. There are two steps to the process. Once the evidence has been documented, the print is developed or visualized using reagents, powders, *alternative light sources (ALS) or other means. The print is then lifted from the surface using adhesive tape and placed on a card or other sturdy support.

ligature The object used to cause *strangulation in a murder, suicide, or accidental death. Ligatures are often ropes or other cords but can be anything that will encompass the neck and to which pressure can be applied. Towels, scarves, belts, sheets, and phone cord have all been used as ligatures and the knots used to tie or secure them can become critical evidence. Ligatures can also produce distinctive impressions on the neck that can be physically matched to the ligature. A ligature is also any cording that is used to bind a victim.

like dissolves like An informal phrase and rule of thumb used to describe comparative solubilities of materials based on their molecular structure and polarities. Polar materials will dissolve in polar solvents (ethanol dissolves in water, salt (NaCl) dissolves in water) and non-polar materials dissolve in non-polar solvents (oil dissolves in hexane). Non-polar materials such as hexane are not soluble in polar materials such as water.

likelihood ratio A quantity useful in the statistical analysis, presentation, and interpretation of forensic analyses that starts with at least two different theories or hypotheses concerning given scenarios. For example, assume a single hair is found on the clothing of a homicide victim and that a suspect has been identified. One hypothesis is that the hair is that of the suspect, while one competing hypothesis might be that the hair is very similar to the suspect's, but came to be on the victim as a result of some random process. The relative likelihood of these two hypotheses can be expressed numerically using a likelihood ratio. The likelihood ratio could take into account several separate probabilities such as the probability that the victim and the suspect came into contact, the probability that a transfer occurred, the probability that the hair remained in place long enough to be detected, and so on. Similar probabilities could be estimated for competing hypotheses and the summation of these probabilities used to create the likelihood ratio that would be expressed as: LR = probability that the suspect is the source of the hair/probability that a random person is the source.

The type of evidence involved and the amount of hard data and databases available are among the many factors that determine the reliability and usefulness of a likelihood ratio. For example, fingerprints or DNA results are supported by much larger databases and knowledge of frequencies than are hairs, fibres, glass, and other kinds of physical evidence. Despite these limitations, likelihood ratios can be useful for examining alternative explanations and encouraging the generation of alternative explanations for forensic findings. *See also* BAYESIAN STATISTICS.

limit of detection (LOD) In an analytical procedure, the smallest amount or concentration of an analyte that can be detected using that protocol. An instrument may be capable of detecting quantities at concentrations that are too low to be reliably quantified. In such cases, the LOD will be a lower concentration than the *limit of quantitation (LOQ).

limit of quantitation (LOQ) In an analytical procedure, the smallest amount or concentration of an analyte that can be reliably quantified using that protocol. This level is usually defined in terms of acceptable precision. The LOQ is the lowest concentration at which an analyte can be reliably quantified with acceptable *precision. The LOQ may be the same as the *limit of detection (LOD), or it may be a higher concentration.

LIMS An abbreviation for a laboratory information management system, a computerized system that tracks evidence, records results and instrument data, and generates reports.

Lindbergh kidnapping A 1932 crime in the United States that generated intense national and international public interest and highlighted emerging forensic science procedures and capabilities. Charles A. Lindbergh became a national and international hero in 1927 after flying the Atlantic alone in the *Spirit of St Louis*. He later married Anne Morrow and their first child, a son named Charles Jr., was 20 months old when he was kidnapped around 9.30 p.m. on 1 March 1932. The child's body was later found in woods close to the home. The arrest of the primary suspect, Bruno Hauptmann did not occur until 1934.

During the time between the kidnapping and murder of the child and Hauptmann's arrest, forensic investigations were undertaken on the physical evidence including the ransom notes (questioned documents), trace evidence, psychological and psychiatric studies, and perhaps most damning for Hauptmann, analysis of the ladder left at the crime scene and used to gain access to the child's second story window. Albert S. *Osborn, a pioneer in the field of questioned documents, performed analysis of the handwriting found in the ransom notes. Arthur Koehler, a wood expert employed by the Forest Service, undertook a meticulous evaluation of the ladder, including the wood, construction techniques, and toolmarks found on the wood. Eventually, he was able to trace the lumber used to a lumberyard and mill located in the Bronx. Marks made by planers on the wood in the ladder matched a planer at the yard. A search of the attic above Hauptmann's apartment revealed a missing floorboard. Nail holes and tree ring patterns from a rail of the ladder lined up perfectly where the floorboard had been. Furthermore, Koehler was able to demonstrate this at the trial as well as to show how the planer marks from the ladder matched Hauptmann's planer. Hauptmann was convicted and after a series of appeals and reviews, including one by the United States Supreme Court, he was executed on 3 April 1936.

line search *See* STRIP SEARCH AND LINE SEARCH.

linguistics, forensic The evaluation of the use of language in forensic applications. Techniques of forensic linguistics are used in such areas as attempting to identify a region where a person is from, determining the author of a document or determining if two documents were written by the same person, and in attempting to clarify the meaning of statements made in court or to law enforcement officials. One of their most common tasks is in the area of speaker or author identification, comparison, authentication, and analysis. Some authors consider forensic stylistics to be a separate specialty focusing on the style of speech (oral or written) characteristic of a group or individual.

linkage equilibrium In genetics, linkage equilibrium means that the frequency of a combination of different types can be calculated by multiplying the frequency of the individual types together. For example, if a person is typed for two different genetic marker systems and the first type is found in one in a thousand people and the second is found in one in a hundred, the frequency for the combined types is one in 100,000 (100 × 1,000). Such combinations are said to be in linkage equilibrium, meaning that the two types are inherited independently of each other—in other words, they are not linked. If in this example the combined types were found to

exist not in 1 in 100,000 but in 1 in 5,000, then the two genetic loci
are not inherited independently of each other and the system is said to
exhibit **linkage disequilibrium**.

lipophilic Substances that dissolve in or associate with lipids
(fats), which are non-polar molecules. The general rule
regarding solubility is that 'like dissolves like', meaning that non-polar
materials such as fats will dissolve in other non-polar materials
such as oils, but not in polar solvents such as water. Substances
that are lipophilic are 'fat loving', meaning that they will
associate with or dissolve in non-polar lipids. *See also* HYDROPHILIC;
HYDROPHOBIC.

lipophobic Substances that will not dissolve in or associate with
lipids (fats), which are non-polar molecules. The general rule regarding
solubility is that 'like dissolves like', meaning that non-polar materials
such as fats will dissolve in other non-polar materials such as oils,
but not in polar solvents such as water. Substances that are
lipophilic are 'fat loving', meaning that they will not interact with
non-polar lipids. Water is lipophobic. *See also* HYDROPHILIC;
HYDROPHOBIC.

liquid chromatography A generic term for a chromatographic
separation in which a liquid mobile phase flows over a stationary
solid phase. The procedure can be carried out in columns or
instrumentally such as in high performance liquid chromatography
(HPLC). *See also* REVERSED PHASE.

liquid/liquid extraction (LLE) An analytical separation
conducted by selective partitioning between two liquid phases.
It is usually carried out in a piece of conical glassware called
a separatory funnel. Two immiscible solvents are placed in the
funnel along with the sample and it is shaken. As the layers
separate, the sample will partition into the phase in which it
is most soluble. This method is widely used in drug analysis
and toxicology.

livor mortis (lividity) The settling of blood that occurs after
circulation ceases. Once the heart stops beating, blood is not reaching the
lungs and is not being oxygenated, and it takes on a bluish-purple tint.
Exceptions can occur if the victim has been poisoned with substances that
alter the colour of the blood such as carbon monoxide (CO). CO imparts
a distinctive cherry red colour that will also alter the appearance
of the lividity stain. Lividity occurs where gravity naturally
causes settling and lividity stains can look similar to bruises. The

only places blood won't settle is in locations where pressure is being applied. For example, if a person dies while seated, pressure is being applied to the buttocks that will prevent blood from pooling there.

The first signs of lividity begin to appear about an hour after death and will reach a maximum after three to four hours. After about twelve hours, no additional lividity will occur. Thus, lividity stains are useful in determining the time since death or the *post-mortem interval (PMI). The stain pattern can also be used to determine if a body was moved during the period in which lividity was developing. If a stain has already formed and the position of the body is altered within the twelve-hour window after death, a new pattern can form while the old stains partially fade. Similarly if the body is moved after twelve hours, the lividity pattern may not match the position in which the body is finally discovered.

Locard, Edmund (1877–1966) A pioneering French forensic scientist who was instrumental in taking new theoretical ideas of what was then called police science and applying them to casework. Locard was trained in both law and medicine and was influenced by the writings of Hans *Gross as well as the fiction of Arthur Conan *Doyle. In 1910, Locard established a forensic laboratory in Lyon, France. The lab was primitively equipped, but even so, Locard was able to establish a reputation and to increase the visibility of forensic science in Europe. Locard was interested in microscopic evidence, particularly dust, and believed that such trace evidence was crucial in linking people to places. Although he apparently never used the exact phrase himself, Locard is most famous for **Locard's Exchange Principle** that evolved from his studies and writings. The principle is stated in terms such as 'every contact leaves a trace,' and reflects his belief that every contact between a person and another person or a person and a place results in the transfer of materials between the entities involved. Most of this *transfer evidence, such as dust, is microscopic, and it may not last long, but the transfer does occur and it is the task of the forensic scientist to find those traces and use them to establish the link. The success of his laboratory and methods encouraged other European nations to form forensic science laboratories after the conclusion of the First World War. He founded and directed the Institute of Criminalistics located at the University of Lyon, where he remained a dominant presence in forensic science into the 1940s.

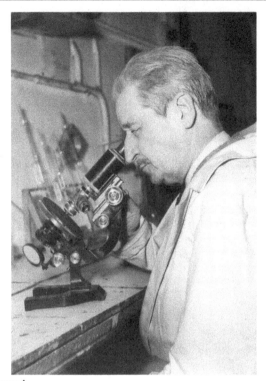

Edmund Locard

locus A physical location on a chromosome. The variants of DNA that are typed forensically are referred to as **loci**.

Lombroso, Cesare (1835–1909) An Italian physician active in forensic medicine who worked at the University of Turin. He subscribed to the theory of *criminal anthropology which held that criminals were inherently and physically different from others and that anthropological methods and physical measurements could be used to distinguish them. *See also* BERTILLON, ALPHONSE.

London subway bombing A terrorist bombing attack on the London Metro system that occurred on 7 July 2005. Fifty-two people were killed and hundreds wounded. The attack was carried out by three suicide bombers and three of the bombs exploded nearly simultaneously inside the tunnels. The fourth bomb detonated nearly an hour later on a bus. The devices were concealed

in backpacks and were estimated to contain between
2 and 5 kg of homemade peroxide-based explosives. *See also* MASS
DISASTER.

lower explosive limit (LEL) The minimum concentration
of vapours in air at which explosion or burning can occur
when a combustion source like a flame is present. Below
the LEL, no combustion can occur. *See also* UPPER
FLAMMABILITY LIMIT.

lower flammability limits The lowest range of concentration
of flammable material in air that can burn if an ignition source is
introduced.

low explosive Explosives that tend to burn quickly rather than
detonate; detonation can occur but requires a confined space.
Accordingly, low explosives are occasionally referred to as burning
explosives. Examples of low explosives include black powder and
*smokeless powder (used as propellants in ammunition),
which are frequently used to make homemade explosives and
pipe bombs. Another low explosive, made infamous by the
Oklahoma City Bombing (in the US) on 19 April 1995, is composed of
ammonium nitrate and 6 per cent fuel oil (ANFO). A similar mixture
of urea nitrate and other materials was used in the first attack on the
World Trade Centre in 1993. The maximum burning speed of
low explosives is around 1,000 metres per second. Low explosives
are sensitive to heat, friction, and sparks and are unstable relative
to high explosives such as TNT. The detonation of a low explosive
generates what is referred to as pushing power, in which large
objects are moved rather than shattered. Fragments of the
container in which the explosive was placed are relatively large and
there are often significant amounts of residues remaining after
the explosion.

low order explosion An explosion in which the speed of propagation
is less than the speed of sound (subsonic). This is also referred to as
deflagration. This contrasts with a high explosive, which *detonates.
*Smokeless powder in a pipe bomb typically results in a low order
explosion.

low velocity impact spatter A bloodstain pattern that
results when blood moving slowly (~1.5 metres per second or less)
strikes a surface. Blood dripping from a nosebleed onto the floor
creates a low velocity impact spatter. These patterns show larger

drops and less secondary spatter than medium and high velocity impact spatters.

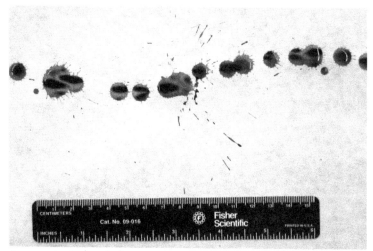

An example of low velocity spatter created by drops falling under the influence of gravity.

LSD *See* LYSERGIC ACID DIETHYLAMIDE.

Lucas, Alfred (1867–1945) An English chemist skilled in forensic and archaeological chemistry who became known as 'Egypt's Sherlock Holmes'. Lucas was trained as an analytical chemist and held several jobs based on this discipline. He began his career at the Inland Revenue Laboratory which analysed imported beer and wine to determine the appropriate custom duty. After contracting tuberculosis, he went to Egypt in 1897 where he performed various analyses and began to work with antiquities. He was named head of the Assay Office in 1912 and he worked closely with the military during the First World War and established his reputation as a forensic chemist and forensic scientist with expertise in handwriting analysis and firearms evidence. He wrote the first English language text on the topic of forensic chemistry, entitled *Forensic Chemistry: Legal Chemistry and Scientific Criminal Investigation* (1921). A second edition followed in 1931. Lucas worked with Howard Carter on the Tomb of Tutankhamun and again with the military during the Second World War. During his career, he published more than 100 articles and books describing his wide-ranging careers and interests.

Alfred Lucas

luminol A presumptive test for blood that is favoured because of its extreme sensitivity, particularly to old blood or traces that have been left after an attempted clean-up of a crime scene. Luminol, unlike other tests for blood, does not work by producing a colour change in the presence of haemoglobin. Rather, the reaction produces light via *chemiluminescence. Since the glow is faint, this test is not appropriate for areas that cannot be made dark such as large outdoor scenes. However, indoors luminol is one of the most useful tests for blood. In addition, the chemicals used in the luminol reagent (3-aminophthalhydrazide, sodium carbonate (Na_2CO_3), and sodium perborate ($NaBO_3$)) do not interfere with any subsequent *DNA typing. Finally, since no colour change need be observed, the colour of the material on which the blood has been deposited is not a limitation as it can be for other reagents.

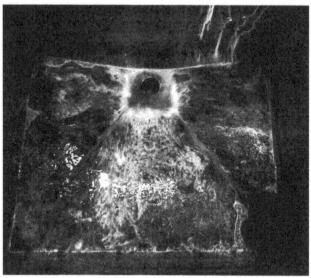

Luminol in a sink in which blood has been poured down the drain

lysergic acid diethylamide (LSD) A potent hallucinogen in the same family as *mescaline (peyote) and *PCP. Doses as low as 25µg can induce alteration of sensory perceptions, hallucinations, a feeling of floating or being 'out of body', and extreme mood swings. LSD is an *ergot alkaloid that is produced from lysergic acid. Lysergic acid is a compound produced by a fungus that attacks grasses, a family that includes grains such as wheat and rye. Another precursor, lysergic acid amide, is found in the seeds of the Morning Glory flower. LSD was first synthesized in 1938 and its hallucinogenic properties unearthed when the chemist who made it (Albert Hoffmann) accidentally ingested a small amount. For a short period, it was used in conjunction with psychotherapy but that use was soon abandoned.

lysis A rupturing such as the rupturing of cells. For example, red blood cells will lyse in distilled water due to ion imbalance. The interior of the cell has a high concentration of ions and water will flow into the cell to equalize the concentration.

McCrone, Walter (1916–2002) An American considered to have been the pre-eminent microscopist of his generation and who founded the McCrone Research Institute in 1960 in Chicago, Illinois. McCrone obtained his PhD from Cornell University in New York in 1942 and worked for a time at the Armour Research Institute. His interests in microchemical analysis led to the formation of the McCrone Associates in 1956 where the emphasis was on this topic as well as on the analysis of crystals and general microscopy. The McCrone Research Institute followed, and it remains a premier training facility for industrial and forensic microscopists worldwide. Of his many publications, one of the best known is *The Particle Atlas* used by forensic microscopists to identify unknown materials. He became familiar outside the scientific community during the analysis of the Shroud of Turin in 1980. The Shroud was purported to be the burial cloth of Jesus. McCrone, along with a group of other scientists conducted numerous tests and concluded that the Shroud was a clever forgery dating not to the 1st century, but to the 14th. He was awarded the American Chemical Society's Award in Analytical Chemistry in 2000 for his numerous contributions to *microscopy and microchemical analysis.

macroscopic crime scene The context or larger setting in which a scene is found; an overall view of the larger scene, for example if a murder is in a bedroom, the macroscopic scene could be the house or even the neighbourhood.

macroscopic examination Assessment of evidence or other materials on a scale compatible with human vision or under low magnification such as with a magnifying glass; most often refers to simple examination without the aid of any tools or instruments. Macroscopic examination precedes microscopic examination.

Madrid train bombing A terrorist attack that took place on 11 March 2004, killing nearly 200 people and injuring nearly 2,000. The attack was targeted at commuters and involved four commuter trains and ten bombs. Three bombs failed to detonate and were later destroyed by police. The bombs were concealed in bags and were detonated remotely by cell phones. One of the consequences of the attack was a false accusation against Brandon *Mayfield, an American Muslim who was incorrectly linked to the attack through faulty analysis of *latent fingerprint evidence. Seven suspects blew themselves up when their apartment was surrounded by police on 3 April 2004. Eventually 29 men were arrested and charged with the attack, one of whom was acquitted.

magazine   In an automatic or semi-automatic firearm, the device that holds cartridge cases so that they can be fed into the barrel prior to firing.

maggots   Larvae of flies that hatch from laid eggs.

magna powder   A magnetic powder used to visualize *latent fingerprints. It is delivered using a magnetic brush.

major axis   In a circular or oval pattern such as seen with blood drops or bullet holes, the major axis is the longest. Calculations using the ratio of the minor axis to the major axis can be used, along with basic trigonometry, to estimate the angle of impact involved in creation of the round feature.

Malphigi, Marcello (1628–94) An Italian botanist who studied plant morphology as a professor at the University of Bologna. He was the first person to use magnification techniques to study the ridge detail and pore structure of human skin. As a result, he is considered one of the early pioneers of fingerprints even though he neither focused on their potential to identify individuals nor their value in criminal investigations. In honour of his work, a portion of skin anatomy was named after him. The Malpighian layer (sometimes called the stratum malpighii) is found in the epidermis (the outer layer of skin) and refers to the combined basal and pickle cell layers (stratum germinativum and stratum spinosum).

malum in se   Literally 'evil in itself': a crime or act that is judged wrong and is illegal because of its inherently immoral, evil, or sinful nature. Murder is considered to be *malum in se.*

malum prohibitum   A crime or act that is prohibited by law or statute, but is not necessarily evil in and of itself.

MAM (monoacetylmorphine; acetylmorphine) There are two forms, 6-MAM and 3-MAM. When both locations (the number 3 and 6 carbons) are acetylated, this is *heroin. 6-MAM is a metabolite of heroin and 3-MAM is a synthetic by-product of the acetylation of morphine to form heroin.

Mandelin reagent   A versatile *presumptive test used in drug analysis that is based on colour formed by a transition metal complex. The Mandelin reagent is prepared by dissolving ammonia meta-vanadate in cold concentrated sulphuric acid (H_2SO_4). Addition of this reagent to cocaine results in an orange colour while codeine yields an olive green, heroin a brown, and amphetamine a bluish green. As with all presumptive tests, the results of a colour test are not sufficient to identify a drug, but it is useful for screening purposes and for directing further analysis.

manner of death The classification of a death as natural, accidental, suicidal, homicidal, or indeterminate, for which the abbreviation NASH is sometimes used. The determination of the manner of death when it is suspicious, questioned, or unattended is usually the responsibility of a *Medical Examiner or *coroner.

mapping, crime scene The process of documenting a scene with a hand-drawn or computer generated map showing the overall layout, perimeter, and key structures or features that define the scene. Reference points and directionality are documented to help locate features and evidence. Mapping is part of crime scene *documentation.

marijuana (marihuana) A general term for drugs derived from the plant *Cannabis Sativa L*, and specifically for the leaves and flowering tops of those plants. Marijuana is classified as a *hallucinogen. The marijuana plant can grow to over 1.5 metres in height and is also used as a source for hemp, the fibres of which can be made into rope or clothing products. The active ingredient in marijuana and its derivatives is Δ^9-tetrahydrocannibinol, usually abbreviated simply as *THC. *Hashish or hash oil is the oily resin excreted by the flowering tops and has a higher concentration of THC, in the range of 10–20 per cent.

Marquis test One of the most widely used *presumptive tests in forensic drug analysis. It works by forming highly conjugated dye with the target drugs. The Marquis reagent is prepared by adding a 40 per cent solution of formaldehyde to concentrated sulphuric acid (H_2SO_4). When added to opiates such as *heroin, a purple dye is formed while amphetamine and *methamphetamine generate an orange coloured dye. Many other drugs react with the Marquis reagent as well. The results of a colour test are not sufficient to identify a drug, but it is useful for screening purposes and for directing further analysis.

Marsh, James (1794–1846) A distinguished English chemist best known for the development of a reliable test for the presence of arsenic in tissues. The test variants were used by forensic toxicologists well into the 20th century, when methods of instrumental analysis such as atomic absorption (AA) eventually replaced it. Marsh was also the first to present the results of an analytical toxicology analysis in court in the year 1836, and his test was used by M. J. B. *Orfila, who is considered to be the father of modern forensic toxicology. The *Marsh test became a powerful and reliable test for arsenic at a time when arsenic poisoning (accidental, suicidal, and especially homicidal) was rampant. *See also* LAFARGE, MARIE; BODLE, JOHN; SEDDON CASE.

Marsh test   The test developed by James *Marsh and designed to detect arsenic in body tissues. The test works on the basis of oxidation/reduction chemical reactions. The test begins by adding solid zinc metal to a glass vessel containing an acid such as hydrochloric (HCl) or sulphuric (H_2SO_4). The tissue or body fluid in question is prepared and added to the vessel, where the reaction of the zinc and the acid has created hydrogen gas (H_2). The hydrogen reacts with the arsenic compound (usually in the form of arsenic trioxide, AsO_3) to produce arsine gas (AsH_3). Heating of the gas results in arsenic metal plating out on the glass or ceramic container into which the gas has flowed. This metal deposit is referred to as the arsenic mirror, which is stable and could be presented to a jury. The test, although reliable, required that the chemist performing it be skilled and practised in the procedure.

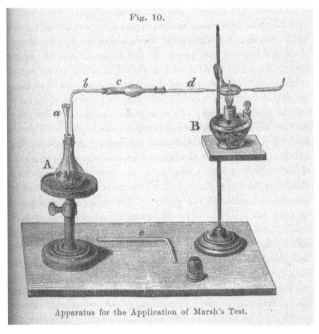

Fig. 10.

Apparatus for the Application of Marsh's Test.

The Marsh test apparatus

Mason, Clyde W. An American pioneer in chemical microscopy. Mason was on the faculty of Cornell University in New York. He taught with Emile *Chamot, who was a teacher to Walter *McCrone, who became an internationally recognized expert in forensic microscopy.

mass disaster (mass fatality) Incidents by a large death toll that exceeds the capacity of local resources. Mass disasters used to be primarily associated with transportation disasters such as airplane or railroad accidents or natural disasters such as the tsunami that struck Asia in 2004. Terrorist attacks such as occurred on 11 September 2001 in the United States or the *Madrid train bombing and *London subway are also mass fatality incidents. From the forensic perspective, mass disasters have two critical aspects: first, recovery and identification of remains, and, second, documentation, recovery, and preservation of evidence necessary for the subsequent investigation.

mass spectrometry (MS) A versatile instrument that separates ions based on their size-to-charge ratio. Mass spectrometry can be utilized for the analysis of organic compounds such as drugs as well as for the analysis of elements such as lead or arsenic. Mass spectrometry as used in forensic science is not a 'stand-alone' technique, but rather a mass spectrometer coupled to different sample introduction instruments or devices, yielding what is called a hyphenated technique. Examples include gas chromatography/mass spectrometry (GC-MS), high pressure liquid chromatography/mass spectrometry (HPLC-MS), inductively coupled plasma/mass spectrometry (ICP-MS), and *pyrolysis mass spectrometry. A slash (/) is often used in place of a hyphen, but the meaning is the same and both notations are used interchangeably.

The sample is introduced through an inlet into a chamber that is kept at a very low pressure, in the range of 1×10^{-5} torr (about one-billionth of normal atmospheric pressure). This low pressure is essential to prevent collisions between ions (charged particles) created by the instrument and atmospheric components. The sample molecule (if it is an organic compound) is then ionized to form charged fragments of the original molecule. The molecular ion (M^+) is the source of these fragments and is created by stripping a single electron away from the original compound. In many cases, the molecular ion is present in the resulting mass spectrum and is used to characterize the molecular weight of the compound. Once formed, all ions are directed into a mass filter, where they are separated by a variety of mechanisms, depending on the instrument type.

A number of different types of ionization schemes are available for mass spectrometers used for organic molecules. The most common is electron impact (EI) in which ionization results from collision with a beam of electrons. Other ionization modes include chemical ionization (CI), particularly useful when a strong M^+ signal is needed; *electrospray (ESI) and atmospheric pressure chemical ionization (API or APCI) sources are used with HPLC systems; and plasmas (ICP) for inorganic samples. Similarly there are many types of mass filters available with a few routinely utilized in forensic science. This includes time-of-flight instruments (TOF), ion traps, quadrupoles, and increasingly, sequential combinations of filters such as quadrupole-time-of-flight (QTOF) and tandem quadrupoles.

Perhaps the most common mass filter type in forensic applications is the quadrupole design used as a detector for *gas chromatography (GC) and as part of tandem detectors for HPLC. In GC, the sample molecules enter the mass spectrometer after being separated on the chromatographic column. Ions are created by collision with a stream of electrons created by a tiny filament. The electrons are drawn toward the target that is positively charged since unlike charges attract. Conversely, since like charges repel, the positive ions are driven into a stack of focusing lenses by the positive charge on the repeller. The ions are focused into a tight beam that enters the quadrupole area, which consists of four metallic rods. Manipulation of the electrical fields allows the ions to be filtered so that only one mass is detected at any given time. The emerging ions are directed into an electron multiplier that amplifies the signal sent to the detector.

Once ions are produced, they are directed into the mass filter, where they are separated out into individual masses and the abundances recorded. The separation is based on size of the ion as well as the charge; this is referred to as the *mass-to-charge ratio designated as m/z. The results are plotted in a mass spectrum that shows the relative abundance of each mass. Ions are filtered in the quadrupole by manipulation of the electrical fields such that only one mass ion is detected at any given time (measured in milliseconds). The electronics are rapidly changed to allow different masses to pass, resulting in the mass spectrum. Typical cycle times for the MS are on the order of a few seconds or less. The quadrupole is nearly standard for GC; ion traps and TOF designs are found in many HPLC systems. There are also MS/MS systems in which fragment ions that emerge from the mass filter are directed into another mass spectrometer that repeats the process and produces another series of smaller fragments. This type of information is useful when attempting to identify a material that was not found in the mass spectral library. Recently, there has been a notable increase in the utilization of multiple mass filter instruments such as triple quadrupoles (QQQ) and quadrupoles linked to TOF detectors (QTOF) in forensic toxicology and explosives analysis. These detectors are usually paired with HPLC systems and utilize ESI or API ionization sources.

See also INDUCTIVELY COUPLED PLASMA TECHNIQUES.

mass-to-charge ratio (m/z) In *mass spectrometry (MS) and related techniques, separation of charged species is based on the size-to-charge ratio of the ion. For example, the mass-to-charge ratio of a sodium cation (Na^+) would be the same as its mass, since the charge is +1. However, the size-to-charge ratio of a calcium cation (Ca^{2+}) would be half the mass since the charge is +2.

matrix controls Samples that are prepared in the same matrix as case samples. These are commonly used in forensic toxicology where sample matrices such as blood and urine are common. An example of a matrix control would be a clean blood or clean urine (which can be purchased commercially) that is analysed at the same time and using the same methods as case samples of blood and urine. The results will show if there are substances in the blood or urine that could lead to *false positive results.

matrix mismatch A condition that occurs when the matrix of a sample (such as blood or tissue) is not the same as that used for the calibration standards.

Mayfield case (2004) A case of mistaken latent fingerprint identification associated with the *Madrid train bombing. Spanish investigators provided the FBI with an image of a partial print found on a plastic bag recovered from the scene. Investigators suspected that the attackers had handled it. Search of the *IAFIS system provided a list of potential matches, and evaluation by experts led to identification of Brandon Mayfield, whose prints were on record because he had served in the US Army. The fact that Mayfield had converted to Islam and had acted as an attorney for a person in Portland, Oregon, who had been accused of operating a terrorist training camp added fuel to the fire, even though the matter he acted on was an unrelated child custody case. Spanish investigators expressed misgivings about the identification and eventually linked the questioned fingerprint to another suspect. Mayfield was released, and the FBI issued a press statement and apology in May 2004, promising to review procedures and practices.

MDMA (3,4-methylenedioxymethamphetamine; ecstasy) A *phenylethylamine stimulant related to *methamphetamine. It is known as a rave or *club drug and can have hallucinogenic and psychedelic effects at high doses.

MDMA

MDMA

measurable quantity A quantity of a substance, usually a seized drug, that can be weighed with acceptable accuracy using an analytical balance.

mechanical fit *See* PHYSICAL MATCHING.

mechanism of death The specific medical, biochemical, and/or physiological process or failure that causes death. For example, in a stabbing, blood loss can lead to shock and often this shock would be the mechanism of death even though it was precipitated by the stab wound.

Mecke test A *presumptive test used in drug analysis based on colour produced by a transition metal complex. The Mecke reagent is prepared by dissolving selenious acid in concentrated sulphuric acid (H_2SO_4). When added to opiates such as *heroin, the reagent turns yellow, fading to a greenish colour. The reagent is particularly useful for identification of *hallucinogens such as *LSD, which produces an olive green colour that turns blackish, and *psilocybin, which produces a yellow-green colour that turns brownish.

Medical Examiner (ME) In the United States, a forensic pathologist appointed by a jurisdiction such as a state, county, or city to oversee death investigations. Medical Examiners did not appear in the USA until 1877, when Massachusetts became the first state to abolish the *coroner system in favour of an ME system. New York City followed in 1915, and many jurisdictions have since converted to the newer system. However, both systems still coexist in the United States. An ME is a physician with specialized training in forensic pathology and who is qualified to conduct an autopsy and tissue analysis. Like a coroner, an ME is charged with determining the cause, manner, and circumstances of a death. At a crime scene involving a death, normally it is the ME's office that has jurisdiction over the body while law enforcement agencies are responsible for the rest of the scene. Similarly, the ME is responsible for collecting any physical evidence discovered during the autopsy and for delivering it to the appropriate forensic laboratory.

medicolegal investigation of death *See* DEATH INVESTIGATION.

medium velocity impact spatter A blood spatter pattern created by a medium velocity blow such as from a fist or club. It is characterized by droplets that are smaller than a simple drip (as in a nosebleed) but larger than the misting produced by a high velocity impact.

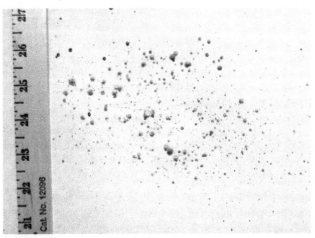

Example of medium velocity bloodstain patterns

medulla In a hair, the central portion that runs lengthwise; it is often likened to a canal running down the middle of a hair. Characteristics of the medulla vary among species and among individuals.

medullary index The diameter of the *medulla relative to the diameter of the *hair. This ratio is sometimes employed during microscopic analysis and comparison of hair.

melanin An organic polymer that forms pigment granules found in hair; these granules impart the colour to hair. Melanin is created by melanocyte cells found in the hair follicle. Melanin is also responsible for skin colour.

melanocyte Pigment producing cells located in the epidermis layer of the skin. The pigment produced is melanin.

mens rea Literally 'guilty mind', the term refers to a perpetrator's state of mind when committing a crime as either having criminal intent or being reckless but without criminal intent.

menstrual blood Blood that is excreted from the womb during a woman's menses. This type of blood contains high amounts of fibrinogen and this characteristic can sometimes be used to differentiate a stain of menstrual blood from stains deposited in other ways.

Merck _Index_ A handbook, available as hard copy or electronically, that contains information and data regarding drugs and related compounds. The _Index_, currently in its fourteenth edition, is published by Merck Sharp and Dohme Research Laboratories and contains data on over 10,000 compounds as well as tables, lists, and extensive cross-referencing information.

( ) SEE WEB LINKS
• Homepage for the well-known reference book. Last accessed May 2011.

mescaline A hallucinogenic compound that is contained in peyote, which is the 'button' located on the top of a cactus found in Mexico and the south-western United States. This button is also called a mescal button and it consists of the flowering head of the _Lophora williamsii_ cactus. The compound was first isolated in 1896 and made synthetically about twenty years later.

metabolism A breakdown product of a substance such as a drug or toxin produced by a chemical transformation process in the body. In drug and poison applications, the ingested substance is called a *xenobiotic or foreign to the body. For example, if someone were to ingest cocaine, that compound is not normally found in the body and is thus considered to be foreign. In other cases, the substance may be found naturally in the body, but in trace concentrations. In forensic toxicology, it is often the metabolites that are the target of analysis in fluids such as blood and urine.

The process of metabolism involves stepwise changes in the molecule using different kinds of chemical reactions. Each stage of the process is catalysed by the actions of *enzymes. When a substance is ingested orally, it is absorbed in the stomach or intestines, where it passes into the bloodstream and into the liver. In contrast, substances that are injected or inhaled are not subject to this 'first pass metabolism'. The first stage metabolites may undergo additional processes, leading to a large number of by-products. Final metabolic products have three principal fates. Volatile products such as carbon dioxide (CO_2) can be exhaled as in the case of the metabolism of alcohol (ethanol). Water soluble products are excreted in the urine or in other body fluids. Products that are fat soluble (hydrophobic) can build up in fatty tissues. Heavy metal poisons such as mercury can produce fat soluble products. Most metabolic processes are concentrated in the liver, but not all. Some metabolism can take place in the stomach and intestines (gastrointestinal or GI tract) and in other organs such as the kidneys.

metadata In a computer file, information regarding the file which is not part of the data itself. Examples of metadata include the name of the person that created the file, dates, when it was accessed, and file size. Some of this information is accessible to a user and thus can be changed; other metadata may be embedded in such a way that it is inaccessible.

metallurgy, forensic The analysis of metal objects and structures in a forensic context, typically part of or closely associated with forensic engineering. Steel is often the subject of forensic metallurgical analysis since steel is so commonly used as a structural component in everything from planes to buildings. Forensic metallurgy was used in the investigation of the crash of TWA flight 800 (in the Atlantic Ocean near New York City) in 1996 where there was considerable doubt early in the investigation as to what caused the centre fuel tank to explode. Potential causes included a bomb or missile, both of which would have left characteristic evidence. For example, if a bomb exploded from within the plane, the metal skin of the aircraft would have been peeled backward and outward, whereas a missile striking the fuselage and exploding would have left a much different signature on the fuselage. In this case, forensic metallurgy pointed to an explosion from within. Other examples where forensic metallurgy is used include the analysis of bombs such as pipe bombs and more traditional forensic engineering analysis such as was used to unravel the sequence of events that led to the loss of the space shuttle *Columbia* in February 2003. Metal fatigue and joint failures (welded, bolted, or other) are often a central concern in many incidents.

metamerism **1.** Occurs when two objects such as fibres appear to be the same colour under one type of illumination and of different colour under another type of illumination.
2. Occurs when two fibres have the same apparent colour when viewed in visible light but actually have different spectral characteristics. Microspectrophotometry using visible, infrared, or fluorescent techniques can be used to differentiate objects that are metameric pairs.

methadone A synthetic *opiate alkaloid that is used to treat heroin addiction and for pain relief.

methamphetamine A synthetic *phenylethylamine that is a stimulant, and at higher doses, a hallucinogen. Methamphetamine is easily synthesized from widely available *precursors and as such presents a significant law enforcement and forensic problem. Methamphetamine is a basic drug with one ionizable centre and is notable for the fact that the *free base form is relatively volatile. There are several means by which methamphetamine can be synthesized including the Nazi or *Birch method, the *'red cook' method, and the *Emde method. *See also* CLANDESTINE LABORATORY.

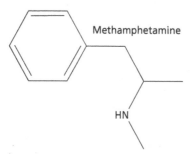

Methamphetamine

method bias A *bias in an analytical method that is constant and reproducible; a reproducible variation between an accepted *true value and an experimentally determined value obtained from the method.

method validation The process of designing, testing, and verifying an analytical method; a process that generates the relevant *figures of merit for an analytical method.

metrology The science of obtaining and reporting measurements; includes the theoretical and practical aspects of estimating the *uncertainty of measurements.

micelle A microscopic structure formed when surfactants such as soap molecules are placed in water. Surfactants are long chain molecules that consist of a non-polar (water-insoluble) portion or tail topped by a polar water-soluble group. When sufficient surfactant is placed in water (exceeding the critical micelle concentration or CMC), micelles will form. Micelles are exploited in a form of electrophoresis called micellular electrokinetic electrophoresis (MEKC).

Michaelis–Menton equation An equation used to characterize the kinetics of enzyme-catalysed reactions such as occur in drug metabolism. Specifically, the equation describes the speed or rate of the reaction relative to the concentration of the substrate to which the enzyme attaches as part of the catalytic reaction. The equation can be presented in several forms, the most common of which is:

$$V = \frac{V_{max}[S]}{K_m + [S]}$$

Where V is the velocity or rate of the reaction; [S] is the concentration of the substrate; and Km is a constant that is unique to each enzyme/substrate combination.

Michel–Levy chart A chart used in *polarizing light microscopy (PLM) that relates colour and sample thickness to *birefringence of samples such as fibres and crystals.

Michelson interferometer A device used in *infrared spectroscopy (IR) which allows many wavelengths of infrared radiation to be directed at a sample simultaneously rather than sequentially. The advantage of this approach is that a sample can be scanned much faster and can be scanned multiple times to improve the quality and sensitivity of the resulting spectrum. An interferometer works based on the principle of interference of coincident light waves. If two beams are in phase, the interference is constructive and the resulting combination has the same maxima and minima at twice the amplitude (height). On the other hand, if the beams are completely out of phase, the resulting interference is destructive and the net result is a cancelling out of both. Between these two extremes, there will be different combinations of constructive and destructive interference occurring. The Michelson interferometer takes advantage of this, coupled to a mathematical operation called a Fourier transform that enables a computer to break a composite pattern down into individual components, in effect undoing the interference and reconstructing the original components. The Michelson interferometer creates an output called an interferogram that is composed of a complex signal generated by multiple wavelengths and multiple cycles moving through the extremes of constructive and destructive interference. The Fourier transform is then applied to the signal to recover the intensity of the original radiation at each wavelength used.

microanalysis The analysis of evidence using magnification ranging from a magnifying glass through *microscopy and *polarizing light microscopy (PLM) to *scanning electron microscopy (SEM).

microbial degradation Processes of decomposition and breakdown of materials by the action of micro-organisms, principally bacteria and fungi. Although the public usually associates this process with the decomposition of human bodies (putrefaction), microbial degradation is an issue for any kind of biological evidence including blood and body fluid stains. Any organic material that a microbe can use as food, from remains to ropes and cloth, is subject to degradation. The rate of degradation depends on the suitability of the environment for the microbes, which generally favour warm, moist conditions. Blood and other body fluids are also subject to putrefaction and, for this reason, bloodstained materials should be dried and stored refrigerated or frozen to slow the process.

microchemical tests Generically, a group of analytical methods performed with small amounts and volumes with results observed using *microscopy. The tests can include colour-based *presumptive tests and tests that involve formation of solids and distinctive microcrystal structures. *See also* CRYSTAL TESTS.

Microchemistry of Poisons, The (1867) A book written by American physician Theodore G. Wormley (1826-1987). It was considered one of the earliest textbooks on forensic microscopy, focusing on toxicology. Microscopists hailed the book for its detail and meticulous illustrations, made from steel engravings which were completed by his wife after Wormley could not find anyone willing to create the complex engravings needed.

microconcentrator A device designed to concentrate via evaporation samples that have a small volume to begin with; typically less than one millilitre. Microconcentrators are often used as part of *DNA typing, and concentration can be affected using heat, vacuum, or gas flow and is often combined with centrifugation.

micrometry The process of taking measurements of objects that are being magnified. This is usually accomplished using a calibrated scale (**micrometer**) in a reticle that attaches to the objective lens.

microsatellite In DNA, a segment that consists of *short tandem repeats (STR) with 2, 3, 4, or 5 nucleotides in the repeated segment. *See also* MINISATELLITE.

microscopy A fundamental tool of forensic science that encompasses visual techniques based on light and electromagnetic radiation as well as techniques based on electrons (scanning electron microscopy (SEM)^). The simplest form of microscopy, still widely used, employs a simple magnifying glass. Other types of forensic microscopy use compound (optical or biological) microscopes, *stereomicroscopes, *polarizing light microscopes (PLM), comparison microscopes, phase contrast microscopes, and fluorescence microscopes.

All optical microscopes are based on magnification as a result of light passing through a lens. A lens can produce two different kinds of images. A real image is one that can be projected onto a screen (like a movie) or onto the retina of the person looking at it. A virtual image is what a magnifying glass produces—an image that is not physically real and can only be seen when looking through the lens. A compound microscope, also called a biological microscope, builds on this design by using two lenses in series, creating two stages of magnification. Although high magnification is possible (800×) using compound microscopes, increasing magnification comes at a cost. The higher the magnification, the smaller the field of view, as was the case with the magnifying glass. Second, as magnification increases, the depth of focus (how deep into a sample the focus remains sharp) decreases. Other variants of microscopy build on this foundation of magnification by lenses.

Microspectrophotometry (MSP), the coupling of microscopes and spectrophotometry, is becoming more widespread in forensic science and the combined instruments are invaluable for the analysis of small and trace amounts of material. Spectrometry is based on the study of how matter interacts with electromagnetic radiation (EMR) or light. Since microscopes exploit many portions of the electromagnetic spectrum, it has proved relatively simple to link the two. In forensic work, the most widespread type of microspectrophotometry uses the infrared region (IR). IR microspectrophotometers are used for the analysis of drugs, paints, dyes and coatings on fibres, and inks. Subtle differences in surface composition can be studied on the microscopic level and can be used to create surface composition maps. Variations of micro-IR include *attenuated total reflectance (ATR) and IR-polarizing microscopy. Microspectrophotometers are also available for the visible region and for ultraviolet (UV) fluorescence and for IR scattering (Raman spectroscopy).

microtransfer The transfer of microscopic evidence between people and/or places as described in *Locard's exchange principle. Dust and fibres are examples of materials that can be part of a microtransfer.

minigel *Electrophoresis apparatus and gels that are significantly smaller than used in traditional slab-gel electrophoresis.

minimum ignition energy (MIE) The amount of energy, typically reported in Joules or mJ, that is required to ignite a combustible mixture of vapours or dust.

minisatellite A genetic locus that is classified as having a *variable number of tandem repeats (VNTR) of *nucleotides. Variations between individuals are based on different numbers of repeats of the same base pair sequence. The sequence in a minisatellite is typically considered to be 10-50 nucleotides. *See also* MICROSATELLITE.

minor axis In a circular or oval pattern such as seen with blood drops or bullet holes, the minor axis is the shortest. Calculations using the ratio of the minor axis to the major axis can be used, along with basic trigonometry, to estimate the angle of impact involved in creation of the round feature.

minutiae The small features of a fingerprint that are critical in matching two fingerprints. Ridge endings, deltas, pores, and bifurcations are examples of minutiae.

mirror image back-up A copy of storage media such as a hard disk drive that is made by copying every bit on the media even if is not being used to represent data. *See also* FORENSIC COPY.

miscible Soluble; for example, ethanol is miscible in water.

misting A bloodstain pattern that is created by a high velocity impact such as a gunshot wound.

mitochondria Cell organelles located outside the nucleus and active in cellular respiration and energy production. The mitochondria have their own DNA (mtDNA) that is separate from the nuclear DNA typed in typical *DNA typing procedures.

mitochondrial DNA (mtDNA) DNA that is found outside the cell nucleus in a structure called the *mitochondria. The mitochondria are key in cell energy production and have their own DNA, which is inherited solely from the mother. Thus, even if a person is not available to provide comparison samples (deceased, missing, and so on), comparison standards can be obtained from anyone in the maternal line. Because it is found in even greater abundance than nuclear DNA, mitochondrial DNA can be used on very small samples, and problems of degradation are reduced. Mitochondrial DNA is found in a loop structure and there are three regions where variations occur called HVI, II, and III for hypervariable regions 1–3, which can be amplified using *PCR techniques.

MNSs blood group system A blood group system conceptually similar to the *ABO blood group system; efforts to type in forensic samples and stains were largely unsuccessful.

mobile phase In chromatography, the phase of material that is moving. In gas chromatography (GC), the mobile phase is the carrier gas while in *high performance liquid chromatography (HPLC), the mobile phase is a solvent or solvent mixture. The mobile phase may be inert as in GC, or it may be active in the separation process, as in HPLC.

modacrylic A type of synthetic fibre composed of polymers based on acrylonitriles $((-CH_2CH[CN]-)$ combined with copolymers such as vinyl chloride.

modes of ingestion Different ways in which drugs, poisons, or other *xenobiotic substances can enter the body. These include swallowing, subcutaneous injection, intravenous injection, smoking and absorption in the lungs, sublingual absorption, dermal absorption, and absorption through the nasal cavity. Mode of ingestion is an important consideration in toxicology.

molecular explosive An explosive in which all the necessary components for *detonation are contained within a molecule; an explosive with both fuel and oxidant present within the molecule. *TNT is an example of a molecular explosive.

monochromatic Literally 'one colour'; refers to light (or other forms of *electromagnetic energy) that is composed of a single wavelength.

morphine A derivative of *opium that constitutes anywhere from approximately 5 to 20 per cent of the extract. Morphine is also a metabolite of some of the *opiate alkaloids such as heroin. The name 'morphine' comes from the name of the Greek god of dreams, Morpheus. Morphine was first extracted from opium in the early 1800s and by the middle of the century was widely used for its potent pain relieving ability desperately needed by the wounded in that conflict. Morphine is classified as a narcotic analgesic (pain reliever) that in large doses can cause respiratory depression and death. It is still used for the relief of severe pain such as that of terminal cancer. Morphine comes in many forms including salts such as morphine hydrochloride and morphine sulphate.

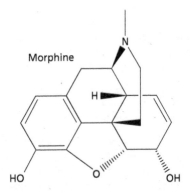

Morphine

morphology Structure or form; characteristics of physical appearance.

Moscow route *See* RED COOK METHOD.

mounting media Substances used to support and hold samples for microscopic examination or for cutting materials into thin sections that are appropriate for microscopy. Mounting media can be temporary or permanent, solid or liquid. For example, fibres can be supported in various types of plastic or polymeric media to support them for cutting to reveal cross-sections.

Mullis, Kary (1944–) An American scientist who played the lead role in developing the *PCR (polymerase chain reaction) technique essential to current methods of *DNA typing using *short tandem repeats. The work was published in 1986 in the respected journal *Nature* and led to a Nobel Prize in Chemistry in 1993.

multi-metal deposition (MMD) A technique used to visualize *latent fingerprints involving the application of gold followed by silver. The general procedure can be used on porous and non-porous surfaces.

Munsell colour system A method and system of describing colour graphically using three dimensions: Munsell Hue (H), Munsell Chroma (C), and Munsell Value (V). The value is the relative lightness or darkness of a colour, the chroma is the vividness of the colour, and the hue is the colour (red, blue, etc.). Standard Munsell colour charts and colour trees can be used to describe the colour of evidence such as soil.

muzzle energy (muzzle velocity) The speed or energy that a bullet has when it emerges from the barrel of a firearm after the cartridge is fired.

m

NA (numerical aperture) A number that measures the size of the 'cone' of light that can be produced by the objective or condenser in a microscope. It is calculated as $n*\sin(\theta)$ where n is the refractive index of the material between the objective lens and the condenser and θ is equal to half the angle between the two edges of this cone of light. The NA is calculated when the diaphragm on the microscope, located below the

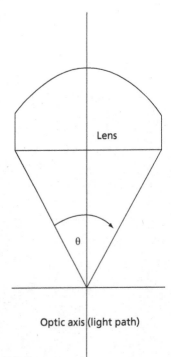

Lens

θ

Optic axis (light path)

Depiction of the numerical aperture

stage and controlling the amount of light reaching the specimen, is completely open. The NA number is related to the resolution, and for maximum resolution, the NA of the objective lens should be matched to that of the condenser.

nandrolone An anabolic steroid of concern in human performance toxicology and doping investigations.

nanoparticles (nanocrystals) Small particles with dimensions that are 100 nm or smaller. Nanoparticles of gold, silver, cadmium selenide (CdSe), and zinc sulphide (ZnS) have been applied in forensic science as visualization agents for *latent fingerprints. The nanoparticles bind preferentially to latent fingerprint residue and can be exploited to develop the fingerprints. The key advantage of this approach is that these tiny particles display intense luminescence that is a function of size rather than chemical composition. Nanoparticle methods can be combined with other techniques such as cyanoacrylate fuming to further improve development. *See also* MULTI-METAL DEPOSITION; PHYSICAL DEVELOPER.

Narborough murders The case in which *DNA typing was used for the first time in a forensic setting. The rape-murders took place in England in the 1980s, not far from the laboratory of Sir Alec *Jeffreys, who would be the one to apply DNA typing to the case. The victims were both 15 years old, one dying in 1983 and the second in 1986. The killings shared enough characteristics to convince investigators that probably one man was responsible. A suspect named George Howard confessed to one of the crimes, but his mental state was questionable and the physical and serological evidence was unconvincing.

Investigators asked Jeffreys to test blood from Howard as well as semen found on the clothing of the two victims and Howard was exonerated and the investigation was stalled. Although a DNA profile had been developed for the killer, there were no population databases available to reference it to. The solution was a *biological dragnet in which police took samples from all local men. None of the approximately 4,000 profiles matched. The break in the case came unexpectedly when a group of people sitting in a pub overheard a conversation in which one man said that he had given his blood in place of another. The man skipping the test was Colin Pitchfork. Police found Pitchfork, obtained a sample for Jeffreys to complete the analysis that was eventually used to convict Pitchfork and sentence him to two life terms. The arrest came in 1987 and the trial in 1988.

narcotic **1.** A drug that affects the central nervous system and causes a reduction in pain, a sense of well-being, and decreases in respiration, heart rate, and blood pressure. Examples are *morphine and *fentanyl. Narcotics have a significant potential for addiction. **2.** Sometimes used generically to describe abused drugs that are addictive such as *cocaine, even though the physiological effects of the drug are not the same as for a narcotic strictly defined.

natural entrances and natural exits At a crime scene, points where a person (suspect or perpetrator) would be likely to enter or leave a room or an area. Identification of these points is an important part of crime scene *assessment.

Nazi method *See* BIRCH METHOD.

negative control A *blank; a sample purposely designed to produce a negative result with a given test.

negative distortion (barrel distortion) In microscopy, an optical aberration that arises from the optics in which the centre of the sample field of view experiences greater magnification relative to the edges; thus the term 'barrel distortion'. This contrasts with a positive or pincushion distortion in which the opposite occurs.

negative impression A type of impression evidence created when contact between two surfaces results in a removal of material where contact occurred. For example, a shoe impression made in mud is a positive impression whereas a shoe print made on a dusty floor would be a negative impression since the sole of the shoe removed dust to create the impression.

Nessler's reagent A presumptive test for urine. It is a solution of mercuric iodide, which detects ammonia that is created by the degradation of urea.

neutral burning powder A type of propellant that is engineered to burn in such a manner that the surface area of the particle decreases at a relatively even rate. This is typically accomplished by placing pores in the particle such that burning can occur inside as well as on the surface. This contrasts with degressive powders that burn from the outside inward and progressive powders that are coated with deterrents that slow the initial burn rate.

ninhydrin and analogues A versatile compound used to visualize *latent fingerprints on porous surfaces such as paper and cardboard. It can also serve as a developing agent for use in thin layer chromatography (TLC) in drug analysis and toxicology. Ninhydrin is also sometimes referred to as triketohydrinhene hydrate. Because of its versatility and sensitivity, it has become one of the primary tools in latent fingerprint visualization and has displaced iodine fuming as the method of choice for porous materials. The first synthesis of ninhydrin is attributed to

Ruhemann in 1910, and the characteristic purple produced by ninhydrin reacting with latent prints is called Ruhemann purple. Ninhydrin reacts with the *amino acids and their degradation products that are part of any latent print. Ninhydrin can be swabbed or sprayed onto a surface, or the entire article can be dipped into a solution. Once ninhydrin is applied to an article, development of the prints can take time (hours or even days), but increasing heat and moisture in the development environment can accelerate it. Ninhydrin analogues are compounds that exhibit similar characteristics to ninhydrin and react with the amino acid component of fingerprints. The most commonly used analogue is DFO, 1,8-diazafluoren-9-one.

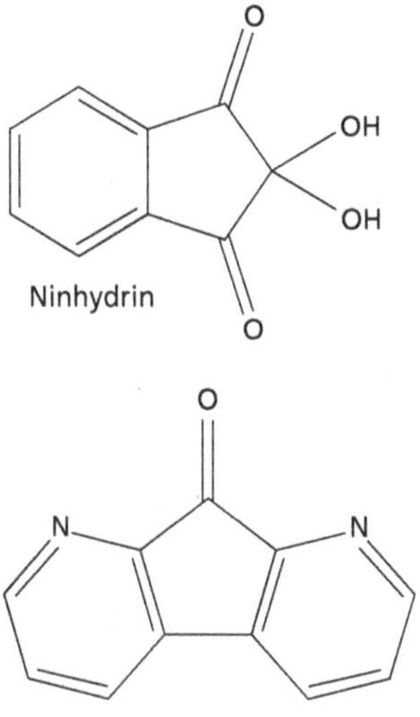

Ninhydrin

DFO (1,8-diazafluoren-9-one)

Ninhydrin

nitrocellulose (NC) A low explosive in smokeless powder, the propellant used in modern ammunition. If nitrocellulose is the only ingredient, the powder is called single base and if it is mixed with nitroglycerin (NG), the powder is called double base. Nitrocellulose is also an ingredient in varnishes and lacquers and was at one time used in automotive paints. There are also formulations of dynamite that use nitrocellulose as an ingredient. When mixed with nitroglycerin in the proper proportions, the resulting mix is a gel that is water resistant and can be used in wet environments. The plastic celluloid is derived from nitrocellulose and camphor. The forensic analysis of nitrocellulose is accomplished principally by thin layer chromatography (TLC).

nitrogen phosphorus detector (NPD) A specialized detector used with *gas chromatography (GC). This detector, also called a thermionic or alkaline flame detector, has a similar design to a flame ionization detector (FID). A sample exiting the GC column enters the detector where hydrogen gas (H_2) and air (containing oxygen, O_2) are mixed in, creating a flame that burns while the detector is operating. An element coated with an alkaline salt such as rubidium sulphate (Rb_2SO_4) is inserted into the reaction area and allows for efficient ionization of molecules containing nitrogen or phosphorus contained in the flame. Once the molecules are ionized, they are attracted to a collector that registers an electrical current that is based on the number of ions that strike it. Since so many pharmaceuticals, illegal drugs, and their metabolites contain nitrogen, the NPD is useful in forensic applications.

nitroglycerin (NG) A shock sensitive material used as an explosive and also as a drug to combat a heart condition called angina pectoris. Nitroglycerin, informally called 'nitro', was synthesized in 1847 and its potential for mining and other operations was immediately realized. However, the instability and sensitivity of the compound caused many accidents and prevented its widespread use until 1867 when Alfred Nobel found that it could be stabilized by mixing it with a diatomaceous earth formulation. Nobel went on to become a wealthy man and a portion of his estate was used to establish the Nobel Prize administered from his native Sweden.

As shown in the figure, nitroglycerin is a relatively small molecule with nitrogen groups substituted for the –OH groups on a glycerine molecule. Glycerine is a common ingredient in consumer products and is used as a moisturizing agent in lotions, an ingredient in soaps, and as a sweetener. It is a thick oily liquid, as is nitroglycerin, and old dynamite is often found with an oily seepage on the outer coating. Nitroglycerin can also penetrate the skin in much the same way that glycerine in cosmetic and lotions does, and for treatment of angina pectoris NG can be administered as an ointment which penetrates the skin and acts as a vasodilator, relieving the chest pain associated with the condition.

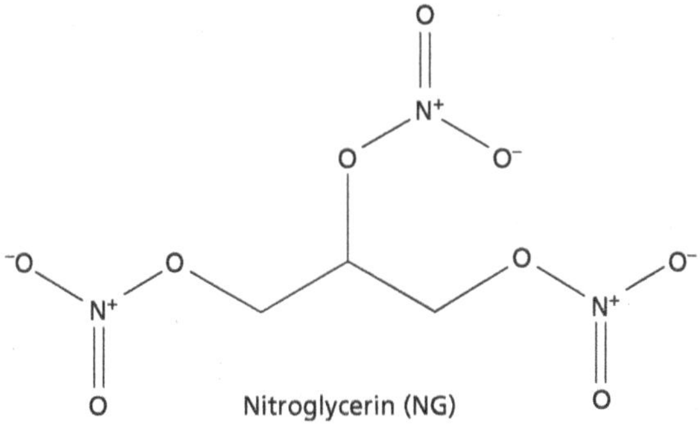

Nitroglycerin (NG)

Nitroglycerin

nitroguanidine An ingredient in triple-base propellants that are typically used in large guns such as artillery pieces. Single-base powders are based on nitrocellulose and double-base powders on nitrocellulose combined with nitroglycerin.

NMR *See* NUCLEAR MAGNETIC RESONANCE.

non-competitive assay (non-competitive immunoassay) A type of immunoassay in which no species are introduced to compete with the antigen-antibody pairing of interest. This is in contrast to a competitive assay in which species that can compete for binding sites are deliberately introduced.

non-impact printing A method of printing such as inkjet printing or laser jet printing that does not involve the impact of a metal pin or surface with the paper or other substrate being printed on. This contrasts with impact printing devices such as typewriters and dot matrix printers.

non-invasive sampling 1. An analysis that can be completed without opening a container or piercing or otherwise penetrating a human body. An X-ray or CT scan is an example of a non-invasive technique.
   2. In medical and toxicological settings, biosamples that can be collected without piercing or penetrating the body. Examples are the collection of hair or saliva samples. This contrasts with an invasive sampling method such as drawing blood.

non-request standard Handwriting samples collected as part of a questioned document (QD) examination. Non-request standards are not collected from the person after the writing in question has taken place; rather, these are samples of previous writing such as notes, cheque signatures, diary entries, and so on that are not created purposely for the investigation.

normal phase In liquid chromatography, *high performance liquid chromatography (HPLC), and *solid phase extractions (SPE), a combination of a polar stationary phase (column) and a non-polar solvent such as hexane. This contrasts with *reversed phase, which is the more widely used of the two in forensic applications.

Norris, Charles (1868–1935) An American and the first appointed Medical Examiner for the city of New York. Norris had trained extensively in Europe (including at Vienna and Edinburgh) and was considered an expert in forensic medicine. He was also a New York native and grasped the problems faced by the city and surrounding areas. His tenure spanned a horrific explosion on Wall Street and the implosion of the stock market in 1927, resulting in many suicides. Gang warfare was rampant, and prohibition came and went, but the seemingly routine deaths dominated the workload. During his tenure, Norris resigned twice and twice returned after the Mayor pleaded with him to do so. In addition to developing a model ME's office, one of his key contributions was the hiring of Dr Alexander *Gettler, who contributed to many advances in forensic chemistry and toxicology.

nuclear magnetic resonance (NMR) An instrumental technique used in organic chemistry and biochemistry to study molecular structure. NMR has also been adapted for medical use in magnetic resonance imaging (MRI). The technique is based on the absorption of electromagnetic energy in the radio frequency range by spinning atomic nuclei. This contrasts with other types of spectroscopy such as IR in which the electrons (outside the nucleus) absorb energy. Any atom that has an odd mass such as hydrogen (mass of 1, indicated as ^1H) is amenable to NMR, as is any atom with an even mass but an odd number of protons. Nitrogen is an example of this type of atom, with 7 protons in the nucleus and a mass of 14. NMR is most often applied to hydrogen and a naturally occurring isotope of carbon, ^{13}C. The bulk (~99 per cent) of naturally occurring carbon is ^{12}C, with 6 protons and 6 neutrons in the nucleus. About 1 per cent is ^{13}C, with 6 protons (an even mass number) and 7 neutrons, leading to an odd mass overall. When NMR targets the hydrogen, it is often referred to as 'proton NMR' since a hydrogen atom consists of one proton. By coupling proton NMR with ^{13}C NMR, the backbone of carbon and hydrogen of an organic compound can be deduced.

nucleoside A unit consisting of a sugar (deoxyribose) linked to a purine or pyrimidine base such as adenine (A), thymine (T), cytosine (C), or guanine (G). The phosphate esters of nucleosides are *nucleotides.

nucleotide A unit consisting of a sugar (deoxyribose), a phosphate group, and a purine or pyrimidine base such as adenine (A), thymine (T), cytosine (C), or guanine (G). Nucleotides are the building blocks of DNA.

null hypothesis A fundamental component of statistical testing and of the scientific method. The null hypothesis (H_0) provides a starting point for the analysis of data and for testing a given idea, assumption, or hypothesis that arises in a given analysis. There are many hypothesis tests such as the t-test of means, each based on a different calculation. However, the generic steps for conducting a hypothesis test are the same. First is the formulation of the null hypothesis that must be stated to include a negative or null value or consideration. For example, if the t-test of means is being used to compare two sets of blood test analysis, the null hypothesis would be that there is no statistically significant difference between the means and that any difference that does exist is the result of small random variations only.

numerical aperture *See* NA.

nursing, forensic The application of nursing skills to legal matters and law enforcement. Nurses are often the first to treat or see people who have been the victims of crime and violence, but they also have contact with those who are suspects in criminal activity. Relatives and friends of both victims and suspects may also be involved in such scenarios, and thus fall under the concerns of forensic nursing. Nurses in these situations need to be familiar with evidence collection both physical and behavioural and in the form of communication, written or other. Clinical forensic nursing (CFN) focuses on nursing in settings such as emergency rooms and other treatment facilities like prison clinics and forensic (psychiatric) hospitals. Forensic nurses may also be associated with Medical Examiners' (ME) or coroners' offices and act as part of death investigations. The types of investigations that forensic nurses can become involved in include civil and criminal cases and span the gamut from crimes of violence to car accidents, workplace accidents, substance abuse, product tampering, neglect, and medical malpractice. A Sexual Assault Nurse Examiner (SANE) is a nurse trained to collect evidence and to counsel victims of sex crimes.

- General information regarding forensic nursing and SANE. Last accessed May 2011.

nylon A common synthetic fibre that is a polyamide. It was the first completely synthetic fibre and was introduced in 1938. Used in women's stockings, which were soon referred to generically as 'nylons', and the word now often refers to a large group of polyamide fibres.

n

objective lens The first component of the imaging system in a microscope. It consists of the lens itself and the mounting. The other lens is the eyepiece or ocular. *See also* MICROSCOPY.

oblique lighting Illumination of the subject from an angle as opposed to having light shine straight down or up through the object being studied. In microscopy, oblique lighting is at an angle to the optical axis of the system.

obliteration 1. In *questioned document analysis, the erasure or other type of removal of writing or printing. Obliteration can be achieved by erasing and overwriting, crossing out or scribbling over, by cutting or scraping the paper surface away, by using erasing substances such as a 'whiteout' compound or correction ribbons on typewriters, and finally by chemical means such as using a bleaching agent to chemically remove the writing from the paper.
2. The purposeful removal of stamped, engraved, or machined serial numbers on evidence such as stolen property or guns. *See also* SERIAL NUMBER RESTORATION.

ocular The eyepiece lens of a microscope. *See also* MICROSCOPY; OBJECTIVE LENS.

odontology, forensic The application of dentistry to legal matters in the areas of personal identification, age determination, bite marks, evaluation of wounds and trauma to the jaw and teeth (particularly in potential child abuse cases), and for evaluation of alleged dental malpractice or negligence. Since teeth are physically and chemically resilient, they endure and are likely to survive the severe trauma associated with mass disasters. Dental identification tasks can fall into one of two categories, identification by comparison to ante-mortem records, and identification where no comparison is available. Odontologists can contribute by estimating age (age-at-death estimation) based on the condition of the teeth and which ones are present.

oil immersion A technique in microscopy in which the specimen is covered in an immersion oil that has the same refractive index as glass. Oil immersion allows for the use of a 100× objective lens, the strongest available in conventional light microscopy while maintaining resolution and brightness. Oil immersion works by eliminating refraction of light passing through a sample, then through the cover slip (glass), then through air, and finally through the glass of the objective lens. In effect, there is no change in the refractive index from the glass of the cover slip to the objective lens. The result is an increase in the effective *numerical aperture (NA) of the lens system.

oligonucleotide In DNA, a short chain of bases on a sugar-phosphate backbone. The primers used in *short tandem repeat *DNA typing are oligonucleotides.

opacity How impervious a sample or object is to the passage of light. Although the term is most often applied to visible light, it is sometimes used and can refer to any form of electromagnetic energy. Certain types of quartz are opaque in appearance but are transparent to ultraviolet radiation.

opiate alkaloids (opiates) Natural, semi-synthetic, and synthetic compounds obtained from, or closely related to, compounds obtained from the opium plant. These compounds are nitrogenous bases and thus are classified as alkaloids. Originally, the term referred only to those compounds directly obtained from opium, but the class now includes completely synthetic compounds such as *methadone and *fentanyl, which produce similar effects and bind to the opiate receptors.

opium A mixture of compounds obtained from the unripened seed pods of the plant *Paperver somniferum*. This poppy plant grows in large areas of Asia, south-west Asia, and Mexico. To obtain opium, the seedpod is cut and a brownish milky substance is extracted. This extract is then dried and can be crushed into a powder that gradually lightens in colour. Opium consists of a mixture of alkaloids including morphine and codeine, and can be consumed directly by ingestion or smoking.

optical isomers Compounds that are isomers of each other and that rotate plane *polarized light in opposite directions. Many drugs have optical isomers such as *d*-cocaine and *l*-cocaine; the *d/l* notation refers to the direction of rotation of the light (to the right or dextrorotatory; or to the left, levorotatory).

optic axis 1. In a crystalline *birefringent material, the direction of propagation of light in which both components of the light travel at the same velocity.

2. In a lens or optical system such as a microscope, the pathway the light follows and around which there is symmetry of structure. For example, in a normal lens, the optic axis runs through the centre.

Orfila, Mathieu Joseph Bonaventura (M. J. B. Orfila)

(1787–1853) Considered the founder of forensic toxicology. Orfila was born in Minorca, a Spanish colony. He moved to France and obtained his MD in 1811, and became Professor of Forensic Chemistry and Dean of the medical faculty at the University of Paris from 1831 to 1848. He was chair of the department of medicinal chemistry at that institution. He began

M. J. B. Orfila

publishing early, with his first paper on poisons in 1814 when he was 26 years old. As a toxicologist, he concentrated on methods of analysis of poisons in blood and other body fluids and tissues. He did not restrict himself to toxicology, but rather participated in a range of medicolegal investigations, including work with maggots and decomposition. He also wrote a foundational book on the topic of poisons and their detection, published during the period 1814–18, in French and subsequent translations. His most famous case was the Marie *La Farge case in which his investigation and analysis of key evidence using the *Marsh test was pivotal in obtaining the conviction.

orthotolidine test (o-tolidine test; tolidine test) A presumptive test for blood that is also referred to by the shorthand notation of *o*-tolidine. This test works similarly to most other tests for blood in that the o-tolidine reacts with haemoglobin in blood in the presence of hydrogen peroxide (H_2O_2) to cause a bluish green colour to form. Like other presumptive tests, the tolidine test is not specific for blood and can produce false positives with substances such as horseradish. Tolidine is also a carcinogenic material and thus this test is not as widely used as the *Kastle–Meyer (phenolphthalein) test.

Osborn, Albert S. (1858–1946) A pioneer of early forensic document examination and author of a text in 1910 that is still considered a foundational work and reference in the field. He was also a founding member of the American Society of Questioned Document Examiners (ASQDE) and served as its first president from 1942 until 1946, the year of his death. Osborn's sons continued in the field, and both Albert and one of his sons were involved in the *Lindbergh kidnapping case.

O'Shaughnessy, Sir William Brooke (1809–89) An English forensic chemist who made notable contributions to the development of colour-based *presumptive tests for drugs. At the request of the editor of the medical journal *The Lancet*, he evaluated various candies for the presence of toxins and identified many; the work was published in 1830. He joined the East India Tea company and went to India in 1833, where his medicolegal work continued. He was an avid user of the *Marsh test and added significantly to the body of knowledge regarding the analysis, classification, and identification of common poisons of the time.

ossification The process of bone formation from tissue such as cartilage. This process begins a few weeks after conception and is generally completed in adolescence.

osteology The study of the structure and function of bone; closely related to forensic anthropology. It is also referred to as skeletal biology.

Otto–Stas method A chemical sample preparation method developed by German chemist Friedrich Julius Otto (1809–70) and Belgian Jean Servais *Stas (1813–91) for the extraction of *opiate alkaloids from tissues and stomach contents. The test was developed to assist in the isolation and identification of poisoning. The multi-step process exploited the basic nature of the poisons to isolate them in an organic solvent.

Ouchterlony, Orjan (1914–2004) A Swedish physician who introduced the test named after him in 1949. The test was widely used in forensic serology before the advent of *DNA typing to determine the species of a blood sample or stain.

Ouchterlony test An immunodiffusion test used to determine the species from which blood or other body fluid originated. To perform the test, agarose is poured into a Petri dish and allowed to gel. A central hole is punched in the gel and sample extract containing antigens is placed in it. A series of other wells are punched into the gel around the central hole a few millimetres away. Antibodies from different species such as human, dog, cat, and so on are placed into the wells. Over a few hours, the antigens in the sample diffuse outward towards the antibodies diffusing inward. If the antigens and antibodies are from the same species, an immunoprecipitate will form in the gel, showing the species of the sample.

overall photo At a crime scene, an overall photo is meant to show evidence in the larger context. It is the first step in the photo documentation of a piece of physical evidence. For example, if a bloody knife is located in a closet, the overall photo would show the knife, but from a perspective that also shows the closet and its location within the hall. *See also* ESTABLISHING PHOTO.

overkill Injuries inflicted during a crime that exceed what is necessary to kill or incapacitate a victim. This type of injury pattern can reveal information regarding the offender and the relationship to a victim.

oxidation and oxidizing agents Oxidation is a coupled chemical reaction characterized by exchange of electrons or electron flow. There are three ways to define oxidation: (1) a loss of electrons; (2) a gain of oxygen; or (3) a loss of hydrogen. Similarly, the other partner in the reaction, the reduction, can be defined as a gain of electrons, a loss of oxygen, or a gain of hydrogen. The oxidizing agent is the compound or material that causes oxidation of another species; the species that is reduced. Oxygen (O_2) is an oxidizing agent, and it causes the oxidation of iron (Fe) to form Fe_2O_3, or rust. Bleach is another common oxidizing agent.

oxycodone (OxyContin®) A narcotic pain reliever made from thebaine, an *opiate alkaloid. Oxycodone acts in the same manner as morphine and codeine and like these substances, abuse can lead to physical and psychological addiction. OxyContin® was introduced in 1995, and contains a time-released form of oxycodone. Since it is time released, the amount of oxycodone in each tablet is much higher, and this has led to increasing abuse and diversion of OxyContin® for illegal use. Abusers crush the tablets and by doing so destroy the time-releasing properties of the drug. This allows them to get a large dose immediately by ingestion, smoking, or injection with effects that mimic heroin.

oxygen balance A method of expressing the amount of oxygen present in an explosive or explosive mixture relative to the amount required to convert all of the carbon in the molecule to CO_2, all of the hydrogen to H_2O, sulphur to SO_2, and metals to metal oxides. If an explosive has an oxygen balance of zero, that means the molecules contain enough oxygen in the structure for this to occur; a negative oxygen balance means more would be needed while a positive oxygen balance indicates that excess oxygen is present. The oxygen balance is calculated from a balanced chemical equation and explosives can be combined to create a mixture with a net zero oxygen balance. As an example, consider the explosive *nitroglycerin (NG, $C_3H_5N_3O_9$). The balanced chemical equation for the complete combustion of this compound is:

$$4C_3H_5N_3O_9 \rightarrow 12CO_2 + 10H_2O + 6N_2 + O_2$$

if there is excess oxygen the oxygen balance will be positive. Since in the balanced equation there are 4 moles NG for every extra mole of oxygen, the oxygen balance can be calculated by converting these values to their weight equivalent:

$$\frac{1 \text{ mole } O_2}{4 \text{ moles NG}} = \frac{32 \text{ g } O_2}{908 \text{ g NG}} \times 100 = +3.5\%$$

Oxygen balance values can also be obtained from tables. *See also* EXPLOSIVES.

p30 A protein that is specific to seminal fluid and detectable for about eight hours after sexual intercourse has occurred. Also known as prostate specific antigen (PSA), detection of this material in a stain shows that it is or contains semen.

paint and paint data query (PDQ) In general terms, paint can be described as a coating of colouring agents suspended or dissolved in a solvent containing other additives such as binders and drying agents. The materials that impart colour (colourants) are *dyes and pigments. Pigments were at one time primarily inorganic compounds such as titanium dioxide (TiO_2, white), ferric oxide (Fe_2O_3, rust), or other compounds made up of cadmium, lead, and other metals. Because of their toxicity, many of these compounds have been replaced with organic pigments. Solvents employed in paint formulations can be organic such as toluene or water based such as used in latex paints. Water-based paints can be cleaned up with soap and water and are popular for interiors of homes. The solvent, be it water or organic, is referred to as the 'vehicle'. Finally, polymers, or materials capable of polymerization (called binders), are included and when dry form a protective coating over the pigments.

There are three ways paint (as physical evidence) can be evaluated. First is via a physical match as would occur when a paint chip can be fit like a puzzle piece into a location from where it originated. Secondly, paint layers can be distinctive even if the top layers of different paint chips appear identical. The layering pattern is referred to as paint stratigraphy. Third, paint can be characterized chemically using methods such as X-ray *spectroscopy, *infrared spectroscopy, and *Raman spectroscopy. Individual layers as well as surfaces can also be characterized.

The PDQ database was developed and is supported by the Royal Canadian Mounted Police (RCMP) and consists of paint data from more than 13,000 automobiles. The database also contains information regarding automotive paint layers that can be useful in comparing paint samples and in narrowing down possible sources of paint chip evidence. The database consists of spectral analysis of the paint samples.

((⊕)) SEE WEB LINKS

• Information regarding the PDQ database and its use. Last accessed May 2011.

palynology A branch of botany that deals with the study of pollen and spores. Forensic palynology is part of forensic botany and is used in a variety of cases where identification of a possible location is of interest given that pollen and spores are easily transferred.

papaverine An opiate alkaloid that was once used as a poison. It is now used medically to treat conditions in which muscle relaxation is necessary such as in high blood pressure.

paper A complex mixture made from slurry containing wood and cotton fibres, binders, glues, bleaching agents and dyes, other colourants, preservatives, and coatings. In general, the finer the paper, the higher the cotton content and such papers are sometimes referred to as containing cotton rag.

papillae (papillary dermis) The boundary layer in skin that separates the dermis from the epidermis. The hill-and-valley pattern of the papillae determines the ridge characteristics of the finger and thus the fingerprint.

Paracelsus (1493–1541) A key figure in the history of toxicology, although he lived well before forensic toxicology as a discipline was recognized. He was a Swiss alchemist, philosopher, and writer with unconventional ideas and enormous experimental skills. He sought to understand why treatments worked so that existing medicines could be improved and new ones developed. He was also a colourful and controversial figure who assumed the name Paracelsus, which means 'greater than Celsus', a physician in Rome during the first century CE. From his early teens, Paracelsus moved frequently between universities gathering knowledge, and moving on, and over the years, he learned and practised medicine. Although his medicinal practice and ideas were mostly judged wrong by today's standards, one of his significant contributions was to upset the foundations of medicine and chemistry, which was still being taught based on Roman texts.

Paracelsus' work in medicinal chemistry led him to state, 'What is there that is not poison? All things are poison and nothing (is) without poison. Solely the dose determines the thing that is not a poison' (quoted in Curtis Klaassen (ed.), *Casarett and Doull's Toxicology: The Basic Science of Poisons* (New York: McGraw-Hill, 2001)). In other words, the dose makes the poison. For its time, this was a revolutionary idea and one that started a chain of events that led to effective tests for *arsenic culminating in the *Marsh test. His writing was among the first examples of what could be called modern science.

Paracelsus

paraffin test *See* DERMAL NITRATE TEST.

paraphernalia Equipment, supplies, or devices associated with ingestion of illegal drugs or substances. These items may be purchased or made from common household items such as bottle caps or light bulbs.

parent drop In blood spatter patterns, a large central drop that, at impact, creates a series of smaller drops associated with it. The smaller drops are sometimes referred to as *satellites or satellite drop-offs of the parent drop.

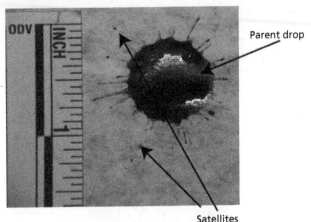

Parent drop

Satellites

The parent drop is in the centre with many satellite drops surrounding it

Parkman case A famous American murder case that had significant forensic aspects and that featured Oliver Wendell Holmes (1809-94) and an eccentric professor, Dr George Parkman, a wealthy physician and surgeon at Harvard University (in the US) who was known as a ruthless financial manager. Parkman had donated most of the land on which the Harvard medical school was located and Holmes held the Parkman Professorship of Anatomy and Physiology. Parkman also owned many of the most downtrodden tenements in the city and had a reputation as a heartless landlord.

Dr John White Webster was a professor in chemistry of average skill and limited financial resources who had borrowed money from many people, including Parkman. By 1849, Webster was deep in debt, his mortgage in Parkman's hands. However, one afternoon in November 1849, Parkman strolled out of his home and never returned.

Suspicion immediately fell on Webster and investigators searched the grounds of the medical school, including the discard pile from the anatomy lab. A custodian reported an altercation between Webster and Parkman the afternoon Parkman vanished. Webster subsequently locked the janitor out of the laboratory and gave him a Thanksgiving turkey, which was unprecedented and out of character. The janitor further noted smoke rising from a chimney the Saturday after Parkman's disappearance and the sound of continuously running water.

The custodian, a man named Littlefield, testified that once Webster left, he entered the laboratory and searched it. Webster had built an indoor toilet in the lab, the shaft of which led to a storage area in the sub-basement. Because the building was located on the Charles River, water would occasionally rise and flush out the area. Littlefield noted that the key to the toilet was gone and the door locked. Littlefield armed himself with a sledgehammer, ventured to the basement, and managed to tear an opening in the toilet shaft. He found bones, a pelvis, and dentures.

Webster's trial began in April of 1850 and turned into an American version of the *LaFarge trial that had taken place ten years earlier in Paris. During courtroom sessions, people were shuttled in for ten-minute periods and hustled out, allowing nearly 60,000 to see at least some portion of the trial. This number represented nearly half the population of the city at that time. The forensic issue was the identification of the bones and teeth found in the toilet. Holmes testified twice about the body parts, but the key testimony came from Dr Nathan Cooley Keep (1800–1875), a physician and dentist who made Parkman's dentures. The dentures recovered had heat damage, making identification nearly impossible. However, Keep was able to show how the dentures fitted the moulds of Parkman's mouth he had in his office. He further explained that the artificial teeth were made of porcelain, which normally explodes when exposed to such high temperature. He suggested that the head itself had protected the teeth. The defence offered their own experts, but none was able to discredit Keep's findings and testimony. The Parkman trial was the first in the United States to revolve around forensic *odontology. The jury needed only three hours to reach a guilty verdict. Prior to his execution in August, Webster admitted the killing but maintained it was unintentional.

partial print A *latent fingerprint that is missing some portion of the expected complete print.

partition coefficient The ratio between the concentration of a compound or *analyte in one phase relative to the concentration in another phase in direct contact. An example is K_{ow}, which is the partition coefficient of a compound in an organic phase such as octanol relative to the concentration of the compound in an aqueous phase:

$$K_{ow} = \frac{[\text{analyte}]_{\text{octanol}}}{[\text{analyte}]_{\text{water}}}$$

passive bloodstain A stain produced by a free-falling drop as opposed to a stain produced by an applied force such as a spatter pattern. Types of passive stains include *wipes, transfer stains (such as a bloody hand on a wall), and flow patterns produced by wounds.

patent fingerprint

200
patent fingerprint The opposite of a *latent fingerprint; one that is visible.

pathology, forensic Pathology is the medical specialty that involves the study of disease and how it effects the structure and function of the body. Forensic pathology is the study of the cause, manner, and mechanism of death undertaken by a medical doctor who has attended a residency in pathology, followed by additional training in forensic pathology and death investigation. Forensic pathologists may work as a Medical Examiner (ME), coroner, or in the offices of one of these officials. The primary job of a forensic pathologist is performing autopsies on questioned or suspicious deaths and determining the *cause, manner, and circumstances of death. This is done based on the autopsy results and also on information gathered as part of the death investigation. The pathologist is also tasked with identification of the body and with estimating the time of death (*post-mortem interval, PMI). Forensic pathologists also serve an important role in public health, such as detecting patterns of death that might be caused by an infectious disease.

pattern evidence, pattern matching, and pattern recognition Broadly defined, pattern evidence is physical evidence that has characteristic patterns that can be used for classification purposes. Examples include *fingerprints, *toolmarks, and *firearms. Pattern matching is a technique used in forensic comparisons in areas such as fingerprints, firearms, bite marks, and toolmarks. Some of these procedures can be automated, such as the one used for fingerprints and firearms evidence; however, many pattern recognition techniques cannot be easily encoded. For example, when an impression of a shoe print is made at a scene and a possible source of the shoe pattern is located, pattern matching techniques are used to compare the two and to determine if that shoe created that impression—i.e., assigning a common source. In most pattern recognition applications some type of 'point comparison' technique is employed in which interesting, significant, or unique features are located on one of the pieces of evidence and then an attempt is made to locate that same feature on the other piece and correlate other features relative to the first point.

PCP *See* PHENCYCLIDINE.

PCR (polymerase chain reaction) A technique used in current methods of forensic DNA identification. The many uses of PCR include *short tandem repeat (STR) analysis, *mitochondrial DNA sequencing, and quantitative PCR (qPCR). The procedure begins by heating the extracted DNA. The heat breaks the hydrogen bonds and unzips the double helix structure into two complementary strands, a process called denaturation. A PCR primer is then added to identify the region or locus of the gene that will be typed. The primer will bind to the base sequences on either side of this region, marking the boundary of the loci of interest. This process is called hybridization and is carried out as the solution is allowed to cool. The final step is to add bases (adenine (A), thymine (T), cytocine (C), and guanine (G)) that will pair with the complementary bases on the isolated regions on the strands. DNA polymerase enzyme is also added which promotes the re-zipping of the strands. The result of this cycle is the production of an exact copy of the region of interest. By the process of this thermal cycling, the original sample is amplified several thousandfold. The PCR technique was developed by Dr Kary *Mullis who was awarded the Nobel Prize in Chemistry in 1993 in recognition of the achievement.

PDQ *See* PAINT AND PAINT DATA QUERY

peer review The process of having written materials such as manuscripts for scientific journals, data for preparation of reports, or proposals reviewed by people with the same level of professional training, experience, and expertise. Publication of scientific methods in peer-reviewed journals is often used in decisions regarding *admissibility of scientific evidence.

pellets Small round projectiles used in shotgun ammunition.

pen lift A characteristic of handwritten documents where a pen, pencil, or other writing instrument has been used. It is demonstrated by a break in a line that indicates that the writing instrument has been lifted off the paper. Pen lift patterns can be useful in questioned document (QD) examination.

perception reaction time (PRT) The time interval from when an object enters a person's field of vision, is recognized as presenting a threat or danger, and when the person is able to react. The term is used in forensic accident reconstruction in cases such as motor vehicle accidents.

perchlorate (ClO$_4^-$) An anion used as an ingredient (oxidizer) in explosives and propellants.

percussive explosive An *explosive that can be detonated by sharp physical contact (percussive force). An example is lead styphnate, which is used in the *primers of firearm ammunition.

perimeter, crime scene The line (either drawn, marked, or defined) that demarcates a crime scene from the surroundings. All areas within the perimeter should be searched and processed for evidence. The definition of the perimeter may change as the scene is processed and more information becomes available.

perimortem Occurring at the time of death or very near to it, such as a perimortem injury.

peroxidase activity Characteristic activity displayed by an enzyme that catalyses an oxidation reaction of an organic compound using a peroxide. A well-known peroxide is hydrogen peroxide (H_2O_2) which is used to sterilize wounds. Most presumptive tests for blood such as the *Kastle–Meyer test are based on the peroxidase-like activity of haemoglobin, which catalyses a reaction that results in a colour change.

persistence The relative length of time that a given type of physical evidence remains unchanged or in the location where it was originally deposited. For example, *gunshot residue (GSR) consists of small particulates and, as such, is not expected to be as persistent as evidence such as a cotton fibre that can become entangled on a surface.

petechial haemorrhages (petechiae, spots, Tardieu spots) In most deaths caused by strangulation, pinpoint haemorrhages called petechiae, petechial haemorrhages, or Tardieu spots are found in the face, particularly in the eyes and on the eyelids. These haemorrhages are caused by capillary rupture brought on by pressure. However, finding petechiae by themselves is not sufficient to determine that death was the result of strangulation. Tardieu spots are named after the French forensic physician Ambroise Tardieu (1818–79), who was particularly well known for his work in uncovering child abuse, sexual abuse, and neglect.

PETN (pentaerythritol tetranitrate) A high explosive used by the military, and in mixtures employed by terrorists. PETN was synthesized in the 1940s and is used by the military as a sheet explosive (a common form is Detasheet), in grenades, and as a propellant in small calibre weapons. Detonation cord, often called 'det cord' or Primacord, contains a core of PETN or RDX covered in cotton and enclosed in a weather-proof casing. Although it is less sensitive than *TNT, PETN must be detonated by a shock wave from some type of initiator such as a blasting cap before it will explode.

Pentaerythritol tetranitrate (PETN)

PETN

petroleum distillate (petroleum hydrocarbons) Hydrocarbon compounds derived or extracted from the distillation of crude oil. Individual hydrocarbons are compounds such as octane or benzene; examples of mixtures include petrol (gasoline) and kerosene. These mixtures are frequently encountered as *accelerants in *arson cases.

peyote *See* MESCALINE.

PGM (phosphoglucomutase) A polymorphic isoenzyme system that catalyses the interconversion of glucose-6-phosphate and glucose-1-phosphate during glucose metabolism. PGM was used as a genetic marker system because of its polymorphism properties. Prior to the advent of *DNA typing, PGM was routinely typed using blood wherever the sample allowed. *See also* CULLIFORD, BRIAN.

pH The scale used to describe the acidity or alkalinity (basicity) of a water-based solution. Water can dissociate into two ions, H^+ and OH^- (hydroxide) and the pH of a solution refers to the balance of those two species. pH is defined mathematically as $-\log[H^+]$ where the $[H^+]$ denotes the concentration of hydrogen ions (also called protons) measured in units of molarity (number of moles H^+ per litre, M). The pH scale centres on 7, which is a neutral solution where the concentration of hydrogen ions equals the concentration of hydroxide at 1×10^{-7}M. A pH of less than 7 is acidic (H^+ in excess) with the lower the number, the more acidic the solution. A pH of greater than 7 is basic (alkaline, excess OH^-) with higher numbers corresponding to increased alkalinity. Lemon juice, which is acidic, has a pH of about 4, skimmed milk about 6.6, blood about 7.4, the stomach, 1.5–2.0, milk of magnesia about 10.5, and lye (NaOH, sodium hydroxide) about 13. *See also* pK_a; IONIZABLE CENTRE.

Phadebas reagents and tests Commercial test kits and reagents
that are used to detect amylase, an enzyme found in abundance in saliva.
The tests are based on a starch-iodine complex and the ability of amylase
to break down starch. These tests are presumptive tests for saliva.

phaeomelanin One of two types of *melanin, the other being
eumelanin, which are found in skin and hair. Phaeomelanin is a yellowish
orange colour and is associated with red and blonde hair.

pharmaceutical identifiers Physical characteristics of commercial
pharmaceuticals useful in classification and identification. For example,
the dimensions, colour, and imprints on a tablet would all be considered
to be pharmaceutical identifiers.

pharmacist's fold *See* DRUGGIST'S FOLD.

pharmacodynamics (toxicodynamics) The study of the effect of
drugs or toxins and their metabolites on the body. Aspects of
pharmacodynamics include interactions with receptors, physiological
effects, and disposition.

pharmacokinetics (toxicodynamics) The study of the movement of
drugs through the body. After a drug or other xenobiotic substance is
introduced, it is absorbed and distributed to tissues in the body by the
bloodstream. Portions of the substance are metabolized and in effect act
as new drugs that enter into the same cycle. As an example, heroin is
metabolized to 6-monoacetyl morphine (6-MAM), which then re-enters
the cycle as another drug substance that may be further metabolized
and/or eliminated. In the case of heroin, the 6-MAM is further
metabolized to morphine. Elimination of the drug and metabolites
follows absorption and distribution, although some portions of some
compounds may accumulate in fatty tissues. Elimination can be by several
routes, principally in urine, but also in sweat, faeces, or breath. Different
drugs have different rates of absorption, metabolites, and speed of
elimination. One measure of how long a drug remains in the system is the
half-life, symbolized by $t_{1/2}$. This information, combined with toxicological
findings, can be useful in determining how much of a drug was taken and
roughly when. This process is also referred to as re-creation of the dose
event. *See also* ADME.

phase (physical states, phase transitions) Generally, the physical
state of a material such as the 'liquid phase'. The three states of matter
are solids (s), liquid (l), and gas (g). In some contexts, plasmas
(as utilized in *inductively coupled plasmas (ICP)) are considered to

be a fourth state of matter. A change in the state of matter is referred to as a **phase change**, i.e. ice → water is a phase change.

phase contrast microscopy A specialized microscopic technique that increases the contrast between items that would otherwise be very difficult to see, such as transparent or nearly transparent materials. Phase contrast techniques are particularly useful in forensic science to visualize sperm cells and fine structure in hair and soil. A phase contrast microscope is similar to a compound microscope in design but includes specialized objectives, lighting, plates, and light condensers. When a specimen and oil (or other mounting medium) have similar refractive indices, it is difficult to see surface relief or to distinguish edges. The purpose of phase contrast techniques is to increase the contrast between the object and the mounting medium, making it easier to discern.

phencyclidine (PCP) An abused drug that is easily synthesized and was at one time used as a veterinary anaesthetic. The compound was synthesized in 1926 and used as a cat anaesthetic in the 1950s. In the early 1960s, it was introduced as a human anaesthetic but soon withdrawn from the market after bizarre behaviour and other side effects were noted. Production of the compound ended in 1979. As an illicit hallucinogen, PCP first appeared in the late 1960s.

phendimetrazine and phenmetrazine Prescription stimulants used for weight control that are abused in ways similar to amphetamine and methamphetamine.

phenolphthalein A weak acid/base indicator that is used in the *Kastle–Meyer presumptive test for blood.

phenotype The outward appearance of a trait as opposed to the genotype, which is the actual combination of genes. For example, in the ABO blood group system, a person inherits one gene from their mother and one from their father. If both genes are A, then the person's genotype is AA and their phenotype is A, meaning that their blood will be type A. If a person inherits an A gene from one parent and an O gene from another, their genotype is AO, but their phenotype will be A and they will have Type A blood.

phenyl-2-propanone (P2P) A *precursor chemical used in the clandestine synthesis of *methamphetamine.

phenylethylamines The class of stimulant drugs based on the phenylethylamine skeleton. This includes *amphetamine, *methamphetamine, and *MDMA.

phenylpropanolamine (PPA) A precursor chemical used in the clandestine synthesis of *amphetamine.

Philips physical developer A form of physical developer (PD) coupled with silver (Ag) which is used to develop and visualize *latent fingerprints. It is particularly useful for prints on paper. It is named after the laboratory where it was developed, the Philips Research Laboratory in the Netherlands.

phonetics, forensic The study of the sound components of speech, usually with the intent of identifying the speaker or to learn things about the speaker. In general, the type of evidence of interest in forensic phonetics is called a 'disputed utterance' or 'questioned utterance' in the same way 'disputed documents' are the subject of questioned document analysis. For example, the speech of a native of the southern United States is usually quite different from that of someone from Edinburgh, Manchester, New Jersey (in the USA), or Toronto, even though all are speaking English. Other aspects of speech of interest include pitch, speed, intonation, emphasis, and accent on syllables. Aside from helping to uncover information, phonetics can be helpful in interpreting meaning from the sound of speech. Again, a simple example would be the difference in meaning between the following statements: *I* like it versus I like *it* versus I *like* it. All three are written the same but spoken quite differently and, because of different emphasis, carry a different meaning.

phosphorescence The emission of electromagnetic radiation (EMR) that occurs at some delayed point after the initial absorption. Phosphorescence is a form of luminescence, and it is characterized by emission that continues after the excitation energy has been removed.

photocopiers Copy machines that use a photographic process to produce a copy of a document. The term 'copier' is generic and usually refers to copiers that work much as laser computer printers (xerographic process) as well as to photocopies. Informally the three terms (copy, photocopy, and Xerox) are used interchangeably although there is a distinct difference between how a photocopier works and how a xerographic copier works. In a photocopy process, an electrostatic charge is placed on a surface and that is selectively discharged by exposure to light, creating a negative image. Projecting light through the negative creates a print, much as 'printing' a negative creates a photograph.

photodegradation The degradation of compounds or formulations (such as dyes or inks) that arise from exposure to light. Usually UV light is the most notable cause of photodegradation.

photography An integral part of the forensic process that has become much more widely used with the advent of digital cameras and imaging systems. The word photography means 'light writing', and in the case of film media, is based on exposure of light sensitive compounds such as silver chloride (AgCl) to light. The light causes the salt to darken and, when developed, the pattern forms a negative of the original image. Colour film photography employs layers of these light sensitive compounds, each of which responds to different colours. Projection of light through the negative is used to create the prints. Film photography is still utilized in a few forensic settings, but is rapidly being replaced with equivalent digital methods.

One of the earliest types of photography was called the daguerreotype, named after its French inventor. These were also known as 'tintypes' because of the backing and by the 1870s daguerreotype portraits were common. By the middle of the same century, photos were being used for identification of cadavers and of criminals. Application of photography to forensic work became commonplace in the latter part of the century and Alphonse *Bertillon was one of its well-known advocates, both for crime scene documentation and for identification of individuals. His early work with identification cards ('Portrait Parlé') could be considered one of the precursors of 'mug shots'.

Digital cameras are based on an array of light sensitive diodes called charged coupled devices (CCDs). The number of megapixels in a camera corresponds to the number of light sensitive diodes in the array, so a six megapixel camera has 6,000,000 photosensitive sites. When light strikes a diode, a charge builds up, with more light creating a bigger charge. A scanning process discharges the diodes, allowing the intensity of light at each diode to be recorded. To create colour images, filters that separate out the red, blue, and green light are used to control which colour reaches a given diode. A processor in the camera creates the images from the CCD and filters.

Forensic disciplines that utilize photography regularly are crime scene *documentation, microscopic analysis and photography (producing photomicrographs), trace evidence analysis (also associated with microscopy), and *latent fingerprint analysis.

photo placard A labelled plastic marker used to identify evidence in crime scene photos. Typically these are yellow with large lettering; some include scaling.

physical anthropology A broad subdivision of anthropology that studies (among other things), primate and human evolution and behaviour. Forensic anthropology is generally considered to be the sub-discipline of physical anthropology that deals with recent skeletal remains as opposed to historical or ancient.

physical developer (PD) Contrary to what the name implies, a chemical method for developing and visualizing *latent fingerprints. Although PD methods can be used alone, they are often coupled to other protocols and developers such as *ninhydrin. The process is similar to that used in black-and-white photography and uses silver chloride (AgCl) or similar metal salts that react with fats and other insoluble constituents of the fingerprint residue. *See also* NANOPARTICLES.

physical evidence Broadly speaking, any type of tangible evidence as opposed to something such as the testimony of an eyewitness. Physical evidence can be anything, from a microscopic trace of dust to a car, but there are some generalizations that can be made. Physical evidence must be documented, collected, marked, transported, and stored in a manner consistent with the type of evidence. It is subjected to a chain of custody to ensure its safety and integrity from the time of collection to use in court.

physical matching The act of linking pieces of evidence together that exist in pieces but once were part of the same item. Reconstructing a broken window is an example of physical matching, as is linking a specific match back to the matchbook from which it was torn based on the unique tearing pattern.

physical properties Characteristics of matter that can be measured by physical means rather than chemical means. Measuring a physical property can be accomplished without changing the chemical composition of the material being studied. On the other hand, chemical properties can only be determined by processes that alter the chemical composition of the sample. For example, the freezing point of water is a physical property since it can be determined by freezing the water and measuring the temperature at which that occurs. The chemical formula of liquid water (H_2O) is the same as the chemical formula of ice, so no chemical change has occurred. The flammability of butane, a chemical property, can only be determined by an experiment that involves the combustion of butane, resulting in the conversion of butane to carbon dioxide and water.

Physician's Desk Reference (PDR) A reference book used by medical doctors that lists prescription drugs, their composition, action, indications, and other important information. In forensic science, the *PDR* is an indispensable reference manual in forensic chemistry (drug analysis), pathology, and toxicology. The first edition of the *PDR* was published in 1946. For identification of prescription drugs seized as physical evidence, the large collection of actual size photographs is invaluable, as is the extensive cross-listing and referencing of the drugs and active ingredients.

picric acid A historically important compound in the chemistry of drugs, dyes, and explosives. Originally synthesized as a dye (it is yellow), it was found to be shock sensitive and explosive and is still used as a reference in explosive power comparisons.

pigment A *colourant that is insoluble in the solvent or *vehicle in which it is suspended. This contrasts with a dye, which is soluble in the vehicle.

pincushion method Also called the polygon method, a technique for comparing *latent fingerprints. In this approach, points of comparison are marked with a point and a line is drawn from one point to the next until a closed shape is created.

Piotrowski, Eduard A Polish forensic scientist who published one of the first textbooks on forensic analysis of bloodstain patterns entitled *Concerning Origin, Shape, Direction, and Distribution of Bloodstains Following Blow Injuries to the Head*. The work, published in 1895, was notable given the extensive experimentation behind it and the scientific approach.

Pitchfork, Colin *See* NARBOROUGH MURDERS.

pK$_a$ The –log of the acid dissociation constant K$_a$:

$$HA \rightleftharpoons H^+ + A^-$$
$$K_a = \frac{[H^+][A^-]}{[HA]}; pKa = -\log(K_a)$$

Where HA is generic for a monoprotic acid. In drug chemistry applications, drugs with *ionizable centres are characterized by the pKa value, even if the drug is basic. From this perspective, the equation is applied as:

$$BT^+ \rightleftharpoons B + H^+$$
$$K_a = \frac{[B][H^+]}{[BH^+]} ; pK_a = \log K_a$$

See also pH.

plain arch One of the common friction ridge patterns in fingerprints along with patterns such as loops and whorls. The other type of arch is a tented arch, which has a more pronounced point at the top than a plain arch pattern.

plain whorl One of the common friction ridge patterns in fingerprints along with patterns such as arches and whorls.

plastic deformation An alteration in the shape of a surface that, once created, does not disappear. Such deformations are called non-elastic, and an example would be a fingerprint created by pressing into soft putty. The resulting pattern has a three-dimensional quality as opposed to a fingerprint on paper which does not have depth.

plastic fingerprint A fingerprint that is an impression or indentation as opposed to a pattern of fingerprint residue left on a surface such as glass.

plasticizer A compound added to a *polymer to change the physical characteristics; typically added to soften. Phthalates are commonly used as plasticizers.

plastics A generic term referring to primarily synthetic polymers that can be encountered as a form of physical, trace, or transfer evidence. Plastics and related compounds are found in storage bags, food containers, bottles, paints, fibres, and automobile parts to name just a few. The term 'plastic' generally is used to refer to synthetic polymers derived from petroleum products. Polyethylene and polypropylene are two examples.

P/M ratio The ratio of a metabolite (M) in a body fluid such as blood to the original ingested substance (parent compound P). Given that metabolism takes place in stages, this ratio can be used to estimate the time that has passed since the substance was ingested.

point of convergence In *bloodstain pattern analysis, a region in space (as opposed to a specific point) where measurements of angles and elevation converge. This area in space is where the blood originated. Strings running from stains or computer programs are used to locate this area.

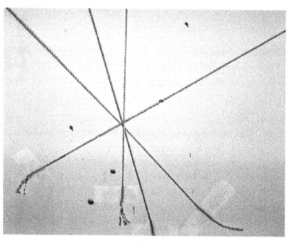

Point of convergence using stringing, two-dimensional

Point of convergence using stringing, three-dimensional

The point of convergence determined using stringing. Notice particularly in the bottom frame that a region in space is defined rather than a specific point.

point of origin **1.** In a fire, the location at which the blaze began. **2.** Occasionally used as a synonym for *point of convergence.

point-to-point search A type of crime scene searching pattern that typically begins with identification of the *primary focal points at a scene. Each point is dealt with sequentially following a cleared line between the points.

poisons Any substance capable of causing a toxic (harmful) response in an organism. 'The dose makes the poison' is an oft-repeated phrase which means that every substance can cause harm depending on how much is ingested and over what period of time. One method of gauging the toxicity of a poison is the LD_{50}, 'lethal dose 50'. The LD_{50} of a substance is the dose (based on body weight) that results in death for half of an experimental population such as laboratory rats or mice. For any given individual, the fatal dose of a poison will depend on general health, age, weight, and a number of other variables. Biological poisons, broadly defined, are those obtained from living organisms such as bacteria or plants. Hemlock, strychnine, venom from snakes, and botulism are examples. Inorganic poisons include hydrochloric acid (HCl), cyanide (both salts and gaseous HCN), lye (sodium hydroxide NaOH), ammonia, mercury, lead, thallium, and arsenic, which is perhaps the most notorious poison of all. The term 'organic poisons' usually refers to organic compounds such as organic insecticides and pesticides such as DDT, toluene and other petroleum distillates, and many drugs. Methanol (wood alcohol) poisoning can occur with homemade or adulterated liquors in which the methanol is substituted for ethanol. Of the gaseous poisons, carbon monoxide (CO), HCN, and forms of arsenic are the most familiar. *See also* PARACELSUS.

polar coordinates An alternative set of coordinates that can be used to document crime scenes in addition to the traditional Cartesian coordinate system with *x-y-z* coordinates. A location in a polar coordinate system is based on a number (the radial coordinate r) which represents a distance from the origin and an angle θ that specifies the direction.

polarimetry A method used to determine if a substance rotates plane *polarized light to the right or left; a means to distinguish *optical isomers of organic molecules such as *pseudoephedrine and *cocaine. A **polarimeter** consists of a light source, a polarizing filter, the sample chamber, and a viewer that measures the direction and angle of rotation of the plane polarized light that has passed through the sample.

polarity **1.** When referring to organic molecules, the degree of imbalance of electron density in a covalently bonded compound measured by the dipole moment. The relative polarity of solvents determines whether they are miscible (soluble) in each other or not. Water and ethanol are miscible because both are relatively polar; water and hexane are immiscible because water is polar and hexane is not.

2. In electrical systems, the location of the *cathode and *anode.

polarized light (plane polarized light) Light that has been filtered such that the waves of electromagnetic radiation (EMR) are oscillating in only one direction. For this reason, the term 'plane polarized light' is often used. One familiar application is in sunglasses; if the lenses have been polarized (have a Polaroid coating), the glare from reflections is eliminated because the light from all but one direction of propagation has been filtered out. Polarization of light is exploited in forensic science in polarized light microscopy (PLM) and in drug analysis principally for the analysis of cocaine. Cocaine that is obtained from extraction of the *coca* plant will rotate plane polarized light to the left ('levorotatory') while synthetic cocaine rotates it to the right ('dextrorotatory'). The two forms of cocaine are referred to as l-cocaine and d-cocaine to distinguish them. The instrument used to determine this is called a polarimeter and the technique is referred to as *polarimetry.

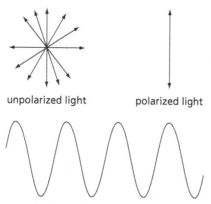

unpolarized light   polarized light

polarized in the plane of the paper

Light that is polarized vibrates in only one direction. The top left frame depicts how unpolarized light behaves when moving towards the observer. There are many directions of propagation but on the top right, all but one direction has been filtered out. The bottom frame shows the propagation of light polarized in the plane of the paper.

polarized light microscopy (PLM) A type of microscopy originally used in geology for the analysis and identification of minerals. Polarizing light microscopes are sometimes still referred to as 'petrographic' microscopes for this reason. The design of polarizing light microscopes is similar to that of a compound microscope with the addition of a few key components. The light that comes from below the sample first passed through a filter called the *polarizer, which converts the beam to plane polarized light. This passes through the sample and then through a second polarizing filter called the *analyser. Initially, these two filters are set such that the light passing through the analyser is polarized in a plane that is perpendicular to the light that can pass through the analyser. As a result, with no sample in the light path, the view appears completely dark, since the analyser blocks all the polarized light from the polarizer. However, when a sample is placed on the stage, the oscillations of light that emerge from it are no longer polarized in one direction. Thus, some of this emerging light will be able to pass through the analyser where the beams can interfere with each other. The result is a viewable image (magnified) with distinctive contrast and which may be highly coloured.

PLM is valuable for studying the optical properties of materials that are anisotropic such as crystals and pseudocrystalline materials. A material that is isotropic for a given optical characteristic will have the same value of that characteristic regardless of the direction from which the light is coming. Solid materials that are made up of molecules that are randomly placed or molecules that are not symmetric will be isotropic. Thus, a material that is isotropic will have the same refractive index regardless of the direction from which the light is coming. In contrast, anistropic materials will display different properties depending on the direction of propagation of the light. The difference in the refractive index of anisotropic materials is the *birefringence, which can be determined quantitatively and used to identify materials. PLM is particularly useful for the analysis of fibre evidence given that many synthetic fibres are pseudocrystalline in nature and thus amenable to PLM methodology. *See also* POLARIZED LIGHT.

polarizer A filter used in *polarized light microscopy (PLM) to filter out all but one direction of propagation of light emerging from the lamp. In the optical train, the polarizer is placed before the sample and the *analyser is placed after. *See also* POLARIZED LIGHT.

pollen A very fine dust produced by plants containing microspores; the male component of reproduction. The study of pollen is called palynology.

polychromatic Literally, 'many coloured'. In forensic science, the term is most often associated with a specimen in microscopy that takes on different apparent colours based on the direction from which it is observed.

polydrug (polypharmacy) 1. A term referring to intoxication by more than one drug.

2. The practice of receiving and taking several types of prescription medicine at one time, and even combining prescription with non-prescription and illicit drugs. Multiple drug intoxication and drug interactions are becoming a concern in forensic toxicology and death investigation.

polyester A generic name for a large class of synthetic fibres in which the monomer units are chemically bonded by ester bonds involving oxygen atoms. Polyesters are versatile and thus widespread; they are also used for insulation. Trade names for polyesters include Ceylon, Dacron, Kodel, and Mylar.

polymers Large molecules (macromolecules) that are created by linking together tens, hundreds, or thousands of subunits called monomers using strong chemical bonds. Polymers are common in nature and include proteins (polymers of amino acids) and carbohydrates (polymers of sugars). For example, cellulose is a glucose polymer that makes up about 90 per cent of the weight of cotton. Collectively, these types of polymers are referred to as biopolymers. Synthetic polymers were first produced in the mid-1800s and included cellulose nitrate and its derivative, celluloid, both of which are readily combustible and thus of limited commercial use. Bakelite, a rigid plastic polymer, was synthesized in 1907 by mixing together urea (the pungent compound that gives urine its characteristic odour) and formaldehyde. Nylon was introduced in 1939, followed by an explosion in the development and utilization of synthetic polymers. In forensic science, polymers are encountered as fibre evidence (nylon, rayon, polyesters, etc.), in building materials (polyvinyl chloride, PVC pipe), paints, plastics, ropes, and many other forms.

polymorphic Literally means 'many forms'; a compound or trait with more than one variant that exists in different forms that are determined genetically, one example being blood type in the *ABO blood group system. The number of repetitions at a *short tandem repeat locus are also polymorphic, which is the basis of current *DNA typing methods.

portrait parlé A card-based record developed by *Bertillon in the late 19th century to record eleven body measurements, a photograph, and physical descriptors of criminals or suspects.

positive control In a chemical or biochemical analysis, a sample known to produce positive results such as a colour change in colour-based presumptive tests. It is used to ensure that the process and reagents are working correctly and is coupled with a *negative control.

post-mortem interval (PMI; PM interval) The time that has elapsed since death. For forensic purposes, the death event is often considered as two processes, brain death and cell death (autolysis) but the time of death generally refers to brain death. Techniques and processes used to estimate PMI include *algor mortis (rate of cooling), *rigor mortis (stiffening), *livor mortis (pooling of blood at lowest points), decomposition stage, and stomach contents. Generally it is difficult if not impossible to pinpoint an exact time of death but combination of evidences can lead to a reasonable estimate.

post-mortem redistribution The change in the relative concentrations of drugs, poisons, and metabolites in different body fluids and tissues that occurs after death. It is thought that the principle driving force of the redistribution is diffusion from a zone of higher concentration to one with a lower concentration, but there are numerous potential contributing factors.

post-mortem toxicology The branch of forensic toxicology that focuses on the analysis of samples associated with a death. Samples are typically collected at autopsy and include matrices such as blood drawn from various locations around the body, urine, *vitreous fluid, and tissue samples such as liver, kidney, or brain. Data from all samples are correlated to assist in determining what substance(s) were taken, when they were taken, and in what amount. Samples are typically screened using techniques such as *immunoassay and then, based on these results, analysed for the presence of typical drugs, poisons, and metabolites. The toxicological analysis is integrated into data from the autopsy to assist determination of the cause and manner of death. *See also* POST-MORTEM REDISTRIBUTION.

postural asphyxia Death by asphyxia (lack of oxygen) brought on by the position of the body or compression of the chest and the resulting inability to expand it to fill the lungs with air. A person trapped in a crushed car may die of this.

precipitin reactions Immunological testing methods in which a positive reaction is signified by the formation of a precipitate or solid (also called an immunoprecipitate) that can be easily seen. In forensic applications the solid typically is the result of an immunological reaction between antigens found in a sample and antibodies contained in purified antisera applied in the test. Diffusion tests for species are an example of a precipitin test. Most of these types of tests have been supplanted by procedures associated with *DNA typing.

precision The agreement between results of quantitative tests performed on the same sample under the same experimental conditions.

It is related to other *figures of merit such as *repeatability and reproducibility.

precursor Compounds or mixtures used as starting materials for the synthesis of drugs. For example, morphine is a precursor to heroin and pseudoephedrine is a precursor for methamphetamine. Ingredients and reagents associated with a synthesis may also be classified as precursors although this is a less formal interpretation of the term.

predator drugs *See* DATE RAPE DRUGS.

Pregl, Fritz (1869–1930) An Austrian chemist who was renowned for his skills in microchemistry. Although not a forensic scientist himself, he developed many tools and techniques that were adopted by, or adapted to, forensic practice. He received the Nobel Prize in Chemistry in 1923.

preponderance of evidence Criteria for degree of proof in a judicial proceeding; arises when the majority of the evidences presented supports one version of events over another. This is a more lenient standard than that of 'beyond all reasonable doubt'.

pressure wave A wave of pressured air produced in an explosion; also called a blast wave. The wave consists of hot expanding gases created by detonation. Explosives are often engineered to maximize the pressure wave over fragmentation, depending on the intended application. The pressure wave is highly compressed and travels at supersonic speed. It dissipates in a fraction of a second.

presumptive tests Preliminary chemical tests widely used in the analysis of blood, drugs, *gunshot residue (GSR), and explosives. A presumptive test does not provide definitive identification; rather, it provides information useful for directing further analysis. Since most of these tests involve addition of a chemical reagent and looking for a colour change, these tests are sometimes referred to as 'colour tests'. Colours are created as a result of a reaction that forms either a dye or a pigment. Other terms used are 'screening tests' and 'spot tests'. Presumptive tests are subject to both false positives and false negatives, but these tend to be limited and recognized.

Tests for blood are based on the ability of the haem group in haemoglobin to act as a catalyst in chemical reactions that involve a colour change. This ability is referred to as peroxidase-like activity in reference to biological enzymes that react with peroxide groups such as are found in hydrogen peroxide (H_2O_2). The *Kastle–Meyer test is widely used in this role. The *luminol test is unique in that the reaction does not cause a colour change but rather results in the emission of light. Sensitivities of these tests vary, but it is usually possible to detect blood that has been diluted several hundred or thousandfold.

Perhaps in no other forensic area are preliminary colour tests used more than in drug analysis. These tests are designed to narrow down the possibilities when an unknown substance is delivered to the laboratory for identification. Examples include the *Marquis test and the *cobalt thiocyanate test. The other large group of screening tests targets the components of gunshot residue (GSR) and explosives, which share many common elements. The *Griess and *diphenylamine tests react with nitrate and nitrite ions (NO_3^- and NO_2^-) found in both.

primary explosive A relatively sensitive explosive that is used to detonate another. An example is *lead styphnate which is used in *primers and is set off by the physical force of the firing pin impact. The resulting combustion sets off the propellant.

primary focal points At a crime scene, the point or points where the initial primary attention of the crime scene investigation is directed. At a homicide, the body is a primary focal point.

primary transfer A direct transfer or the first transfer to occur. For example, if a person owns a dog, the dog will shed hairs onto the furniture and this is called a primary transfer. If the owner sits on the furniture and as a result, dog hairs are transferred to their clothing, this is an example of a secondary transfer.

primer **1.** A small percussive explosive used to ignite *propellant in ammunition. Primers consist of a shock sensitive explosive (typically *lead styphnate, also called lead trinitroresorcinate), an oxidizing agent such as barium nitrate ($BaNO_3$), and a fuel such as antimony sulphide (Sb_2S_3). This is the same combination of ingredients used in combustion and the ignition of a primer which produces an intense flame that is directed through vents into the chamber of the cartridge case where the propellant is stored. This flash ignites the propellant and results in the acceleration of the bullet down the barrel of the weapon. In addition to the initiator, fuel, and oxidizer, primers can also contain many other ingredients including sensitizers (to make the initiator more sensitive to shock), binders, and traces of other explosive materials. The compounds used in primers are important components of *gunshot residue (GSR). The two types of primers in use are centrefire and rimfire.

2. A short segment of nucleotides used to recognize regions in DNA. The primer binds to the complementary strand of the area of interest and isolates it for replication. *See also* PCR; DNA TYPING.

principal focus With a lens, such as used with a microscope, a term used to describe its behaviour. If an object is placed an infinite distance away from a lens, the image will appear at the principal focus point. Conversely, if an object is placed at the principal focus point, its image would form an infinite distance away from the lens. The symbol 'f' is used to indicate the location of each principal focus, one on each side of the lens.

probability of discrimination *See* DISCRIMINATION INDEX.

probe, DNA A sequence of bases that is used to detect or identify a labelled strand of DNA that hybridizes with its RNA or monoclonal antibody that combines with a specific protein.

proficiency testing The testing of laboratory analysts as part of obtaining or maintaining a certification from a professional association. For example, to obtain certification from the American Board of Criminalistics (ABC), a person must complete written tests as well as laboratory proficiency testing in their area of specialization.

profiling Behavioural evidence (broadly defined) applied to the study of criminals at crimes and crime scenes. Although there are no standards for profiling, the process normally includes examination and review of physical evidence and crime scenes in an attempt to delineate the motives and fantasies of the perpetrator. Profiling may also incorporate a psychological evaluation of victims (victimology). Like other forensic disciplines, a large part of profiling is seeking of patterns such as consistent elements of crimes, the modus operandi (MO), and any signature behaviours shown during the commission of a crime.

progressive burning powder A type of propellant engineered to burn relatively slowly at first and then at faster rates. This is accomplished by coating the particles with materials that discourage burning (deterrents).

projected bloodstain pattern **1.** Generally, a bloodstain pattern that is created when blood is forcefully ejected or pushed outward from a point of origin. For example, blunt force trauma can project blood away from the victim onto an impacting surface.

2. A bloodstain pattern created when a victim forcefully exhales blood such as by coughing; also called an expired bloodstain (in contrast to aspirated or inhaled blood).

propellant A low explosive material used to generate hot expanding gases to propel a projectile forward. Known informally as *gunpowder, propellant is placed in a cartridge case packed between the primer and the projectile. Black powder (a mixture of charcoal, potassium nitrate, and sulphur) was used from ancient times until about the mid-1800s when it was replaced by smokeless powder. Modern smokeless powder propellants are either 'single base', consisting of nitrocellulose, or 'double base', consisting of cellulose nitrate and nitroglycerin. The impact of the firing pin on the primer cases causes a flash, which ignites the propellant. The rapid combustion that follows creates large volumes of hot expanding gas resulting in high pressures that are confined within the barrel, forcing the bullet forward at high speeds. The burn speed can be altered by physical manipulation of the shape and surface area as well as chemically by the use of deterrents. *See also* PROGRESSIVE BURNING POWDER; NEUTRAL BURNING POWDER.

Propellant. Note the variety of shapes of propellant particles in this commercial mixture.

prostate specific antigen (PSA) *See* P30.

proximate cause The event or action nearest to the event in question. This phrase is most often used in relationship to a death investigation, where the proximate cause is the physiological event precipitating the death event. For example, if a stabbing victim arrives at the hospital and dies of shock, the shock is the proximate cause while the stabbing is the legal cause.

pseudoephedrine *See* EPHEDRINE AND PSEUDOEPHEDRINE.

pseudoscience Theories, ideas, or explanations that are represented as scientific but that are not derived from science or the scientific method. Pseudoscience often springs from claims or folk wisdom or selective reading without independent data collection or validation. Scientific statements are specific and well defined while pseudoscience is vague and variable. One of the key differences between science and pseudoscience is that a scientific statement or theory is stated in such as a way as to be falsifiable. In contrast, pseudoscientific statements are usually not falsifiable using objective experimental or observational evidence. Pseudoscience provides no room for challenge and tends to dismiss contradictory evidence or to selectively decide what evidence to accept. Thus, pseudoscience is usually nothing more than a claim, belief, or opinion that is falsely presented as a valid scientific theory or fact.

psilocin and psilocybin Hallucinogens found in mushrooms located principally in Mexico. In this respect, these compounds are similar to *mescaline, which is obtained from the peyote cactus. Psilocybin can also be synthesized from psilocin, but most seizures are of the naturally occurring materials. In mushrooms, there is more psilocybin than psilocin but the psilocin is about twice as potent. The drugs are taken by chewing the dried mushrooms and the effects start within an hour and can last for hours. Psilocybin is one of the few drugs with a phosphate group in the molecule.

psychoactive substance A substance that when ingested, causes a change in brain function as a result of crossing the blood-brain barrier.

psychological autopsy An informal term that usually refers to an evaluation of a person's psychological state and behaviours as related to criminal activity. The subject of such an 'autopsy' need not be dead; typically the usage refers to an analysis of past activities regardless of the state of the subject.

putrefaction A stage in the *decomposition process. Putrefaction begins with a greening of the skin along with a surge in microbial degradation leading to bloating and purging of gases and fluids from the body. Putrefaction is marked by the characteristic foul odours of decomposition. The stage ends when all soft tissue has disappeared.

pyrolysis Literally, 'fire cutting'; an analytical method in which a sample is burned (typically in an anoxic environment) and the gases produced by the decomposition are analysed using a gas chromatograph (GC). Forensic applications include characterization of fibres and plastics.

quadrupole mass spectrometer *See* MASS SPECTROMETRY.

qualitative analysis An analysis designed to identify a substance or substances present in a mixture.

quality assurance (QA) **and quality control** (QC) Inclusive terms for procedures and protocols used in forensic analysis to ensure that any data or results produced are reliable and relevant. Although the terms are often used interchangeably, quality assurance is usually defined as those measures taken within a laboratory whilst quality control measures are those imposed by an outside entity. However, these definitions are not always strictly applied. Often, the term quality assurance is used to describe the foundations in place to ensure acceptable laboratory performance. In this scheme, QA refers to things such as training, documentation, laboratory policies and procedures, and *method validation. Quality control reflects all of the actual practices used to ensure the trustworthiness of data.

quantitative analysis Testing that leads to the determination of how much of a given component or components are present in a sample. This is in contrast to *qualitative analysis in which only the identity of components present is necessary, not including in which amounts or concentrations. Quantitative analysis is most often an issue in *toxicology and *seized drug analysis, where the amount of an illegal substance present may be critically important. For example, in the analysis of blood alcohol levels, the first stage is the definitive identification of ethanol (qualitative analysis) followed by an accurate determination of the quantity of alcohol present.

quantitative polymerase chain reaction (qPCR) *See* PCR.

quantitative transfer The transfer of a sample from one container or vessel to another such that none is lost; a complete transfer.

quantum dots Also referred to as photoluminescent nanoparticles, these are used to visualize *latent fingerprints. The types of quantum dots used for this purpose include cadmium selenite (CdSe) and cadmium sulphide (CdS). A quantum dot is composed of a nanoparticle with a size of between 1 and 100 nanometres of a semiconductor material such as CdSe, CdS, and InAs that is luminescent when found in such small crystals. The nanoparticle is then coated or encapsulated with various materials that impart capabilities such as the ability to bind to certain surfaces or materials. Changing the size of the quantum dot changes its absorbance (excitation) and emission characteristics.

quartz wedge In microscopy, a tool that can be used to determine the *birefringence of a fibre, in conjunction with a polarizing microscope and a *Michel–Levy chart.

questioned documents (QD) The forensic specialty dealing with suspicious, questioned, or damaged documents, be they handwritten, typed, printed, FAXed, copied, or computer-generated. The examination of questioned documents began to emerge as a forensic discipline around 1870 and an early practitioner in Europe was Alphonse *Bertillon. Albert S. *Osborn, an American, is considered to be a pioneer of document examination in the United States and wrote a book entitled *Questioned Documents* in 1910, along with a later revision. The analysis of questioned documents includes the analysis of papers, inks (or other marking material), and the devices or processes used to generate the document. As an example, questioned documents examiners might be asked to examine a copy of a document made on a typical office copy machine. While analysis of the paper is likely of little value, an examination of the copier itself might be critical. If the glass on the copier is scratched, that marking could be reproduced in some fashion on documents copied while resting on the glass. This is a form of *pattern evidence that under ideal conditions might link a document to a specific copier.

   QD analysis also includes handwriting analysis, which is also approached as a type of pattern recognition. Samples of handwriting (also called exemplars) can be collected under supervised conditions or from documents written in the past by the person of interest. Signatures are frequently the subject of handwriting analysis, but numbers, notes, and letters are also studied. The analysis of inks, dyes and papers is conducted using instruments such as a Video Spectral Comparator (VSC) in which samples are illuminated with particular wavelengths of light while the reflected and emitted light is examined through a filter. For example, illumination of some inks with UV light will result in fluorescence in the visible region. Other instruments used in document analysis include *ESDA, *Raman spectroscopy and *infrared spectroscopy.

   QD also includes the analysis of currency and credit cards, both of which are the targets of counterfeiters. Governments utilize elaborate methods of generation of currency to thwart counterfeiting, but the advent of high resolution scanners and printers has made it easier to make simple copies. Features of currency include specialized printing techniques that lend texture to a bill, elaborate fine patterning of printing that is difficult to copy, specially formulated dyes and pigments that may fluoresce, *watermarks, colour-shifting inks, and holographic features. Many of these same features are now incorporated into credit cards and are also studied in questioned document cases.

questioned sample (Q) The sample in question, the one that was collected as evidence; compared to a known sample. For example, a questioned fingerprint would be one collected at a crime scene and it would be compared to standards or exemplars collected from suspects or other persons that might have deposited it.

q

racemic mixture A sample of a single compound that contains a mix of *stereoisomers. This is important in cases such as the clandestine synthesis of *methamphetamine, in which the composition of the stereoisomers can provide information regarding the synthetic method used to prepare it.

racial determination In forensic anthropology, the determination of racial origin of evidence such as hair or bones based on morphology, measurements, or other characteristics.

radial fracture The roughly linear fractures that form at an impact site in glass and move outward. These are accompanied by *concentric fractures, which form circular shapes around the impact.

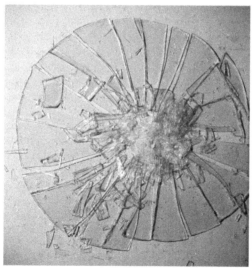

The radial fractures are radiating up and out from the central point of impact in the glass.

radial loop A loop pattern in fingerprints that opens toward the thumb.

radioimmunoassay (RIA) A type of *immunoassay in which the label attached to the drug is radioactive and is detected by the emission of radiation.

radiology, forensic The application of medical and dental imaging techniques (generally) and X-ray techniques specifically to forensic work. Forensic radiology is considered a branch of forensic medicine that is related to forensic *pathology. While many autopsies are accompanied by X-ray imaging, forensic radiology is often considered to be a closely related but separate specialty. Although the most frequently used tool in the field is the familiar X-ray film, all radiological techniques are available, including ultrasound; magnetic resonance imaging; fluorescent imaging; CT scans (computated axial tomography or CAT scans); and nuclear imaging techniques in which radioactive materials are utilized. Forensic radiology plays an important role in the response to *mass fatality incidents.

RAM 1. The abbreviation for the dye combination Rhodamine 6G, Ardrox, and MDB (7-(*p*-methoxybenzylamino)-4-nitrobenz-2-oxa-1,3-diazole). RAM is used to visualize *latent fingerprints.

2. An abbreviation for random access memory (volatile memory) of computers or related devices.

Raman spectroscopy A spectroscopic technique that probes vibrational interactions. It is related to *infrared spectroscopy (IR) and is finding forensic use in the analysis of drugs, explosives, dyes, and even fingerprints and blood. Unlike traditional infrared spectroscopy, which relies on measuring how much infrared radiation is absorbed, Raman spectroscopy is based on scattering interactions. Since this scattering behaviour is specific to a given molecule, Raman spectroscopy (like IR spectroscopy) produces a unique spectrum for each compound. Thus, Raman spectroscopy can be used to identify specific molecules or for the qualitative analysis of complex mixtures.

For a compound to be infrared active, it must have a dipole moment, which in simple terms means an imbalance or unevenness in the electron cloud that surrounds the molecule or compound. However, for Raman activity, these bonds must be polarizable by incoming electromagnetic energy. Furthermore, the degree of polarizability must change as the bonds stretch and contract. Interestingly, this leads to a 'mutual exclusion' property—a bond that is IR active will be Raman inactive and vice versa. One of the advantages of Raman methods is that they can be performed on and through glass and are widely used as microspectrophotometers in the analysis of evidence such as fibres.

random error An error in a measured value (deviation from and accepted true value) that is attributable to unpredictable and typically small variations over replicate measurement events. *See also* ACCURACY; BIAS; TRUENESS.

random man (random match, random man not excluded (RMNE)) A measurement most often used in *DNA typing (but applicable to other types of evidence) that states how likely a given combination of frequencies is to occur in a population. It provides a method of expressing a probability-based inference in an easily understandable way. If a bloodstain is typed for several different DNA loci, it is important to know how common that particular combination of types is. In other words, if a 'random man' were selected from the same population, how likely would it be that this man would have the same combination of types and thus not be excluded as a possible source? The value of this probability of a random match is determined using population genetics and population frequencies. As an example, assume that a bloodstain is typed for four DNA loci and that the combination of frequencies is 0.080, 0.068, 0.041, and 0.080 in European populations. The likelihood of finding this combination in a random selection from that same population is expressed as the product of these four, or 1.78×10^{-5}. This means that this combination of types would be found in about eighteen people out of a million that belong to the parent population, here Europeans. Another way to phrase it would be to say that using the same population, there would be eighteen chances in a million that any one man (or person) selected at random would have the exact same combination of types.

random sample A sample selected from a larger population such that the particular sample has an equal chance of being selected.

rape kit A generic descriptor for kits used to collect evidence in sexual assault cases. Generally, rape kits consist of a whole blood sample, swabs of any dried secretions, and swabs of the vagina, genital area, thighs, anus, and mouth. In addition, smears on slides are made from these swabs and all must be air-dried. A vaginal rinse may also be collected. Any visible hairs and fibres are collected and the victim may be asked to undress over a large sheet of paper so that any *trace evidence that falls off in the process can be collected and preserved. All clothing worn also becomes part of the physical evidence.

rayon One of the first synthetic fibres manufactured, although it is not based on synthetic polymers. Rather, rayon is classified as a regenerated fibre because it is made from cellulose, which is derived from plant material such as cotton. Rayon was originally developed in the late 1800s as a replacement for silk. The term 'viscous rayon' refers to rayon made by a specific process involving sodium hydroxide.

RDX A *high explosive used commercially and in the military. The chemical name for the compound is cyclotrimethylenetrinitramine, and it is also known as 'cyclonite' and 'hexogen'. The origin of the abbreviation is unclear, variously reported as 'Royal Demolition Explosive' or 'Research Department Explosive'. RDX is a secondary high explosive meaning that it is shock insensitive and must be detonated by a primary high explosive. It is the principal component (~90 per cent) of C4, a military explosive that is mouldable and is sometimes referred to generically as 'plastic explosive' or 'plastique'.

1,3,5-trinitro-1,3,5-triazinane

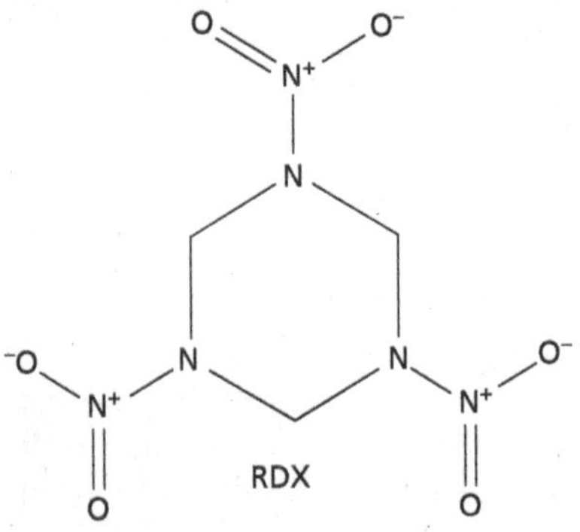

RDX

RDX

reaction order In a process or chemical reaction, the order relates to the kinetics or rate of a reaction. The rate of a first order reaction depends solely on the concentration of one component while second order reactions depend on two concentrations. Reaction orders are frequently used to describe metabolic reactions. Mathematically, the reaction order is defined as the power to which a concentration is raised in the equation that describes the reaction rate. Generically this is expressed as rate = k[A] where [A] is the concentration of substance A, raised to the first power.

real image In microscopy, an image that forms on a screen or other surface as the result of the convergence of light rays. Lenses and lens combinations can be used to form and manipulate a real image. *See also* VIRTUAL IMAGE.

receiver operating characteristics (ROC) A mathematical relationship applied in forensic science, particularly in cases of computer-aided comparisons and identifications. A typical ROC application would be to plot the rate of false positives obtained by a given technique or test on the x axis and the rate of false negatives on the y axis for the same test.

recoil The backward momentum created when a weapon such as a handgun is fired.

recoverable regions In automated fingerprint analysis algorithms, a method that uses a series of filters to identify regions in a *latent fingerprint that are most likely to be genuine and that are best suited for enhancement.

rectangular coordinates The familiar x, y coordinate system based on an x baseline and a y line perpendicular to it. Rectangular coordinates are used to document and locate evidence at crime scenes using a *grid method and measurements from a reference *baseline or baselines. *See also* POLAR COORDINATES.

recurving ridges A fingerprint pattern (friction ridge pattern) that has significant curvature.

red cook method A common method used in the clandestine synthesis of *methamphetamine. The precursor is usually *pseudoephedrine and the ingredients needed are a source of iodine and red phosphorus and water. The phosphorus is used as part of a procedure to generate hydroiodic acid (HI) in situ and the process results in the reduction of the precursor to methamphetamine. Red cook method is also known as the Moscow, *hypophosphorous route, or hypo route.

reducing agent A chemical compound that promotes the reduction of another compound. In an oxidation/reduction reaction, one compound is oxidized and one is reduced. The compound that is oxidized is the reducing agent.

reduction A chemical process that is the companion of oxidation. Such paired reactions are referred to as oxidation/reduction (redox), and one reaction cannot occur without the other, just as acid/base reactions are paired. Reduction can be defined, based on the situation, as the gain of electrons, the gain of hydrogen, or as the loss of oxygen. If CO_2 is converted to CH_4, the carbon dioxide is reduced.

reductive amination A description of a generic chemical transition, usually used in reference to the clandestine synthesis of methamphetamine. The process involves a chemical reduction (elimination of an oxygen) and the addition of an amine group (NH_2) to a molecule.

reference material (RM) A material or sample that has been determined to be acceptably stable, homogeneous, and well characterized and that is used as a basis for evaluation of the performance of a method in some capacity.

reference points In the examination and comparison of latent prints, a point or points selected on one that serve as a reference point. The locations of other features are characterized relative to the reference point. Reference points are also used in crime scene documentation.

reflection spectroscopy Spectroscopy that is performed by the interrogation of reflected electromagnetic radiation in contrast to absorbed or transmitted radiation. In forensic science, the analysis of inks and paints is often accomplished using reflective spectroscopy techniques. For example, to perform a colorimetric analysis of an ink on paper, the source is directed onto the surface and the reflected light is characterized.

refractive index (RI) A quantity that measures the bending of light as it travels from one medium into another. Mathematically, the refractive index is defined by the following formula:

$$RI = \frac{velocity\ of\ light\ in\ a\ vacuum}{velocity\ of\ light\ in\ medium} = \eta$$

The symbol η also stands for the refractive index. The speed of light in a vacuum is the maximum achievable, so the RI is a quantity that is greater than 1.00 since light is always slower in a medium than in a vacuum. *See also* BIREFRINGENCE; GLASS ANALYSIS; POLARIZED LIGHT MICROSCOPY.

regenerated fibres Fibres such as rayon and triacetate that are made by processing of cellulose derived from plants. Thus, while such fibres are technically synthetic, they are not manufactured from man-made polymers such as polyesters and nylon.

regression line A best fit line generated through a set of points. *Calibration curves are examples of regression lines in which a series of standards of increasing concentrations are analysed to obtain an instrument response. The best fit line to these points is called the regression line and is generated through linear regression techniques. One common method of defining the line is through minimizing distance between each point and the generated line; this is called the least squares approach since distances are squared.

Reinsch test A test developed by Adolf Reinsch (1862–1916), a German physician. The test was roughly contemporaneous with the *Marsh test, although variations of the Reinsch test were still used relatively recently. The test targets heavy metals such as arsenic (As) and antimony (Sb) and is simple to execute. A piece of copper foil or wound copper wire is inserted into an acidic solution of the sample of interest. If a greyish discoloration is noted, this is an indication of the presence of metals. Further heating applied to the copper can generate a deposit containing the metal on a glass surface such as the inside of a test tube. The test is also sensitive to mercury and bismuth.

Reiss, R. A. (1875–1929) A professor at the *University of Lausanne in Switzerland who was instrumental in advancing early work in forensic photography. Prior to working at Lausanne, he studied under *Bertillon, who used photography as part of his Bertillonage criminal identification system. In 1902, Reiss taught a course in what he called 'judicial photography'. Reiss's efforts and interest in forensic science led to the formation of the Lausanne Institute of Police Science. This was the first known university programme devoted to forensic science, as opposed to the institutes of legal medicine found in Europe by that time. The school was renamed School of Criminal Sciences, and it remains a hub of forensic science education in Europe.

repeatability The precision (closeness of agreement) of successive measurements collected under identical or nearly identical conditions.

replicates Repeated measurements obtained from the same sample or sample preparation. For example, if a blood sample is extracted, repeated tests on that extract would be considered replicates. *See also* DUPLICATES.

representative sampling The process of obtaining samples for testing that will accurately reflect the composition of the bulk material in question. This is an issue any time evidence is collected and subject to forensic analysis. For example, if an analyst needs to compare a cotton fibre found at a crime scene with jeans recovered from a suspect, they must obtain a representative sample of fibres from the jeans since fibres will vary in appearance depending on where they are taken from. Samples should be both representative and random meaning that any one item has an equal chance as any other item to be selected as a sample. Sampling plans are used to design representative sample selection. *See also* HYPERGEOMETRIC SAMPLING.

request standards Samples of handwriting that are requested of a person for the purposes of *questioned documents examination. These samples are collected while the writer is being observed so there is no question as to their origin.

residual data *See* AMBIENT DATA.

resolution 1. The density of collected points in a digital image, photo, copy, or printout in dots per inch (dpi) or megapixels.
   2. A measurement of the degree of separation that is achieved in a chromatographic separation such as in gas chromatography (GC). The greater the separation between components achieved by the chromatographic column, the higher the resolution. For any two adjacent peaks, the resolution can be calculated by the following formula:

$$R = \frac{t_{r2} - t_{r1}}{\frac{1}{2}(W_2 - W_1)}$$

where t_{r1} and t_{r2} are the *retention times of the two peaks and the W values are the widths. If R = 1.5, there is very little overlap (~0.1 per cent or less) and the peaks are said to have baseline resolution.

restriction enzyme An *enzyme that is used to locate a specific segment of DNA and to break the molecule specifically at that point. These enzymes are often informally referred to as 'molecular scissors', and are used in *DNA typing.

restriction fragment length polymorphism (RFLP) One of the first methods of *DNA typing applied to forensic casework. RFLP typing targets tandem repeats in the DNA, but the length of the repeating segments is longer that the *short tandem repeats (STRs) now used. Sir Alec Jeffreys was instrumental in developing this technique. The procedure begins with the use of a *restriction enzyme on a DNA sample, followed by binding to probe molecules, separation using *gel electrophoresis, and visualization. *See also* AUTORADIOGRAM.

retardation The degree of difference in the speed of propagation of light moving through a medium with a high *refractive index (RI) relative to the speed of propagation of light moving through a low RI material. Devices referred to as retardation plates are used in *polarizing light microscopy to enhance this difference and, for example, make it easier to see materials with low *birefringence.

retention time (t_r) In a chromatographic analysis such as gas chromatography (GC) or HPLC, the time at which a component of a mixture elutes from the chromatographic column. A compound with a short retention time emerges from the column quicker than a compound with a longer retention time. Retention times are often expressed relative to standard compounds (the relative retention time).

reticular dermis One of two layers into which the structure of human skin can be divided. It is the lower layer and contains connective tissues.

reversed phase In chromatographic techniques where a liquid mobile phase interacts with a solid stationary phase (for example, *high performance liquid chromatography (HPLC)) analytical conditions in which the stationary phase (the chromatographic column) is composed of non-polar materials while the mobile phase (the solvent) comprises a polar solvent or solvents. The alternative arrangement is called normal phase, with a non-polar mobile phase and a polar stationary phase.

rhodamine A group of dyes that are used to enhance the visualization and development of *latent fingerprints. Rhodamine dyes are often coupled with cyanoacrylate fuming (Super Glue) techniques. Types of Rhodamine include Rhodamine 6G (also called R6G), and Rhodamine B.

ridge characteristics (ridge detail) Detailed features of the friction ridge patterns found on the hands and feet. Collectively, these details are referred to as *minutiae. Their characteristics, number, direction, location, and location relative to each other are used in *latent fingerprint analysis and comparison.

ridge count The number of ridge features found in a designated area of a *latent fingerprint. This term is most often used in conjunction with automated fingerprint identification systems (AFIS).

ridge endings The ending or termination point of a ridge feature in a *latent fingerprint.

rifling *See* LANDS AND GROOVES.

rigor mortis The stiffening of a body that occurs shortly after death and that can be used to estimate the *post-mortem interval. Rigor begins to set in 2–6 hours after death, starting in the small muscles of the jaw and progressing through the trunk and out to the arms and legs. The stiffness remains for 2–3 days and then releases in the reverse order. The rate of stiffening is temperature dependent, with colder temperatures accelerating it and warm temperatures slowing it. The rate can also be influenced by physical activity before death. If a person ran or engaged in strenuous activity right before death, the rate of stiffening increases. Rigor mortis is not the same thing as cadaveric spasm, which can lock a joint in the position it was in at the moment of death.

rimfire cartridge A type of ammunition in which the *primer is contained inside a roll of metal that wraps around the base of the cartridge. This is typical with small calibre handguns such as 0.22.

roadmapping A photographic and documentation technique used at crime scenes to record bloodstain patterns. This is accomplished by identifying distinctive or natural but separate patterns and documenting these in *overall photographs. A series of labels are used to identify the patterns and individual feature within. For example, there may be a group of stains associated with *cast-off high on a wall and a separate wipe pattern on the floor; in this case the two would be treated as separate groups.

robustness A description of the reproducibility of a given test or assay in the presence of small and deliberate changes in the method parameters. Robustness helps to describe the reliability of a given analytical method. *See also* RUGGEDNESS.

rohypnol (flunitrazepam) A *date rape drug that produces a sedative effect and can lead to short-term amnesia.

round robin A quality control process in which several laboratories participate in the analysis of test samples as part of comparisons or proficiency testing.

ROYGBIV An abbreviation for the spectral colours in the range of ~400–700 nm. From 400 (near the ultraviolet region) moving to 700 (near the infrared region), the colours are *v*iolet, *i*ndigo, *b*lue, *g*reen, *y*ellow, *o*range, and *r*ed.

RSD (%RSD) Per cent relative standard deviation, also known as the coefficient of variation (CV). The %RSD is calculated by dividing the standard deviation of a set of data by the mean and multiplying it by 100. The quantity is used to gauge precision or reproducibility of replicate measurements.

Ruhemann purple The coloured compound that forms when *latent fingerprints are treated with *ninhydrin. It is named after S. Ruhemann, who reported the first synthesis of triketohydrindene hydrate that would come to be known as ninhydrin.

Ruybal test *See* COBALT THIOCYANATE TEST.

ruggedness A description of the reproducibility of a given test or assay obtained under a wide variety of conditions, such as different analysts, different laboratories, different stock reagents, and different instrumentation. Ruggedness helps to describe the reliability of a given analytical method.

Sacco and Vanzetti case A landmark case involving *firearms evidence. On 20 April 1920, a robbery took place in South Braintree, Massachusetts, in the United States. The robbery was perpetrated by five men and during the course of the crime a paymaster and guard were killed. A month later, two men, Nicola Sacco and Bartolomeo Vanzetti, both Italians, were charged with the crime. A .38 pistol was recovered from Vanzetti, but it could not be conclusively tied to any of the evidence recovered. Bullets were recovered from the body (0.32 ACP calibre), and Sacco had a .32 pistol in his possession when arrested. Numerous experts, including Calvin *Goddard testified and the trial was surrounded by controversy. The men were convicted and executed.

Sacco and Vanzetti

saline (isotonic saline) A solution of sodium chloride (NaCl) in distilled water that has the same concentration of salt as in blood, 0.9 per cent (w/v).

saliva A common form of *body fluid evidence used for *DNA typing and as a matrix for testing in forensic *toxicology. For toxicological analysis, saliva is considered to be a filtrate of the blood, similar to urine.

saltpetre A historical term for potassium nitrate (KNO_3), used as an oxidizer in *gunpowder.

sampling plan A predetermined approach to obtaining a sample for analysis from a larger bulk sample or from a larger population of items requiring analysis. For example, if a forensic laboratory receives a case that contains several hundred individual packages of tablets or powder, a sampling plan is needed to ensure that an appropriate number of samples are collected to support the conclusions drawn and results reported. *See also* HYPERGEOMETRIC SAMPLING.

Sam Sheppard case Sheppard was a physician convicted of murdering his wife in 1953 in Ohio (USA). Although Sheppard was eventually released from prison, the continuing controversy was the inspiration for the 1960s television series *The Fugitive* and the 1993 movie of the same name. One of the most notable types of physical evidence in the case was *blood and *bloodstain patterns and one of the notable forensic participants was Paul *Kirk.

SANE Abbreviation for a Sexual Assault Nurse Examiner, a certification obtained through the International Association of Forensic Nurses (IAFN).

(SEE WEB LINKS)

• General information regarding forensic nursing and SANE (sexual assault nurse examiner). Last accessed May 2011.

saponification Informally, the type of reaction that forms a soap; specifically it is the hydrolysis of an ester by an aqueous base to form soap, a molecule with a long hydrocarbon chain that terminates with a carboxylate group. The substance *adipocere is created by a saponification reaction of human fat.

satellite drops (satellite pattern) In bloodstain patterns, smaller blood droplets that are ejected from a larger volume drop when that drop hits a surface. The thin tail-like portion of the satellite points backward toward the parent drop.

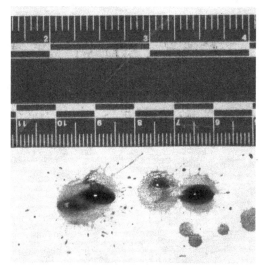

Satellites of the parent drop are located around its periphery

scale cast (**scale patterns**) A method used to capture the pattern of scales found on the surface of *hair. The medium is often clear nail polish and a hair is placed into the liquid polish. As the polish sets, the scale pattern on the hair is captured and preserved.

scallop pattern A type of edge pattern seen in blood drops and blood spatter patterns. The higher the height that a droplet falls, the more exaggerated and elongated the scalloping will be.

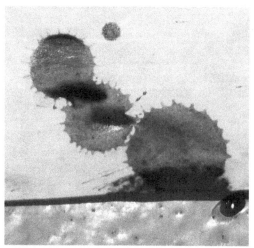

Scalloping around the perimeter of a blood drop

scanning electron microscopy (SEM) A form of *microscopy that uses beams of electrons instead of beams of light to image a sample and is able to achieve very high magnification up to 1,000,000 × (magnification by a factor of a million). SEM also has high *depth of field, meaning that a large portion or depth of the image remains in focus no matter how high the magnification. This contrasts with traditional light microscopy, where the higher the magnification, the shallower the depth of focus. Because the process of bombarding a surface with electrons creates X-rays characteristic of the electronic structure of elements, SEM and the associated X-ray *spectroscopy techniques (electron dispersive spectroscopy (also called energy dispersive) or *X-ray diffraction (XRD)) are used for elemental analysis.

To visualize the sample, an electron gun supplies a tightly focused beam of incident electrons that interact with the sample in a vacuum chamber. Although many types of interactions result, it is the emission of backscattered and secondary electrons that is used to create an image. On the sample's surface, elements with higher atomic numbers will scatter more incident electrons and appear brighter than elements of lower atomic numbers. This difference will be discernible in the final image. Secondary electrons, which are actually emitted from the sample rather than scattered, are used to obtain information about surface features (topography). To generate an image, the electron beam is moved over the surface, scanning it as the backscattered and secondary electrons are collected. The image displayed shows the relative intensity of the electrons collected at a given location.

scene integrity (crime scene integrity) The degree to which a crime scene has been protected and preserved in the state that it was when the crime occurred. Steps taken to preserve the integrity of a scene include establishing a perimeter and limiting access. Because the integrity of the scene degrades naturally over time, processing is undertaken as quickly as is feasible and appropriate to the conditions.

scientific method The procedures and framework in which science is practised. The starting point is a hypothesis, an idea offered to explain an observation or the result of an experiment. Once the preliminary hypothesis is formed, the next step is to gather data either by experiments (empirical data) or by observation. This data is then analysed, and based on this the initial hypothesis is confirmed or modified as the data suggests. If needed, an entirely new hypothesis might have to be generated. If no reasonable hypothesis can be made, then the cycle jumps back to the beginning for the collection of additional information. A key element of any hypothesis is that it must be testable or falsifiable. Other critical characteristics of the scientific method are that it is objective (versus subjective), based on experiment, observation, and fact, includes testable ideas, and is quantitative. Science is often described as 'self-correcting' in that current theories are constantly open to study, revision, and review. It is also governed by *peer review in which scientific findings are reviewed by knowledgeable scientists in the field before publication. When findings are published, other researchers usually attempt to reproduce the experiments and confirm the findings. In this way, the scientific method is designed to be self-correcting and to constantly move in a forward direction, albeit at a sometimes methodically slow pace. While it might appear that the method described above would not apply to a forensic analysis per se, elements clearly do. For example, forensic reports must be stated in such a way that the results are clear, complete, and sufficiently detailed to be falsifiable. *See also* NULL HYPOTHESIS.

scientific working groups (SWG) (technical working groups (TWG)) Groups of forensic practitioners, often international, that are appointed by various agencies and entities to address specific topic areas in forensic science. Examples include the Scientific Working Group on Seized Drug Analysis and the Scientific Working Group for Materials Analysis.

(⊕) SEE WEB LINKS

• Example websites for scientific and technical working groups. Last accessed May 2011.

screening test *See* PRESUMPTIVE TESTS.

sebaceous sweat Sweat produced by the sebaceous gland, which is one of the three glands that contribute to the composition of sweat and in turn to the composition of latent fingerprints. These glands are found in association with hair follicles as well as on the face and secrete oil. The material secreted from the sebaceous glands is called sebum.

secondary crime scene A scene related to a crime, but not where the crime itself occurred. If a person is killed in one location and dumped in another, the dump site is a secondary scene.

secondary explosion An explosion caused by another initiating explosion.

secondary explosive A relatively insensitive explosive, the detonation of which is initiated by another explosive.

secondary transfer A transfer of physical evidence once removed from the original transfer of interest. For example if a person owns a dog and transports it in a car, anyone who subsequently sits in the car can pick up dog hairs on their clothing; this would be a secondary transfer.

second order reaction A reaction, such as involved in drug metabolism, that is governed by second order kinetics. The rate of such a reaction depends on the concentration of two different reactants or on the concentration of one reactant squared. The rate law expression is given by:

$$\frac{1}{[X]_t} = kt \frac{1}{[X]_0}$$

Where [X] refers to the concentration of a substance as the reaction begins (t = 0) and at subsequent times (t).

secretors The roughly 80 per cent of the population that secretes antigens from the ABO blood group system into their body fluids. Prior to the ascendance of *DNA typing, secretor status was an important consideration in forensic serology, particularly in sexual assault cases. As was discovered in the 1930s, a person's secretor status is under genetic control and is an inherited characteristic. Depending on the population studied, approximately 75–85 per cent are secretors. *See also* HOLZER, FRANZ JOSEPH.

securing the scene In the initial phases of crime scene investigation, it is critically important to protect the scene and preserve it (*scene integrity). Securing a scene is typically accomplished by law enforcement personnel and involves creating a marked boundary with strictly controlled access.

Seddon case A famous arsenic poisoning case that took place in Britain in 1912 that was notable for the use of the *Marsh test and the participation of Sir Bernard *Spilsbury. The Seddons owned a rooming house and one of their elderly residents died shortly after changing her will in the Seddons' favour. After suspicion was raised, the body was exhumed and Spilsbury performed the test. At trial, the jury was able to view the arsenic deposit on the apparatus and a conviction resulted.

seized drug analysis The subdiscipline of forensic science that deals with the analysis of drugs as physical evidence. This is in contrast to drugs as biological evidence as is the case with forensic toxicology. Examples of seized drug evidence include pills, powders, and plant material. What drugs are considered illegal varies from country to country.

seizure disk A computer disk that, when inserted into the computer, prevents any alteration or deletion of data.

selected ion monitoring (SIM) A technique used in *mass spectrometry (MS) to increase the sensitivity of the analysis for a selected compound or small set of compounds. In the most common form of mass spectrometer operation, the mass detector scans through a large range of atomic masses, collecting fragment ions at a given mass for only a fraction of a second before moving to the next mass. The wider the mass range scanned, the less time spent collecting ions of each individual mass. When SIM is employed, the detector collects data at only a few masses, or a single mass. As a result, the detector collects ion fragments at the targeted masses for longer times, increasing the sensitivity, and allowing for detection of smaller quantities. However, since only a few fragments are collected, identification of unknown compounds, which require a large range of mass fragments, is more difficult.

selectivity A term that refers to what certain procedures or instrumentation will detect. A highly selective procedure, such as an immunoassay, responds to only one compound or a small set of compounds. A less selective procedure, such as a colour test, may react with or detect many compounds. Although often confused, selectivity is not synonymous with sensitivity, another *figure of merit used to describe analytical methods.

semen and seminal fluid (sperm) The fluid ejaculated by a man during sexual intercourse. Older presumptive tests for seminal fluid targeted such compounds. A single ejaculation typically consists of a few millilitres (2–6) of fluid that, like blood, has a serum component (seminal plasma) and a cellular component (sperm cells or spermatozoa). The number of sperm cells found in a millilitre of the ejaculate is variable but is usually in the range of 100,000,000. The cellular component composes about 10 per cent of the volume of the ejaculate. Semen is a thick milky liquid that dries as a crusty, somewhat shiny material that will acquire a slight yellowish tinge as it ages. *See also* P30.

semi-automatic firearm A firearm that automatically ejects a spent cartridge and inserts a fresh one into the firing chamber. This is accomplished by exploiting the hot gases created when the cartridge is fired.

semi-synthetic drugs Drugs that are (or can be) prepared using naturally occurring starting materials. For example, *heroin can be considered to be a semi-synthetic drug that is made starting from *morphine. This terminology has become less common as the ability of industry to synthesize drugs has improved.

SEMTEX A high explosive that is a combination of *PETN and *RDX.

sensitizer A compound or compounds added to the primers used in ammunition to make them more shock sensitive, thus ensuring detonation and firing of the cartridge when the trigger is pulled and the hammer strikes the primer.

sequence polymorphism A genetically controlled variation in the sequence of base pairs in DNA. This contrasts with the type of polymorphism seen in STRs, which is based on differences in length of the sequence.

serial number restoration The process of revealing serial numbers that have been filed, scraped, polished, or otherwise obliterated. Although most common in firearms cases where serial numbers on weapons have been removed, any metal object with a stamped serial number such as engine blocks, tools, or equipment can be treated in a similar manner. When a serial number is stamped into a metal object, the force of compression is transferred to the metal below the indentation, causing damage and strain to the metal. The depth of this strain can be several times the depth of the original impression. This damage to the metal makes it more susceptible to attack by oxidizing agents such as strong acids.

serology, forensic Serology is a subdivision of *immunology, the discipline that focuses on the reactions between antigens and *antibodies which are found in the ABO blood group system. The word 'serology' arises from the serum portion of the blood, where the antibodies are found. Forensic serology generally refers to ABO blood group typing and isoenzyme typing. As *DNA typing has all but replaced traditional forensic serology, the more inclusive term of forensic biology is being used to describe characterization of blood and body fluids. *See also* LANDSTEINER, KARL.

Serturner, F. W. (1783–1841) The German chemist who first isolated morphine in 1804. He utilized acetic acid to convert the basic drug to a water-soluble form which he then converted to salts. He named the substance *morphium* in honour of the God of dreams.

serum *See* BLOOD.

serum proteins *Polymorphic proteins that are found in the serum portion of blood. Serum proteins are genetic marker systems that were occasionally used to help individualize bloodstain and some types of body fluid evidence. Haemoglobin is one example of a polymorphic serum protein; others that have been used in forensic serology include haptoglobin (Hp), transferrin (Tf), and group-specific component (Gc). With the advent of *DNA typing techniques, serum protein typing is rarely used.

sex determination (sexing) The analysis of blood, bloodstain, body fluids, or skeletal remains to determine the sex of the person who was the source of the evidence. Current *DNA typing methods use the *amelogenin loci to identify the sex of a donor. Prior to this, immunological methods were utilized. If DNA evidence is unavailable, bones can be used to assign sex based on the morphology and size of bones and, in most cases, determining sex is based on pelvic bones and cranium structures. The program FORDISC, created by the Department of Anthropology at the University of Tennessee, Knoxville, is widely used for this purpose.

sexual asphyxia (autoerotic death) An accidental death that is a form of strangulation. Usually the victim is a male that uses a noose or other type of ligature to decrease blood flow to the brain to increase sexual pleasure.

Sheppard case *See* SAM SHEPPARD CASE.

shock wave A pressure wave (sensed as sound) produced by something moving through the air at a speed faster than the speed of sound. These waves can be produced by explosives and also by high powered firearms. Many rifles and some smaller weapons fire bullets that travel this fast and thus produce a shock wave or sonic 'boom'. Silencing such guns often involves decreasing the propellant such that the bullet exits at a slower speed, eliminating the characteristic cracking sound.

shoe bomber The nickname given to Richard Reid, who attempted to blow up an American Airlines flight in December of 2001 by igniting explosives hidden in his shoe. The explosive was *PETN. *See also* IMPROVISED EXPLOSIVE DEVICE.

shoe impressions A type of *impression or *pattern evidence created by a shoe. Footwear impressions can be two dimensional (such as a shoe print seen on a dusty floor) or three dimensional, such as a shoe print in mud or snow. The former are treated much the same as latent fingerprints while the latter are treated similarly to tyre impressions using dental stone casting.

An example of a shoe impression in soft soil

shored exit wound An exit wound created by a bullet that has an altered appearance due to clothing or other support. Shored exit wounds generally appear smaller than might otherwise be expected. For example, if a person is shot through the back of the neck and the exit wound is through a tight necktie, the tie can support and cradle the skin, lessening the damage done as the bullet exits.

short tandem repeats (STRs) A pattern where two or more nucleotides in DNA are repeated and the repeated sequences are next to each other. STRs serve as the basis of current *DNA typing methods. The number of repeats of the sequence is genetically determined (*polymorphic) with the total length of the sequence being about 400 base pairs. Since they are small, degradation is not as serious a problem as it is for longer fragments and *PCR can be used to amplify the sample. STRs are abundant in DNA, and although each locus has only a few variants, typing several loci at once dramatically increases the discriminating power. Loci that are used include TH01, D7S820, and D3S1358. Typing three systems leads to a discrimination power of about one in 5,000, while typing thirteen pushes this number into the trillions. An added advantage is that commercial STR kits include the *amelogenin gene, a gene which codes for dental pulp and is found on both the X and Y chromosomes, although the gene in the Y chromosome is six base pairs shorter on the X. This makes the amelogenin gene a sex determining marker. Women, who are XX, will show one type, since both variants are the same, but a male (XY) will show two, one shorter than the other. An added advantage to sexing a stain or other evidence is that the results eliminate approximately half the population as a potential source with one test.

shotgun A type of firearm that fires collections of pellets rather than a single projectile. Shotguns do not have rifled barrels and they fire shotgun shells, which are a distinctly different type of ammunition compared to that used by rifles and handguns. Shotguns are identified by their *gauge.

signature analysis 1. In questioned documents, the analysis of a person's handwritten signature or characteristic written individual identification.

2. In the analysis of crimes and crime scenes, a signature consists of actions that are consistent across all crimes in a series and is an element that is unique to one perpetrator. This is in contrast to the modus operandi (MO), which can change or evolve. Identification of a signature can help investigators determine if the same person is likely to have committed several crimes or if the crimes are unrelated.

significant figures In recording the result of a measurement such as a weight or data from an instrument, all of the digits that are certain plus one. This last digit may be displayed digitally, estimated from markings on a scale, or in the case of a calculated quantity, derived from the values used in the calculation. For example, mass of an exhibit of evidence may be recorded directly from a digit display as 1.234 g. There are four significant figures in this number. Significant figure considerations are crucial when reporting data obtained from instrumentation, and rules for handling significant figures must be followed in any calculation based or related to data obtained from an instrument.

Simon test A colour-based presumptive test used in seized drug analysis, typically to differentiate amphetamine from methamphetamine or to detect other *phenylethylamines. The test consists of two reagents, one containing sodium nitroprusside ($Na_2Fe(CN)_5NO$) and acetaldehyde dissolved in water, and the other an aqueous solution of sodium carbonate.

single-base powder A type of *smokeless powder used as a *propellant for ammunition. Single-base powder consists of nitrocellulose

(NC) (made by treating wood shavings or cotton with nitric and sulphuric acids, HNO_3 and H_2SO_4), diphenylamine, and other additives. The amount of nitrogen in the nitrocellulose is reported by weight; 'guncotton' is 13.3 per cent nitrogen by weight. To prepare the single-base powder, an emulsion is made with solvents, which is dried and further treated before it is ground or otherwise powdered for use.

single nucleotide polymorphism (SNP) A polymorphic variation in a single nucleotide at a given location.

skeletal remains A body that has been completely stripped of flesh and soft tissue; the final stage of decomposition.

skeletonized stain A bloodstain pattern that can arise if a blood drop is allowed to partially dry and is then wiped. Since the blood tends to be thinner at the edge of the drops, this portion dries first, leaving liquid in the middle. This liquid can be wiped away, leaving a hollowed area in the centre.

sketch, crime scene *See* DOCUMENTATION, CRIME SCENE; MAPPING, CRIME SCENE.

slippage **1.** A stage in decomposition in which skin slips away from the underlying tissue.

2. A type of toolmark that can be imparted to a bullet as it travels down the barrel of a firearm.

small particle reagent technique (SPR) A group of techniques used to visualize latent fingerprints. In this approach, tiny particles with various properties are suspended in a solution that is applied to the print. The particles adhere to the oils in the print and help make it visible. *See also* NANOPARTICLES.

smear pattern A type of bloodstain pattern in which blood on a surface is smeared by moving contact with another surface or object.

smokeless powder A low explosive that is used as the propellant in ammunition and as a component of pipe bombs and other homemade explosive devices. Smokeless powder was a military innovation introduced in the late 1800s to replace black powder, which created large amounts of smoke that obscured battlefields. As a propellant, black powder is now used principally in historical weapons owned by collectors and hobbyists. There are two kinds of smokeless powder, single base and double base. Single-base powder consists of nitrocellulose (made by treating wood shavings or cotton with nitric and sulphuric acids, HNO_3 and H_2SO_4), diphenylamine, and other additives. The amount of nitrogen in the

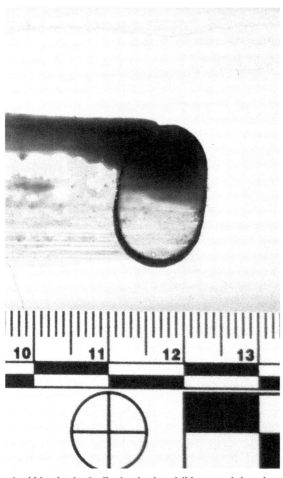

A skeletonized bloodstain. Scalloping is also visible around the edges of the drop.

nitrocellulose is reported by weight; 'guncotton' is 13.3 per cent nitrogen by weight. To prepare the single-base powder, an emulsion is made with solvents, which is dried and further treated before it is ground or otherwise powdered for use. Double-base powder consists of nitrocellulose and nitroglycerin along with various additives. In addition to use as propellants, smokeless powders are encountered in the forensic context as a component in an incendiary device or homemade bomb such as a pipe bomb.

smudge ring *See* BULLET WOUNDS.

Snell's Law An equation that describes the changes in *refractive index (RI) that occur as a result of light moving from one medium into another:

$$\frac{n_1}{n_2} = \frac{sin\Theta_2}{sin\Theta_1}$$

sodium rhodizonate A *presumptive test reagent used to detect *gunshot residue (GSR). The rhodizonate anion forms a coloured solid with barium and lead. The reagent is used as part of *distance determinations.

solid phase extraction (SPE) A group of related techniques used to extract compounds from sample matrices. Solid phase methods are used for sample preparation drug analysis and toxicology. SPE works through selective absorption and solubility with the sample placed in a liquid phase and delivered to a column containing the solid phase. The solid phase typically consists of tiny beads to which chemical functional groups are attached. For example, a C8 column consists of an eight-carbon chain bonded to the solid support. There are numerous phases including ion exchange resins that are useful for analytes such as drugs that possess *ionizable centres. In a typical SPE method, an aqueous or other liquid phase containing the analytes of interest is loaded into the column via vacuum or pressure. The analytes associate with the solid phase and a series of washing stages are used to strip all other components out of the column. An elution solvent is then used to draw the analytes off the column and into a collection vessel. This solution is typically evaporated to dryness and then reconstituted in a solvent suitable to the instrumental method to be used, typically *gas chromatography (GC) or *high performance liquid chromatography (HPLC).

solid phase microextraction (SPME) A variant of a *solid phase extraction (SPE) in which a thin capillary column is coated with a solid absorbent. This needle-like device is inserted into a vial either above the surface of the sample to collect *headspace vapours or into a liquid sample to allow for analytes to selectively absorb into the sorbent. SPME is commonly used for *arson analysis in which accelerant vapours that collect in a heated vial of fire debris are absorbed onto the SPME fibre. The fibre is then placed into the injection port of a *gas chromatograph (GC) where desorption occurs and the sample is introduced into the GC column.

solvent extraction A sample preparation method frequently used in forensic chemistry and toxicology to isolate compounds of interest from a complex sample matrix. The principle of solvent extraction is based on *selective partitioning between two different phases or solvents based on relative solubility of the analytes in each. In solvent extraction, a sample such as urine can be extracted with an organic solvent such as chloroform or methylene chloride (dichloromethane) to selectively isolate compounds in the organic layer. Other solvents commonly used are hexane, acetone, alcohols, and ethers. Acid/base extractions are also extensively used to isolate drugs that have acidic and basic forms. In recent years, *solid phase extraction (SPE) techniques have replaced many traditional solvent extractions since they can often yield a cleaner extract with fewer extraneous materials. This is particularly valuable for toxicology where the sample matrix itself, particularly blood, complicates solvent extraction.

Southern blotting A method for transferring DNA fragments from a gel to another type of support such as a film where it can be visualized. It was used in early *DNA typing methods and is named after the man who invented it, and not a region.

speciation 1. The process of determining the species from which a body fluid stain originated. Blood, saliva, and semen are the body fluids most commonly tested for species. Prior to the widespread adoption of *DNA typing using PCR amplification, immunological tests such as immunodiffusion and crossed-over electrophoresis, an immunoelectrophoresis method, were employed for speciation. These tests involve the use of antisera created to react with blood or body fluids of other species such as human, cat, or dog. In DNA typing procedures using PCR, one step of the procedure requires determining how much human (higher primate) DNA is present in the recovered sample. In so doing, the test confirms the presence or absence of human DNA.
   2. Determination of the oxidation state of a metal or atom. For example, the metal arsenic has several oxidation states that are important in determining how it bonds and in determining its toxicity; for example As^{3+} versus As^{5+}.

spectrometry, spectrophotometry, and spectroscopy
Generically, spectrophotometry is the study of the interaction of electromagnetic energy (EMR) with matter. The interaction can be measured and used to determine what is present (qualitative analysis) and how much (quantitative analysis). The simplest form of spectrophotometry and also the first developed is colorimetry, in which the visible portion of electromagnetic energy is used. Spectrometers

consist of an energy (light) source, a mechanism or device to filter the source energy and select the wavelength(s) of interest, a device or method to hold the sample, and a detector system, which converts electromagnetic energy (light) to a measurable electrical current. Other kinds of spectrometry used in forensic science include infrared spectrophotometry (IR), colorimetry (VIS), and ultraviolet/visible (UV/VIS). Recently, forensic science has widely adopted instrumentation that combines spectrometry with *microscopy (MSP), particularly for infrared, Raman, and UV/VIS spectroscopy.

sperm (sperm cells, spermatozoa) The cellular component of semen, the male ejaculate fluid. A typical ejaculation contains on the order of 10^8 sperm cells per mL, with 3–4 mL ejaculated. Sperm cells are the male sex cells and carry 23 chromosomes that pair with those from the female egg when fertilized. *See also* CHRISTMAS TREE STAIN.

spike A compound or material purposely added to a sample to test the efficiency of its recovery using an analytical method. For example, to test the efficiency of a method to detect cocaine in urine, an analyst can spike a known clean urine sample with a known amount of cocaine and then compare the amount recovered to the amount spiked. This recovery is often expressed as a percentage of the original amount spiked.

Spilsbury, Sir Bernard (1877–1947) An English physician who made numerous contributions to death investigation. His colourful career was the subject of several books, including *The Scalpel of Scotland Yard: The Life of Sir Bernard Spilsbury*. His public life was one of fame, his private later life one of tragedy. Two of his sons, also doctors, died during the war period.

Spilsbury began training in medicine in 1899 at St Mary's hospital in London, one of the key facilities associated with legal medicine. He was able to study under some of the most famous forensic pathologists and toxicologists of the day, men who were themselves representative of the first and second generations of forensic scientists who emerged after *Orfila. By 1809, he was senior pathologist and the Home Office pathologist at St Mary's. His celebrity status was launched with a famous murder case in 1910. The accused was a fellow physician named *Crippen whose wife had been reported missing in early January. The badly decomposed body was found in July, buried in their cellar. His work was hampered because the killer had removed the head, bones, limbs, and sexual organs from the body. All Spilsbury had to work with was a decomposed torso. Analysis of the tissue revealed the presence of a compound called hyoscine (scopolamine). This drug is a naturally occurring alkaloid that is readily absorbed through the skin, but it is not as toxic as other poisons common in the day. Spilsbury's testimony centred on the difficult task of identification which he was able to do using a scar found on the abdomen. Crippen was convicted. In 1923, after several more high profile cases and convictions, he became Sir Bernard Spilsbury.

One of the most ironic and interesting cases Spilsbury worked on occurred in 1924. A woman named Emily Kaye was killed inside a small house on the south-eastern coast of England. Her body was dismembered by a saw, the parts further chopped and then boiled, and parts including the head were never located. The bloody saw was found in a suitcase belonging to Patrick Mahon. Spilsbury arrived on the scene and managed to find a few bone fragments in the room that he concluded were from a large woman who was pregnant at the time of her death. The remains also showed evidence of violent blows inflicted at the time of death. Spilsbury's testimony was crucial in convicting Mahon, who was subsequently executed by hanging. Spilsbury performed the autopsy on Mahon. Based on his findings in this and subsequent autopsies of executed criminals, Spilsbury made several recommendations to make death by hanging more humane. He committed suicide in 1947 using carbon monoxide gas. *See also* Brides of Bath case; Coventry case; Seddon case.

spiral search (circle search) A pattern used for searching areas at crime scenes. The spiral can begin at a specific point and spiral outward or start on a perimeter and spiral inward. The width of the spirals depends on the circumstances but should be narrow enough to ensure complete visual coverage.

spoliation The destruction of evidence, whether by incorrect preservation or deliberate action. The term is often used to describe decomposition or degradation of biological evidence such as blood and body fluid stains.

spontaneous ignition temperature A temperature at which a fuel/air or fuel/oxidant mixture that is combustible will spontaneously ignite.

spot plate A ceramic (or sometimes plastic) plate that contains several wells or depressions in which samples and reagents are added to perform *presumptive tests (also called spot tests).

spot tests *See* presumptive tests.

spurious minutiae *Minutiae generated in the image of a *latent fingerprint that are not present in the fingerprint but are rather generated by problems in the development or imaging processes.

squalene An oil secreted on the skin that forms an important component of *latent fingerprints.

SSRIs (selective serotonin re-uptake inhibitors) A class of drugs used to treat depression, anxiety, and other related disorders. Paxil and Prozac are examples of SSRIs.

stabilizer A compound such as *diphenylamine (DPA) added to *propellants to chemically stabilize and preserve the mixture and to prevent accidental ignition.

stable isotope An isotope of an element that is not radioactive. Deuterium is a stable isotope of hydrogen that contains one proton and one neutron in the nucleus. Tritium, which contains three protons, is radioactive and thus not a stable isotope. Stable isotopes can be used in *profiling of evidence such as seized drugs. *See also* ISOTOPE RATIO MASS SPECTROMETRY.

staining A family of techniques used in microscopy to aid in the visualization of otherwise hard to see features. For example, sperm cells are often stained with a pair of reagents collectively called *christmas tree stain to make the cells easier to see. Some of these stains have been adapted to other uses such as in the visualization of latent fingerprints.

standard addition A method of *calibration used in instrumental analysis. In a standard addition quantitative analysis, a known amount of the target substance is added to the sample in increasingly larger portions. From a standard addition curve, a plot of amount of substance added versus signal, the original concentration in the sample can be determined.

standard methods (standardization) Practices and procedures used in laboratories to ensure that a method or instrument will produce accurate and reproducible results under specified standard operating conditions. Standardization is a vital part of quality assurance/quality control (QA/QC). Standard methods are tested, validated, approved, and used routinely in the laboratory. The use of standard methods ensures that results obtained are as accurate and reliable as possible. The use of standard methods also facilitates comparison of results between labs.

standard observer curves Plots and data that are used as part of the characterization of colours, such as comparing colours of fibres and paint. The standard observer curves are part of the CIE colour analysis system first formalized in 1931 by the International Commission on Illumination. In forensic applications, the CIE system is used to ensure objective colour comparison and characterization based on instrumental data rather than on human perception. The standard observer curves express a colour on the basis of combining red, green, and blue.

(⊕) SEE WEB LINKS

• The homepage of the International Commission on Illumination. General information about colour, colour perception, and colour measurements can be found here. Last accessed May 2011.

standard operating procedure (SOP) A procedure that has been *standardized and validated and that should be followed each time a procedure is executed.

standards Reagents or materials of known or verified composition. These can be prepared within a laboratory or purchased from a vendor.

starburst dendrimer (PAMAM) A particular type of CdS *quantum dot (*nanoparticle) used to visualize fingerprints. The dot is bound chemically to the dendrimer (branched chemical structure) which in turn attaches to residues in the fingerprint.

starches Generically, a polymer of glucose $(C_6H_{12}O_6)$. In the forensic context, starch gels are used as support media for *electrophoresis and may be encountered as a diluent in seized drugs or as type of trace evidence.

Stas, Jean Servais (1813-91) A Belgian chemist who studied under *Orfila and who developed methods for detection of alkaloid poisoning. In his most famous case, he was able to identify nicotine poisoning in 1851.

stationary phase In a chromatographic method of separation, the phase that does not move in contrast to a mobile phase of gas or liquid.

stature estimations Considered primarily a task of forensic anthropology, the determination of the likely height of an individual based on skeletal remains. This is accomplished by measurements of the long bones such as those found in the arm and the leg (femur for example). Based on these measurements and databases of information, the anthropologist can estimate the height of the individual. Stature estimates are difficult if not impossible if only partial skeletal remains are recovered.

stellate pattern (star pattern) **1.** Features seen in contact gunshot wounds to the head. When the barrel of a gun is placed in contact with the skin over the skull, firing the weapon results in gases ejected below the skin and an outward rupture that can create a roughly star-shaped injury in the skin.

2. In severe burns, a pattern of sharp, star-like projections emanating from a split in the skin. *See also* BULLET WOUNDS.

stereoisomers Compounds that share the identical molecular formula and order of connection of atoms but that differ in the three-dimensional arrangement of these atoms. If two stereoisomers are mirror images of each other, they are called *enantiomers; otherwise they are referred to as *diastereoisomers.

stereomicroscope A type of microscope that uses two eyepieces, relatively low magnification, and reflected light. The term 'microscope' is generally taken to be synonymous with stereomicroscope or stereoscopic microscope.

steroids Compounds derived from cholesterol and chemically characterized by the presence of four linked cycloalkanes. Of most direct forensic interest are the *anabolic steroids, which are used in body building and are an issue in sports doping and *human performance toxicology.

Stielow case A landmark case in the United States involving firearms evidence. In 1915, a double murder occurred in New York involving a pistol. Charles Stielow was a hired helper on the farm where the crime took place. A recent immigrant, he did not speak English well. He was arrested and interrogated, using questionable practices (at best), and eventually confessed. He never signed a written confession and retracted the oral version in court. The first firearms 'expert' to testify was later ridiculed, but was sufficient, along with the confession, to obtain a conviction. A prison guard took up Stielow's cause, convinced that the man was too simple-minded to have committed the crime. In 1917, the Governor of New York ordered an independent investigation. Charles *Waite worked for a New York State prosecutor and quickly became involved in the investigation. Waite initiated another firearms examination that included microscopic comparison. The examination clearly demonstrated that the patterns of lands and grooves in the bullets could not possibly have been made by Stielow's weapon. Stielow was immediately pardoned and released.

stimulants Drugs that affect the central nervous system (CNS) and cause elevated heart rate, breathing, and increases in blood pressure. Ingestion of stimulants produces a feeling of wakefulness, decreased fatigue, decreased appetite, and general well-being. Cocaine, amphetamine, methamphetamine, Ritalin, caffeine, and nicotine fall into this category. In higher doses, many stimulants can also act as hallucinogens.

stippling Also referred to as tattooing, a pattern in skin that can result from a gunshot wound in which burning powder hits the skin and causes small burns or stippling patterns. *See also* BULLET WOUNDS; STELLATE PATTERN.

STR *See* SHORT TANDEM REPEATS.

strangulation Death by asphyxia that is brought about by compression of the neck. The cause of death is lack of blood flow to the brain. Strangulation can be performed manually with the hands ('throttling') or by use of a ligature. Hanging is a form of ligature strangulation in which body weight is used to generate the compression.

striation Marks that are made in a surface as the result of motion of one surface across the other. Scratching, sliding, and scraping motions all can produce striations on one or both surfaces. In the case of metal-to-metal contact, the softer metal yields to the harder metal and will show striations.

strip search and line search A pattern used to search relatively large areas at crime scenes. In a line search, a square area is divided into parallel strips or lanes with one searcher per lane. The searchers slowly walk a roughly straight line through the middle of the lane and visually cover the full width of their lane. In a strip search, one person walks the lanes, starting for example with the lane to the far left, searching it, then turning around and moving into the next lane and repeating the process.

strychnine A poisonous substance that can be extracted from the seeds of the plant *Strychnos nux vomica* L. or synthesized. It is an ingredient in rodent poisons.

subcutaneous injection A mode of ingestion in which the substance is injected beneath the skin. This contrasts with intravenous injection in which the substance is directly introduced into a blood vessel.

sublingual absorption A mode of ingestion in which the substance is absorbed while in the mouth and under the tongue.

succession and succession patterns A natural process that involves advancement along defined pathways. Ecological succession is a concept that is used to help find clandestine graves and occurs when a patch of ground is disturbed to dig the hole. When the hole is filled in and the dirt replaced, all existing plants have been destroyed, leaving essentially bare earth. Ecological succession occurs as grass or moss colonizes the

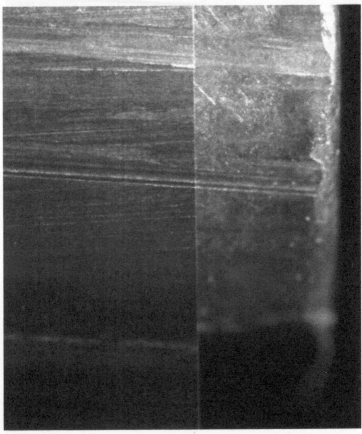

An example of striations created by drawing the blade of a screwdriver through a soft media.

bare soil, followed later by larger plants. Similarly, forensic entomology takes advantage of the succession of insect species that can colonize a body after death.

swipe stain A type of blood spatter (bloodstain) pattern created by a swiping motion through an existing wet stain. Often swipe patterns are created by hands or hair.

synergistic effect A combination of two or more effects in which the result is greater than what would be expected by summing the individual effects. Drugs that are mixed can have a synergistic effect; for example, alcohol increases the drowsiness produced by medications such as antidepressants.

synthetic drugs Drugs that are synthesized from relatively simple precursors. This is in contrast to drugs such as heroin that are frequently made from *opiate alkaloids extracted from the opium plant.

systematic error An error that influences all results in the same way; a reproducible error or *bias. For example, an improperly calibrated analytical balance is a source of systematic error.

S

taggant Materials or compounds that are placed in a product that can be chemically identified and linked back to a source, time of manufacture, etc. As an example, taggants were once placed in many inks and when detected, could be used to identify the ink by what company made it and when.

Takayama test (haemochromogen test) A test that was once widely used to test for the presence of blood. The test is based on the formation of distinctive haemochromogen microcrystals when the sample is treated with pyridine. The test was developed in 1912 by Masao Takayama in Japan and was widely used prior to the advent of *DNA typing and other presumptive tests for blood such as luminol.

tandem mass spectrometers Instruments in which more than one mass filter (*mass spectrometer) exists in series. Examples of tandem mass spectrometers include Q-TOF (a quadrupole followed by a time-of-flight detector and a 'QQQ' or triple quadrupole system in which three quadrupoles are organized end-to-end in the detection system. Tandem mass spectrometers are being rapidly adopted in forensic toxicology.

tape lift A method of recovering *latent fingerprints from physical evidence. This can be accomplished at a crime scene or in the laboratory. Prior to lifting, the fingerprint is visualized using powders or other means. Adhesive tape is placed over the print, pressed down, and then transferred to a sturdy backing such as an index card.

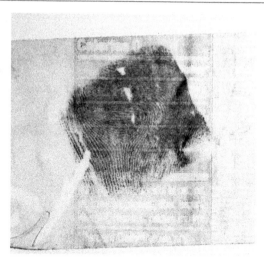

Tape lift. A latent print was dusted with black powder and recovered from a glass surface.

taphonomy The systematic study of 'death assemblages' and *decomposition applied to forensic science. Taphonomy is a sub-discipline of anthropology and archaeology that has found increasing use in forensic cases over the past twenty years. Strictly defined, taphonomy focuses on the process of death and the aftermath that ultimately led to the fossilization of remains, but in the forensic context, the time frame of interest is much shorter.

Taq polymerase An enzyme that catalyses the addition of nucleotides to DNA and a key component in *PCR amplification and *DNA typing.

Tardieu spots *See* PETECHIAL HAEMORRHAGES.

TATP (triacetone triperoxide) An explosive synthesized from acetone and hydrogen peroxide.

Taylor, Alfred Swaine (1806–80) An English physician and forensic practitioner who was involved in many cases and who authored a key early reference in the field, *Medical Jurisprudence*, first published in 1843. His work was inspired by the work of *Orfila and Taylor is known to have attended lectures given by him. In 1831, he assumed the position of lecturer in medical jurisprudence at Guy's Hospital in London and began his forensic career. Many of his ideas and beliefs were ahead of his time, such as the understanding that chemical tests common in that era were problematical and multiple types of analyses, coupled with clinical findings, were essential in forensic casework. He was an early advocate of chain-of-custody procedures and laboratory controls. He worked on several poisoning cases and used the *Marsh test as well as the *Reinsch test, which also targeted heavy metals but was based on the use of copper wire. Like many forensic practitioners of that age, Taylor did not restrict himself to medical matters but also worked with other types of evidence such as hair and bloodstain pattern analysis.

Alfred Swaine Taylor

Teichmann test (haematin test) A confirmatory test for blood based on the formation of distinctive haematin crystals that are viewed under a microscope. The reagents typically used are sodium chloride and glacial acetic acid. The test was developed in 1853 by Ludwig

Teichmann and is identified with both the Teichman and Teichmann spellings. *See also* TAKAYAMA TEST.

telogen phase The final phase of the growth cycle of hair, during which the hair sheds naturally. Most hairs found as evidence, unless forcibly removed, are in the telogen phase.

terminal ballistics The behaviour of a bullet after it ends free flight and impacts a target.

testosterone The principal male sex hormone. Testosterone has androgenic effects such as the ability to increase muscle mass and decrease recovery time between workouts. For this reason, it has become a primary focus of anti-doping forensic toxicology. Other related compounds include *nandrolone and stanolone. Because testosterone is *endogenous, it is often a difficult analytical challenge to detect doping. Methods used to test for testosterone include *isotope ratio mass spectrometry (IRMS) and *mass spectrometry, focusing on the relative ratios of testosterone and related compounds. *GCMS and *LCMS have both been used to measure ratios, a process referred to as steroid profiling.

(⊕) **SEE WEB LINKS**

- The website for the World Anti-Doping Agency which combats doping in sports and overseas analyses at accredited laboratories. This website is the primary source of information for athletes and coaches on sports doping and prohibited substances. It lists prohibited substances, discusses rules and regulations, and many other aspects of the topic. Last accessed May 2011.

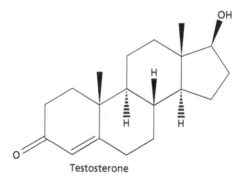

Testosterone

Testosterone

tetramethylbenzidine (TMB) An older *presumptive test for blood made by dissolving TMB in glacial acetic acid. Like other similar tests such as the *Kastle–Meyer (KM) test, TMB changes colour in a reaction that is catalysed by haemoglobin. The TMB test is an alternative to the benzidine test, which has been abandoned due to the carcinogenic properties of that compound.

textiles A generic term for materials that are woven or knitted into flexible batches. Textiles are made up of yarns or filaments of natural or synthetic fibres.

THC (Δ^9-tetrahydocannabinol; Δ^1-tetrahydocannabinol) The primary psychoactive ingredient in *marijuana. THC is classified as a hallucinogen. It is found in the oily resin, flowering tops, and leaves of the plant, with the highest concentrations found in the oil. Two naming conventions have been used to describe this compound and the related cannabinols. The Δ^1 convention arises from using monoterpine as a reference point and the Δ^9 convention is based on a pyran system. The latter is the more common description.

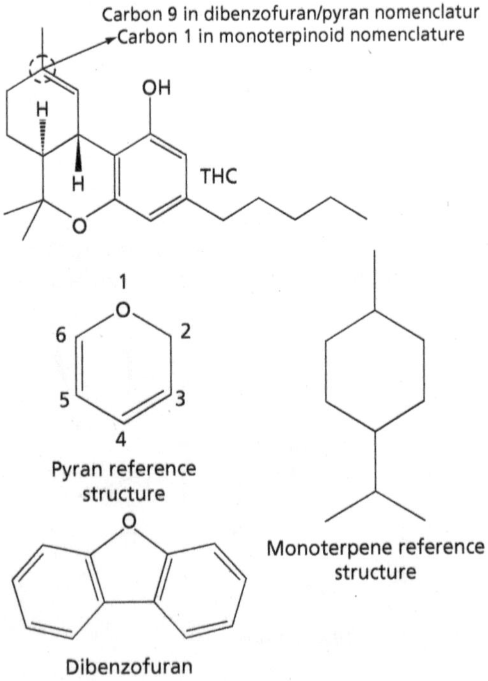

Carbon 9 in dibenzofuran/pyran nomenclatur
Carbon 1 in monoterpinoid nomenclature

THC

Pyran reference structure

Monoterpene reference structure

Dibenzofuran

THC

theophylline A xanthine alkaloid found in chocolate and coffee. It is used to treat asthma and can have effects similar to the phenylethylamines such as ephedrine.

thermal cycler A device used in PCR amplification of DNA. A thermal cycler carefully controls temperature through successive heating and cooling essential to the copying DNA.

thin layer chromatography (TLC) A simple form of chromatography that separates mixtures by exploiting solvents travelling over a solid support phase and the resulting chemical interactions between the solvent, solid support, and the molecules of interest. Tiny spots of dissolved sample are placed in a line across the bottom of a plate or paper. The plate is coated with a thin layer of silica or a related powdery material. The line is called the origin. The plate is then placed in a shallow solvent bath so the level of the solvent is below that of the origin. The solvent can be as simple as water (used for ink analysis) or may consist of two or more organic solvents such as benzene, ethanol, or acetonitrile. Capillary action draws the solvent up the plate where it encounters the sample at the origin. Depending on the solubility of the sample in the solvent, some or all of it dissolves and begins moving along with the solvent front as it is drawn up the plate. Some components in the mixture will interact with the silica material causing it to fall behind components that interact less. Eventually, all separable components will be spread out in spots across the plate. Any components that are not soluble in the solvent will remain at the origin. In the case of ink analysis, spots are clearly visible; however, in many cases a developer must be sprayed or otherwise applied to visualize the spots.

three-dimensional impression An impression that has depth as well as pattern. For example, a shoe on a dusty floor will create a two-dimensional (flat) pattern in the dust but the same impression made in mud will have depth and will thus be a three-dimensional impression.

threshold weight A quantity, typically of a seized drug, that if present in this quantity or above, results in legal and judicial consequences. For example, possession of 1 gram or more of an illegal drug could result in a more severe penalty than possession of a quantity of less than 1 gram.

throttling Strangulation that is accomplished by the hands and not by use of a *ligature such as a rope or cord.

thymine (T) One of four *nucleotide bases that comprise DNA and RNA. It is the complementary base to *adenine.

time of death *See* POST-MORTEM INTERVAL.

time resolved imaging (time resolved spectroscopy) A technique of collecting images over a time period to collect different information. The technique is exploited in detection of fingerprints using special treatments such as *quantum dots. For example, a fingerprint may be on a surface that fluoresces under UV light so brightly that the fingerprint image is washed out. By using treatments that phosphoresce (similar to fluorescence but longer lasting), this can be avoided by delaying collection of information until after the fluorescence is gone. Data and information is resolved by exploiting time.

Tiselius, Arne (1902–1971) A Swedish scientist who is credited with developing modern methods of *electrophoresis and methods of separating large molecules. He was awarded a Nobel Prize in chemistry in 1948.

TNT (2,4,6-trinitrotoluene) A secondary *high explosive used extensively in the Second World War as a military explosive. It is prepared by treating toluene (a common solvent used as a paint thinner) with nitric and sulphuric acids (HNO_3 and H_2SO_4). A related compound, 1,3,5-trinitrotoluene can also be prepared, which is often used as a standard in forensic analyses. A secondary high explosive, TNT must be detonated by a primary high explosive and thus is relatively shock insensitive.

toner Materials that are used in laser printers and copiers to produce the image or document. Toners are powdery materials that adhere to static charges on the paper that are then fixed by heat and pressure to the paper. Most toners are granular with a waxy consistency.

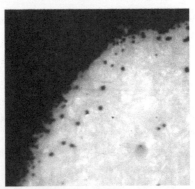

Toner particles are visible under low magnification

toolmarks A form of *impression evidence created when a metal tool comes into contact with a softer metal or materials such as wood or paint. The most common source of toolmark evidence are burglary cases. Tools can create indentation or compression imprints, scraping or *striations, or a combination of the two. Through two factors, grinding during

manufacture and *wear patterns, toolmark impressions can often be
linked to a specific tool if the quality of the impression is good enough and
the suspect tool is recovered for comparison.

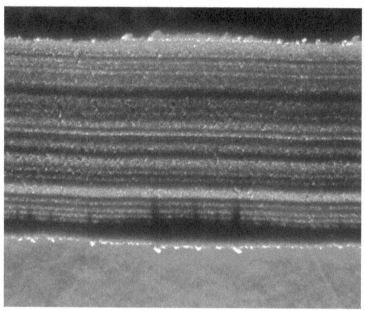

Striations from a screwdriver blade captured in clay

total quality management (TQM) A general term and acronym
describing plans or procedures that laboratories put in place as part of
quality assurance/quality control.

toxicity The degree of harm that a substance can do to an organism.
Toxicity is a function of the substance, the amount present, and the span
of time over which it is ingested. The adage 'the dose makes the poison'
applies to toxicity; even common substances such as aspirin and table
salt can be toxic if a large enough amount is ingested over a short
period of time. The size of the person also plays a role and dosages
are often cited in amounts such as mg/kg to reflect this. Measures
of toxicity include the *LD_{50}, which refers to the dose that is lethal
to half of a specified population and species. One method of
categorizing toxicity is based on immediate short-term ingestion
of a relatively large dose (acute toxicity) versus long-term ingestion
of smaller amounts (chronic toxicity).

toxicology, forensic The analysis of drugs, poisons, and other *exogenous substances (and their metabolites) in blood and body fluids. The forensic toxicologist works with biological samples and must consider absorption of the material, distribution in body tissues, metabolic conversions (metabolites), conjugates, protein binding, movement through the system (pharmacodynamics and pharmacokinetics), persistence of the drug and modes of excretion. The most common test carried out by forensic toxicologists is that to determine *blood alcohol (BAC) levels.

The history of toxicology traces back to the late 1700s and early 1800s when incidents of arsenic poisoning were rampant. James *Marsh, an English chemist, developed a reliable test for determining the presence of arsenic in body tissues that was first used in a legal setting in 1840. In that case, M. B. *Orfila, an Italian credited with being the father of forensic toxicology, performed the analysis. Although in modern practice, toxicology is more focused on drugs, detection of poisons is still an important component of the field. Forensic toxicology includes post-mortem toxicology, drug testing (such as urine screening for employment or athletics), and human performance toxicology (including blood alcohol).

traceability The ability to link a measurement or value to an unassailable source through an unbroken chain of connections. For example, a laboratory may own a set of standard weight sets that are traceable to an internationally accepted standard such as those kept by the Bureau International des Poids et Mesures (International Bureau of Weights and Measures) in Paris. Assuming acceptable performance, any weight obtained on that balance would be traceable.

trace evidence Physical evidence that is found in very small or trace quantities. Common forms of trace evidence include hair, fibres, soil, dust, and glass. The primary tool for the analysis of trace evidence is microscopy including light microscopy, *polarizing light microscopy, and microspectrophotometry (*see* MICROSCOPY). The term is often used synonymously for transfer evidence. *See also* LOCARD, EDMUND.

tracing forgery (traced forgery) In *questioned documents cases, a forgery of writing such as a signature that is accomplished by tracing the original.

tranquilizers An older term used to describe compounds that reduce anxiety and assist in sleeping. Examples include *benzodiazepines and *barbiturates.

transferability A term sometimes used to describe how easy it is for evidence such as fibres or particulates to be dislodged from the position in which they were originally deposited. For example, shed head hairs and dust would have high transferability relative to carpet fibres still woven into the carpet.

transfer evidence (trace evidence) Materials that are transferred from one person or place to another person or place. The evaluation of transfer evidence is at the heart of traditional forensic science and is often conducted using microscopy. Edmund *Locard (1877–1966) was credited with developing what has become known as Locard's exchange principle, paraphrased as 'every contact leaves a trace'. Locard was particularly interested in everyday materials such as dust that are among the most common forms of transfer evidence. Other ubiquitous types of materials found as transfer evidence are hairs, fibres, glass, soil, and paint chips.

transfer pattern A type of *bloodstain pattern created by the contact of a bloodied object or appendage with a surface. If a person has bloody hands and places their palm on a wall, the palm print is considered a transfer pattern.

transient evidence Evidence that is easily lost, destroyed, or liable to decomposition; evidence that does not persist.

transitory effect A form of evidence or information found at a crime scene that has a limited lifetime and must be recognized immediately for documentation and evaluation. Examples include the odour of cigarette smoke in the air or fresh ice in a glass.

trash mark In *questioned documents, imperfections, scratches, dirt, or other foreign matter on the glass surface of a photocopier. These marks can be imaged and placed on the copies and can be used to link a copy to another copy or to a specific copier.

Trauring model A mathematical model proposed in 1963 that describes the probability of coincidental matches of latent fingerprints being obtained during automated searching routines. This model was proposed well before automated fingerprint identification systems (AFIS) were widely available. The algorithm utilizes reference points and the location of *minutiae relative to that reference point.

triangulation A method of measurement used to record the location of evidence found at a crime scene. Triangulation can be accomplished using a single baseline as the reference or as part of a grid system. In the case of a one-reference baseline, reference marks are placed at set intervals along the baseline and the distance from evidence to two adjacent marks forms a triangle that is used to record the location of the evidence. In a grid system, triangulation is utilized to ensure that junctions within the grid are at 90° angles. Once this is established, when physical evidence is found within a grid square, measurements from it to the two closest intersections can be used to show exactly where the evidence was located within that grid square. The location is typically reported in *rectangular coordinates.

tricyclic antidepressants *See* BENZODIAZEPINES.

trigger pull The amount of force needed to pull the trigger of a firearm, usually measured in pounds.

trilobal A type of cross-sectional shape seen in synthetic fibres such as those based on *nylon and *polyester.

triple-base powder A *propellant formulation used in large calibre weapons such as artillery. The three ingredients referred to in the name are *nitrocellulose (NC, guncotton), *nitroglycerin (NG) and nitroguanidine. It is a smokeless powder, along with single-base and double-base formulations used in smaller weapons.

tristimulus values (XYZ) In the *CIE colour system, there are values that correlate to the relative amount of red, green, and blue primary colours that must be combined to create a given perceived colour. These values are calculated starting from a visible light spectrum (reflected light) and utilize *standard observer curves. The tristimulus values can be used to generate *chromaticity coordinates that can be plotted in two dimensions. The system allows for colour representation that is objective and based on instrumental data rather than human perception and description.

(((⊕))) SEE WEB LINKS
- Website of the International Commission on Illumination. Lots of information on colour and colour measurement across many fields. Last accessed May 2011.

tropane alkaloids Alkaloid compounds based on the tropane skeleton, which is a bridged ring. This family includes *cocaine, and the poisons atropine, hyoscyamine, and scopolamine.

Tropane alkaloids

trueness The calculated difference between an experimentally determined value in quantitative analysis and an accepted true value. It is usually expressed in terms of a *bias and is the systematic component of accuracy.

tryptamines Alkaloid compounds based on the tryptamine structure, which is in turn derived from the amino acid tryptophan. These compounds are derived from plants and have hallucinogenic effects. Serotonin, a key neurotransmitter, is a tryptamine compound, as are *mescaline, *psilocybin, and *psilocin.

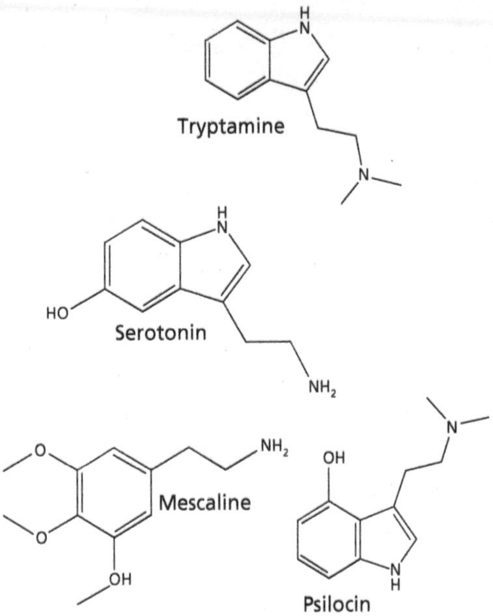

Tryptamine

Serotonin

Mescaline

Psilocin

Tryptamine alkaloids

TWA 800 An airline flight that crashed in 1986. Although the cause of the accident was ultimately linked to a fuel tank explosion, the incident came at a time when there were heightened fears of terrorism. The crash occurred off the coast of Long Island after the flight departed from John F. Kennedy airport in New York. All aboard were killed and the wreck was scattered across several square miles of ocean bottom. Initial concerns focused on the possibility of a bomb or missile strike but forensic and investigative analysis eventually ruled out this possibility.

twelve-point rule In fingerprint comparisons, debate continues as to how many individual points (features or *minutiae) on one print must match those of another before a match is declared. The twelve-point rule is a historical one that is widely accepted.

twin loop pattern A *friction ridge pattern found in fingerprints that is often considered to be one of six fundamental classes of patterns found in fingerprints along with whorl, loop (left and right), arch, and tented arch.

two-dimensional impression An impression such as a fingerprint on glass that lacks depth. This is in contrast to a three-dimensional impression such as a shoe print in mud.

Tylenol tampering An incident that occurred in Chicago in 1982 that ultimately led to tamper-proof packaging for many consumer items. In this case, powdered cyanide was added to several bottles of Tylenol (paracetamol), killing seven people. The perpetrator was never caught.

type I error A classification of error used in statistical nomenclature. A type I error is an incorrect exclusion or a false negative. It is the incorrect rejection of the null hypothesis.

type II error A classification of error used in statistical nomenclature. A type II error is an incorrect inclusion or a false positive. It is the incorrect acceptance of the null hypothesis.

typeface A collection of printed letters with the same pattern; similar to font styles used in word processing and other computer applications. Typewriters typically have the Pica or Elite typeface.

tyre impression A form of *impression evidence. A tyre print in soil, mud, or snow is created by compression and is sometimes referred to as compression evidence or as an indentation. Tyre prints can also be created without compression, such as when black tyre marks are left on the concrete floor of a garage. When indented tyre prints are discovered, they must be protected and preserved until documentation and casting can be performed. Further analysis is conducted on the cast.

Uhlenhuth, Paul (1870–1957) German immunologist whose research was foundational for immunological species testing prior to DNA methods. These methods are based on immunological reactions in which serum from one species (such as human) is introduced into another such as rabbit, provoking an immunological reaction and the ability to consequentially produce antisera. *See also* SPECIATION

ulnar loop A fingerprint pattern named for its directionality. The ulna is the lower arm bone that is aligned roughly with the little finger. Accordingly, an ulnar loop pattern flows out toward the ulna.

ultraviolet light spectroscopy (ultraviolet-visible (UV/VIS) spectroscopy) In the *electromagnetic spectrum, ultraviolet energy lies on the high energy side of visible light. Since many of the analytical techniques that utilize the UV range also work in the visible range, the term 'UV/VIS' is often used in the description. The UV range encompasses wavelengths from 200 nm to 400 nm, at which point the energy can be detected visually as violet light. Many organic compounds can absorb UV/VIS light and it is this behaviour that is the basis of UV/VIS spectroscopy. In addition, UV illumination has many forensic applications. In *questioned documents analysis, UV light can be used to stimulate *fluorescence in inks. Similarly, drugs such as LSD fluoresce under UV light.

unallocated space On a computer hard disk drive or related media, areas that do not contain easily accessible data. Unallocated space is created when files are deleted and will exist until that same space is overwritten with new or other data. This arises out of the typical mechanism of file deletion. When a user deletes a file, the data is not erased, just the means to access it; the space where the data is found is designated as unallocated.

uncertainty The range within which the value of a measured parameter is expected to fall. Any measurement made in a laboratory has uncertainty associated with it that in turn depends on factors related to the method or procedure used, the instrumentation and equipment, and the analyst. For example, if an analyst needs to report the weight of a sample of cocaine, the weight will have an uncertainty associated with it that arises from the weighing device (analytical balance), the procedure used by the analyst, and the analyst's skill and training with the method and equipment. Uncertainties may also be reported with quantitative data such as concentrations of drugs or metabolites detected in blood or urine. An uncertainty is typically reported as a +/- value. There are many methods that can be used to estimate uncertainties such as *uncertainty budgets and *control charts.

uncertainty budget A method of estimating the uncertainty of a quantitative measurement. Each contributor to uncertainty in a measurement is identified and the contribution from that step or stage is quantified. These individual contributions are restated as standard deviations and summed as in a budget-like spreadsheet. To complete the calculation, the value of the combined uncertainties is usually multiplied by a coverage factor (k) with a value of 2 or 3. In the example shown, if the coverage factor of $k = 2$ was used, the uncertainty estimated by the budget would be

$$U_{final} = \sqrt{1.77 \times 10^{-5}} \times 2 = 0.0069 \quad \text{grams}$$

( ) SEE WEB LINKS

- The homepage for Eurachem, which is an umbrella organization for a group of analytical organizations in Europe. It has many useful guides and documents, including those related to the estimation of uncertainty. Last accessed May 2011.

Table 1 Example uncertainty budget for a weighing

Contributing factor	Value (grams)	Type of distribution	Standard uncertainty (u)	u^2	Relative contribution (%)
1. Linearity of the balance	0.002	Rectangular	1.16×10^{-3}	1.33×10^{-6}	8
2. Repeatability of the balance	0.0040	Normal	0.0040	1.60×10^{-5}	90
3. Readability of the balance	0.001	Rectangular	5.77×10^{-4}	3.33×10^{-7}	2
Sum of standard uncertainties			5.74×10^{-3}	1.77×10^{-5}	100

uncorrelated techniques Measurement or identification techniques that produce uncorrelated results. To be considered uncorrelated, the techniques must rely on different fundamental properties or mechanism of action. For example, *infrared spectroscopy (IR) and *thin layer chromatography (TLC) are uncorrelated techniques because IR probes vibrational interactions within molecules while TLC is based on selective partitioning of an analyte between a solid and mobile phase.

University of Lausanne A university in Switzerland which is home to the oldest forensic science educational program in the world, founded in 1909.

(((●))) SEE WEB LINKS

• The homepage for the University of Lausanne, home to the oldest academic forensic science programme. Last accessed May 2011.

upper explosive limit (UEL) *See* UPPER FLAMMABILITY LIMIT.

upper flammability limit (UFL) The upper limit concentration of a gas that will be flammable. This depends on the concentrations of the flammable gas and air present, as oxygen is necessary for combustion to occur. Above the UFL, the concentration of flammable gas relative to air is too high to support combustion, i.e. the mixture is too rich. This limit is sometimes referred to as the **upper explosive limit** (UEL).

urea A compound found in urine and known for its distinctive urine-like odour. One *presumptive test for urine involves heating a stain to determine if the odour of urea is detected.

urea nitrate explosive An improvised explosive mixture created from urea and nitrate salts such as potassium nitrate (KNO_3) or fertilizers such as ammonium nitrate (NH_4NO_3).

usable quantity A minimum amount of a drug that must be present for prosecution to proceed. This is a legal limit that varies by location and jurisdiction.

u

vacuole A region in a bloodstain that is formed where a bubble existed; also called a bubble ring. For example, if there is an air bubble in a pool of blood, as the blood dries, the bubble will burst, leaving behind the characteristic pattern.

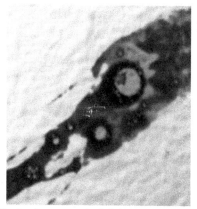

A vacuole or bubble ring is seen to the left in this image

vacuum metal deposition (VMD) A technique used to recover *latent fingerprints on many different types of surfaces, but most often applied to non-porous surfaces such as plastic bags. In general, the object to be examined is placed in a chamber that is subjected to a vacuum by means of a pumping system. A small amount of gold is evaporated out of a container and disperses into the chamber where a thin invisible layer settles on the surface. Typically, the gold will penetrate the fingerprint residue to a small extent. A small amount of zinc is then similarly introduced and settles on the gold layer but it does not penetrate the fingerprint residues in the same way the gold does. As the gold layer is not visible and the zinc layer is, the fingerprint is usually developed as a negative image. VMD can be combined with other development techniques such as *cyanoacrylate in which the cyanoacrylate is applied first, followed by VMD.

vaginal acid phosphatase (VAP) A type of phosphatase enzyme found in vaginal secretions that originates from the cells that line the vagina.

validation studies A series of analytical experiments designed to determine characteristics of a particular method including accuracy, precision, limits of detection, limits of quantitation, interferences, and the limitations of its use as a tool of forensic analysis. The method can be validated internally (within the lab) or across numerous different laboratories. Similarly, validation can be applied to a single analyst, who must show that he or she is capable of performing the test correctly and obtaining acceptable results. Even procedures such as documentation can be validated. The goal of validation is to ensure that reliable results are obtained when proper procedures are followed.

van Deen, J. Isaac (Izaak) (1805–69) A Dutch scientist credited with the development of one of the earliest *presumptive tests for blood. The test was based on a substance called guaiac, which was obtained from a shrub. A similar test, the stool guaiac test is still used today to detect blood in stools.

Van Urk test *See* EHRLICH TEST.

Vanzetti case *See* SACCO AND VANZETTI CASE.

vapour pressure The vapour pressure of a substance (at equilibrium) is the pressure of that substance above the surface. A high vapour pressure correlates to relatively large amounts of evaporation relative to substances with low vapour pressures. Vapour pressure is dependent on temperature.

variable number of tandem repeat (VNTR) In DNA, a locus that has a base pair sequence that repeats a variable number of times. Thus, variation within a population is not generated by what bases are found but how often a given sequence is repeated. Both current STR and older RFLP techniques target VNTR sites.

vegetable alkaloid An older term for a basic drug that is extracted from a plant. Examples include *cocaine and *morphine, which are both extracted from plants.

vegetable fibres Fibres that are obtained from plants and are high in cellulose. Examples include cotton and kapok. The other category in this classification scheme is animal fibres such as wool. Mineral fibres such as asbestos may also be considered as a fibre type.

vehicle In a paint or ink formulation, the compound or compounds that act as the solvents.

victimology In forensic behavioural sciences and profiling, a detailed study of the victims of crimes undertaken to reveal information about the perpetrator. For example, the reason behind victim selection which if ascertained can reveal important information regarding the perpetrator, including possible locations, proximity, and their state of mind.

video spectral comparison (video spectral analysis (VSA)) A technique used principally for the analysis of inks. The technique spans the ultraviolet-visible-infrared ranges and exploits variable illumination, filters, digital imaging, and *fluorescence to evaluate inks. For example some inks will fluoresce in the IR range after being illuminated with higher energy electromagnetic wavelengths such as those in the visible or UV range. This behaviour can be used to differentiate inks that appear identical under normal illumination and observation conditions.

vinyon A type of synthetic fibre that is high in polyvinyl chloride.

virtual image A point in space where the optical paths of rays traced backwards from an object converge. A *real image is formed at a point where light paths converge whereas a virtual image occurs at a point in space where the rays appear to have converged. A virtual image is not an imaginary image as the contrast with the term 'real image' might suggest even though a real image can be viewed on a screen and a virtual image cannot.

Vitali test An older *presumptive test for drugs that involves adding a drop or two of fuming nitric acid (HNO_3) to a small amount of the material in question. Any colour change is noted and then the sample is evaporated to dryness where a second colour change may be noted. Finally, alcoholic potassium hydroxide (KOH) is added and any additional colour changes are recorded. Vitali's test is used for morphine and heroin (yellows), LSD (brownish purple), and mescaline (reddish browns).

vitreous humour The fluid inside the eyeball that is frequently used for post-mortem toxicological analyses. Since this fluid is contained and fairly isolated, it degrades more slowly than other fluids such as blood and urine and thus is usually preferred for cases in which any significant decomposition has begun.

void pattern In bloodstain patterns, a void is an area that is somehow shielded and thus does not show staining that would otherwise be expected. Also called a shadow pattern, a void pattern can be seen when a person's body, shoe, hand, etc. intercepts blood in flight, blocking it from reaching a surface such as a wall or floor.

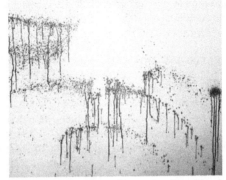

A void is created in the pattern where the source of the blood was blocked by a person or object in its path.

void volume In chromatography, the volume of liquid or gas that a column can contain at any given moment.

voir dire A legal proceeding commonly used to assess the admissibility of an expert's testimony through an evaluation of their qualifications and competencies relevant to the matter at hand. The questioning can be directed at a forensic scientist but is not limited to them; a prospective juror can also be subject to the voir dire process.

Vollmer, August (1876–1955) An American police officer instrumental in linking university scientists to the analysis of evidence and in developing forensic science laboratory systems in the United States. In 1907 he recorded the first use of the scientific analysis of evidence in a case in the United States, involving the analysis of blood, soil, and fibres. He is best known for establishing the first forensic science laboratory in the United States while he served as Chief of Police in Los Angeles in 1923–4. Back in Berkeley in 1930, he established the first criminology and criminalistics programme (Police Science) in the United States at the University of California, Berkeley, which later became a separate school in 1950.

volume of distribution (apparent volume of distribution) (V$_d$) A descriptor used in forensic toxicology that describes the relative solubility of a drug. Mathematically, it is defined as:

$$V_d = \frac{D}{C_p \times \text{body weight}}$$

Where d is the dose, C_p is the peak plasma concentration of the drug, and the body weight of the person is reported in kilograms. The units of dose and C_p are not standardized but are usually reported in units of µg and µg/L or mg and mg/L respectively. The volume of distribution represents the total volume of fluid that would be required for the drug to be distributed in to generate the desired concentration in the plasma. It provides a means of describing the relative distribution of the drug, with larger values of V_d corresponding to wider distribution throughout the body. It is important to realize that V_d has no physical equivalent but rather represents a useful descriptive and comparative value.

Vucetich, Juan (Ivan) (1858–1925) An Argentinian (born in Croatia) who was a pioneer in the use of fingerprints in criminal investigation and is credited with the first case solved according to their use. He worked for the Central Police Bureau in La Plata and was involved in implementing *Bertillonage as the preferred system of criminal identification. In 1892, a woman murdered her two sons and in an attempt to deflect suspicion, injured herself. However, Vucetich was able to locate her bloody fingerprint on a doorjamb, leading to a confession. Vucetich had read Sir Francis Galton's book (*Finger Prints*) and created a large collection of prints by 1891. This early collection still included Bertillon measurements, although fingerprints would soon supplant them. By 1896, he had developed and instituted a fingerprint classification system that is still extensively used in Latin America called 'vucetichissimo'.

wadding A plug made of plastic, cardboard, paper, or felt that is used to separate the propellant from the shot in shotgun ammunition. An older term for wadding is 'overpowder wadding'. In newer ammunition, a one-piece plastic cup and wad combination is typically used. The wadding material is blown out of the barrel when the ammunition is fired, and the position of the wadding at a shooting scene can sometimes be helpful in distance estimation.

Waite, Charles E. (1865–1926) An American active in early work with *firearms evidence. He worked in New York with other noted firearms experts Philip O. *Gravelle and Calvin *Goddard in an organization called the Bureau of Forensic Ballistics. Waite was the founder. He became interested in firearms evidence as a result of the *Stielow case. In 1917, Waite was working for the New York State Prosecutor's Office when he joined an inquiry into the case called by the Governor. Waite was instrumental in uncovering false testimony regarding key firearms evidence used to convict Stielow. He was eventually pardoned and released. After the Second World War ended, Waite built up a large collection of firearms from the United States and Europe and he founded the Bureau in 1924. He died shortly after.

Walker test A presumptive test for *gunshot residue (GSR) useful for clothing. The Walker test detects the nitrite ion ($NO_2{}^-$) found in propellants in ammunition. The test works by transferring the residues to inactivated photographic paper that has been pre-treated with sulphanilic acid and 2-napthylamine (or similar reagents). Development of an orange-red colour is indicative of nitrates and thus possible existence of GSR.

Washing Away of Wrongs, The (*Collected Writings on the Washing Away of Wrongs*) An ancient Chinese text considered to be the first known published work relating to forensic death investigation. Authorship is attributed to Song Ci and publication in 1247. It primarily deals with forensic pathology and death investigation and was remarkably advanced. The text was eventually translated into many languages and was used into the 18th century. It is still in print and available.

watermarks A physical mark made in some types of paper that is created by thinning the material in a set pattern. Watermarks can be seen when the paper is held up to the light, since the thinner areas will pass more light than thicker ones. Watermarks can be used to identify and in some cases date paper. Some word processors also can create digital watermarks in printed documents.

wavelength *See* ELECTROMAGNETIC ENERGY.

Wayne Williams case A pivotal murder investigation that took place before the advent of modern *DNA typing methods and was notable for a lack of physical evidence aside from trace evidence such as hair and fibres. Starting in 1979, young black males were disappearing in Atlanta, Georgia in the US. The bodies were later discovered dumped in wooded areas or near highways and streets. Significant amounts of hairs and fibres were recovered from the bodies and when a local paper published information relating to the fibre findings, the killer began stripping his victims completely or down to their undershorts and dumped some of the bodies into the Chattahoochee River. Investigators began observing bridges over the River.

During the early morning hours of 22 May 1981, a car passed slowly over a bridge being watched by a surveillance team. A splash was heard as he drove over the bridge. Police stopped the vehicle and arrested the driver, Wayne Williams. Subsequent searches of his home and vehicles led to the discovery of the probable sources of the fibres and hairs (a family dog) and a greenish carpet fibre with the unusual cross-section similar to those found on some of the victims. Additional research eventually led to the probable manufacturer of the carpet and allowed the forensic analysts to estimate that this type of carpet would be found in only one in approximately 8,000 homes in the Atlanta area. When the particular combinations of fibres were considered, the odds of a *random match were even smaller. Williams was tried and convicted.

wear characteristics Patterns acquired in or on an object as a result of normal usage. Wear patterns are found in objects ranging from clothing to tools and can be distinctive enough to allow individualization.

weathering 1. Degradation and other changes brought about from exposure to the environment; in relation to arson, weathering refers to the loss (through evaporation) of lighter hydrocarbons found in accelerants such as gasoline.
2. Degradation of colourants in substances such as paint and ink.

Weiner, Alexander (1907–76) An American forensic scientist who worked with the New York City Medical Examiner's Office. He played an important role in implementing forensic serological techniques such as ABO blood group typing in the United States. He also extended serological methods to other body fluids.

wet origin impression An impression, usually from footwear, created when a person steps in something wet such as a puddle of water or mud, and then steps on another surface, leaving an impression made by deposition of the water or mud.

wheelbase measurement A measurement of the distance between the front and rear axles of a motor vehicle; used in accident reconstruction.

whorl (whorl pattern) One of the main fingerprint patterns in which the ridge pattern is roughly circular and has a central core.

Widmark, Erik (1889–1945) A Swedish toxicologist best known for his work with blood alcohol and related topics. Among his many accomplishments was the development of the first reliable blood test for alcohol (ethanol) in 1922. He also elucidated much of the metabolic pathway of ethanol. The method he developed for ethanol in blood was based on an oxidation reaction. A small portion of blood was placed in a vessel over a solution containing sulphuric acid (H_2SO_4) and dichromate (CrO_4^-). With heat, the ethanol evaporated and diffused into the oxidizing solution, consuming dichromate in proportion to the alcohol concentration. The amount of ethanol present in the blood could be calculated indirectly by determining how much oxidizer remained. In the 1920s Widmark published papers that documented the link between blood and breath alcohol, and the equations he developed are still used.

William West case A case in the United States in 1903 that marked the beginning of the end of *Bertillonage as a means of criminal identification. West was booked into the federal prison at Leavenworth, Kansas, and, as was the custom at the time, had several bodily measurements recorded. These were found to match measurements of another inmate in the prison, also called William West. The two bore a striking resemblance to each other, but their fingerprints were different. This incident helped to speed the widespread implementation of fingerprints for individual identification.

wipe pattern A type of blood spatter pattern produced when a bloody object such as a hand, clothing, or hair, is wiped across a surface like a wall.

working distance In microscopy, the distance between the outer surface edge of the objective lens and the top surface of the sample under observation. Typically, the higher the magnification of the objective lens, the shorter the working distance.

wound biomechanics (wound ballistics) The study of wound patterns and forms, principally by forensic pathologists, to determine such things as what type of weapon was used, what movement took place during the struggle, when the wounds were inflicted, and whether wounds might have been defensive or self-inflicted.

woven fabric A textile fabric made by weaving two separate yarns together in an over and under pattern. These two yarns are typically at right angles to each other, but this is not universal.

Wraxall, Brian (1943–2012) A forensic serologist who developed several electrophoretic methods for blood and body fluid typing that were widely used until the advent of *DNA typing. He, along with Brian *Culliford developed a method for typing the serum protein haptoglobin in 1966 and in 1974 he helped develop a sensitive fluorescence-based method for the detection of seminal fluid using methylumbelliferyl phosphate. He remained active in the field of forensic biology into the DNA era.

xanthine alkaloids A class of *alkaloids that contain compounds such as caffeine and theophylline. These compounds occur naturally in coffee, tea, and chocolate.

X-chromosome A sex chromosome and location of the *amelogenin gene locus. A female has the XX *genotype and a male the XY genotype.

xenobiotic (xenobiotic substance) A substance introduced into the body such as a drug or poison that is not normally there; a foreign substance such as a drug or poison.

X-ray crystallography *See* X-RAY DIFFRACTION.

X-ray diffraction (XRD) A technique used to characterize solid crystalline compounds. Crystals possess a regular and orderly structure where the distances separating the atoms are in the same order of size as the wavelengths of X-ray radiation. As a result, X-rays can interact with the atoms in the crystals, resulting in the bending (diffraction) of the radiation in ways that are characteristic of the particular crystal. The principle of diffraction is based on constructive and destructive interference patterns created by reflection and the scattering of radiation within the crystal.

X-ray fluorescence (XRF) An analytical technique frequently paired with *scanning electron microscopy (SEM). When X-rays interact with the electrons surrounding an atomic nucleus, inner shell electrons are sometimes caused to be ejected from the atom. This creates instability that is remedied when an electron from an outer shell moves in to fill the vacancy. When an electron 'falls' into an empty orbital, energy is released in the form of an X-ray. The emitted X-ray is of a longer wavelength (therefore of a lower energy) than the original incident X-ray. If a filling electron comes from one shell away, the process is referred to as an (alpha) transition; from two shells away as a (beta) transition; and from three shells as a (gamma) transition. Because more than one electron can be ejected simultaneously and more than one electron can change shells during the refilling process, each atom can give off more than one wavelength of radiation. The pattern of emitted X-rays is therefore characteristic of each individual element.

There are two principal methods for implementation of XRF, energy dispersive and wavelength dispersive. These techniques are sometimes referred to as energy dispersive spectroscopy (EDS) and wavelength dispersive spectroscopy (WDS). In EDS, the detection system differentiates between X-rays emitted from elements based on the different energies produced. In WDS, this differentiation is achieved by separating and detecting the various wavelengths of the X-rays emitted from the sample. The most common use of XRF in forensic science is in the analysis of *gunshot residue (GSR).

yarn A continuous strand of fibres that are often twisted. Yarn can be made of natural fibres such as cotton or synthetic fibres such as polyester. Yarns are used to construct fabrics.

Y-chromosome A sex chromosome and location of the *amelogenin gene locus. A female has the XX *genotype and a male the XY genotype.

zone search One of many types of search patterns that can be used at crime scenes. Zone methods work well in restricted spaces such as small rooms or cars where other patterns (*grid, *spiral, etc.) are not feasible. Rooms in a house can also be divided up into zones for purposes of a search. Zone searching can also be applied to large crime scenes as a means to subdivide them into manageable sectors.

Z-twist A type or direction of twist used in the production of *yarn and rope. A Z-twist is to the right while an A-twist is to the left. When two or more fibres are joined by twisting, different directions of twist may be combined.

Zwikker reagent *See* DILLE–KOPPANYI TEST.

zymogram (activity stain) A method for visualizing enzymes through their activity. Zymography utilizes *electrophoresis for separation of the components, typically on a gel. This gel contains a substrate that will react with a particular enzyme once separation is complete if it is present. This enzyme is activated by the use of a buffer. Any reaction between the enzyme and the substrate will generate a detectable response.

Appendix 1 Common Abbreviations

Abbreviation	Definition	Category*
AAS	atomic absorption spectroscopy/spectrometry	Instrument/analytical method
AAS_1	anabolic-androgenic steroids	Toxicology
ABI	Applied Biosystems	Company or Corporation
ACSII	American Standard Code for Information Exchange	General terminology
ADH	alcohol dehydrogenase	Toxicology
ADME	absorption, distribution, metabolism, and excretion (or elimination)	Toxicology
AES	atomic emission spectroscopy	Instrument/analytical method
AFIS/IAFIS	Automated Fingerprint Identification Systems/Integrated AFIS	Fingerprints
AFLP/AmpFLP	amplified fragment length polymorphism	Forensic biology/DNA
AMFLP	amplified fragment length polymorphism	Forensic biology/DNA
ANFO	ammonium nitrate-fuel oil	Explosives
AP	acid phosphatase	Forensic biology/DNA
ATR	attenuated total reflectance	Instrument/analytical method
BAC	blood alcohol concentration	Toxicology
BrAC	breath alcohol	Toxicology
CBD	cannabidiol	Chemical or drug structure
CBN	cannabinol	Chemical or drug structure
CCD	charge coupled device	General terminology
CE	capillary electrophoresis	Instrument/analytical method

EOF	electroosmotic flow	Instrument/analytical method
ESD	esterase D	Forensic biology/DNA
ESI	electrospray ionization	Instrument/analytical method
F	bioavailability	Toxicology
FAR	false acceptance rate	Fingerprints
FCR	false classification rate	Fingerprints
FID	Fame ionization detector	Instrument/analytical method
FRR	false rejection rate	Metrology/QA/QC/Accreditation
FTIR	Fourier transform infrared spectroscopy	Instrument/analytical method
GBL	gamma butyrolactone	Chemical or drug structure
Gc	group specific component	Forensic biology/DNA
GC	gas chromatography	Instrument/ analytical method
GHB	gamma hydroxybutyrate	Chemical or drug structure
GSR	gunshot residue	Firearms/toolmarks
Hb	haemoglobin	Forensic biology/DNA
HLA	human leucocyte antigen	Forensic biology/DNA
Hp	haptoglobin	Forensic biology/DNA
HPLC	high performance liquid chromatography	Instrument/analytical method
IAFIS	Integrated Automatic Fingerprint Identification System	Fingerprints
ICP	inductively coupled plasma	Instrument/analytical method
ICP-MS	inductively coupled plasma mass spectrometry	Instrument/analytical method

IDE	improvised explosive device	Explosives
IDL	instrument detection limit	Metrology/QA/QC/Accreditation
IED	improvised explosive device	Explosives
IEF	isoelectric focusing	Forensic biology/DNA
IEP	isoelectric point	Chemistry, general
IMS	ion mobility spectrometry	Instrument/analytical method
IR	infrared spectroscopy	Instrument/analytical method
IRMS	isotope ratio mass spectrometry	Instrument/analytical method
K	known sample	General terminology
KM	Kastle-Meyer test	Forensic biology/DNA
LA or LAB	laser ablation	Instrument/analytical method
LCL	lower control limit	Metrology/QA/QC/Accreditation
LC-MS	liquid chromatography-mass spectrometry	Instrument/analytical method
LD_{50}	lethal dose 50	Toxicology
LDIS	Local DNA Indexing system	Forensic biology/DNA
LEL	lower explosive limits	Arson/combustion
LFL	lower flammability limit	Arson/combustion
LIMS	laboratory information management system	General terminology
LLE	liquid-liquid extraction	Instrument/analytical method
LOD	limit of detection	Metrology/QA/QC/Accreditation
LOQ	limit of quantitation	Metrology/QA/QC/Accreditation
LR	likelihood ratio	Metrology/QA/QC/Accreditation
LSD	lysergic acid diethylamide	Chemical or drug structure

LWL	Lower warning limit	Metrology/QA/QC/Accreditation
m/z	mass to charge ratio	Chemistry, general
MAM	monoacetylmorphine	Chemical or drug structure
MDMA	3,4 methylenedioxymethamphetamine	Chemical or drug structure
MEKC	micellular electrokinetic capillary chromatography	Instrument/analytical method
MMD	multi-metal deposition	Fingerprints
MS	mass spectrometry	Instrument/analytical method
MSD	mass selective detector	Instrument/analytical method
MSP	microspectrophotometry	Instrument/analytical method
mtDNA	mitochondrial DNA	Forensic biology/DNA
NA	numerical aperture	Microscopy
NASH	natural, accidental, suicide, homicide (for manner of death)	Pathology/Death Investigation
NC	nitrocellulose	Explosives
NG	nitroglycerin	Explosives
NMR	nuclear magnetic resonance	Instrument/analytical method
NPD	nitrogen phosphorus detector	Instrument/analytical method
P/M	parent to metabolite ratio	Toxicology
P2P	phenyl-2-propanone	Chemical or drug structure
PCP	phencyclidine	Chemical or drug structure
PCR	polymerase chain reaction	Forensic biology/DNA
PD	physical developer	Fingerprints
PDQ	paint data query database	Chemistry, general

PDR	Physician's Desk Reference	Toxicology
PGM	phosphoglucomutase	Forensic biology/DNA
PLM	polarizing light microscopy	Microscopy
PMI	post-mortem interval	Pathology/Death Investigation
PPA	phenylpropanolamine	Chemical or drug structure
PRT	perception reaction time	Forensic Engineering
Q	questioned sample	General terminology
QA	quality assurance	Metrology/QA/QC/Accreditation
QC	quality control	Metrology/QA/QC/Accreditation
QD	questioned document	Questioned documents
qPCR	quantitative polymerase chain reaction	Forensic biology/DNA
QQQ	triple quadrupole mass spectrometer	Instrument/analytical method
QTof	quadrupole - time of flight mass spectrometer	Instrument/analytical method
RBC	red blood cell	Forensic biology/DNA
RFLP	restriction fragment length polymorphism	Forensic biology/DNA
RI	refractive index	General terminology
RIA	radioimmunoassay	Toxicology
RM	reference material	General terminology
RNA	ribonucleic acid	Forensic biology/DNA
ROC	receiver operating characteristics	General terminology
ROYGBIV	red-orange-yellow-green-blue-indigo-violet	General terminology
%RSD/CV	per cent relative standard deviation or coefficient of variation	Metrology/QA/QC/Accreditation

SANE	Sexual Assault Nurse Examiner	General terminology
SAO	single action only	Firearms/toolmarks
SEM	scanning electron microscopy	Microscopy
SNP	single nucleotide polymorphism	Forensic biology/DNA
SOP	standard operating procedure	Metrology/QA/QC/Accreditation
SPE	solid phase extraction	Instrument/analytical method
SPME	solid phase microextraction	Instrument/analytical method
SRM	Standard Reference Material	General terminology
SSRI	selective serotonin reuptake inhibitors	Chemical or drug structure
STR	short tandem repeat	Forensic biology/DNA
$t_{1/2}$	half-life	Toxicology
t_r	retention time	Instrument/analytical method
TATP	triacetone triperoxidase	Explosives
Tg	glass transition temperature	Chemical or drug structure
THC	Tetrahydrocannabinol	Chemical or drug structure
TLC	thin layer chromatography	Instrument/analytical method
TNT	trinitrotoluene	Explosives
TOF	time of flight	Instrument/analytical method
TQM	total quality management	Metrology/QA/QC/Accreditation
UCL	upper control limit	Metrology/QA/QC/Accreditation
UEL	upper explosive limit	Arson/combustion
UFL	upper flammability limit	Arson/combustion
UPLC	ultra high pressure liquid chromatography	Instrument/analytical method

UV/VIS	ultraviolet-visible	Chemical or drug structure
UWL	upper warning limit	Metrology/QA/QC/Accreditation
VAP	vaginal acid phosphatase	Forensic biology/DNA
Vd	volume of distribution	Toxicology
VNTR	variable number of tandem repeats	Forensic biology/DNA
VSC	video spectral analysis/visual spectral comparison	Questioned documents
WBC	white blood cell	Forensic biology/DNA
WDS	wavelength dispersive spectroscopy (X-ray)	Instrument/analytical method
XRD	X-ray diffraction	Instrument/analytical method
XRF	X-ray fluorescence	Instrument/analytical method

*The field of forensic science with which the term is most closely associated.

Appendix 2 Selected Forensic Journals

Journal Name	Web link*
Forensic Science International	http://www.sciencedirect.com/science/journal/03790738
Journal of Analytical Toxicology	http://www.jatox.com/
Journal of the Canadian Society of Forensic Science	http://www.csfs.ca/csfs_journal.aspx
Journal of Forensic Sciences	http://www3.interscience.wiley.com/journal/118519059/home?CRETRY=1&SRETRY=0
Science and Justice	http://www.scienceandjusticejournal.com/
Drug Testing and Analysis	http://www.wiley.com/bw/journal.asp?ref=1942-7603&site=1

*Last accessed May 2011.

Appendix 3 Selected Forensic Professional Organizations

Abbreviation	Organization or Group	Web link*
AAFS	American Academy of Forensic Sciences	http://www.aafs.org/
ABC	American Board of Criminalistics	http://www.criminalistics.com/
AFTE	Association of Firearm and Toolmark Examiners	http://www.afte.org/
ANSI	American National Standards Institute	http://www.ansi.org/
AOAC	Association of Analytical Communities, International	http://www.aoac.org/
ASCLD	American Society of Crime Laboratory Directors	http://www.ascld.org/
ASCLD/LAB	American Society of Crime Laboratory Directors Laboratory Accreditation Board	http://www.ascld-lab.org/
ASQ	American Society for Quality	http://www.asq.org/
ASQDE	American Society of Questioned Document Examiners	http://www.asqde.org/
ASTM	American Society for Testing and Materials International	http://www.astm.org/
CAC	California Association of Criminalists	http://www.cacnews.org/
CIE	International Commission on Illumination	www.cie.co.at
CSFS	Canadian Society of Forensic Science	http://www.csfs.ca/
ENFSI	European Network of Forensic Science Institutes	http://www.enfsi.eu/
EURACHEM	European Analytical Chemistry	www.eurachem.org
FSS	Forensic Science Society	http://www.forensic-science-society.org.uk/
IAFN	International Association of Forensic Nurses	http://www.iafn.org/
IAI	International Association for Identification	http://www.theiai.org/
ISO	International Organization for Standardization	http://www.iso.org/iso/home.htm
IUPAC	International Union of Pure and Applied Chemistry	http://www.iupac.org/

NAFE	National Academy of Forensic Engineers	http://www.nafe.org/
SOFT	Society of Forensic Toxicologists	http://www.soft-tox.org/
SWGDRUG	Scientific Working Group for the Analysis of Seized Drugs	http://www.swgdrug.org/
SWGFAST	Scientific Working Group on Friction Ridge Analysis, Study, and Technology	http://www.swgfast.org/
SWGGUN	Scientific Working Group for Firearms and Toolmarks	http://www.swggun.org/

*Last accessed May 2011.

Appendix 4 Further Reading

Agrawal, J. P., and R. D. Hodgson. *Organic Chemistry of Explosives*. Chichester, UK: John Wiley and Sons 2007. ISBN: 978-0-470-02967-1.

Akkavan, J. *The Chemistry of Explosives*. 2nd edn. Cambridge, UK: RSC 2004. ISBN: 0-854-04640-2.

Baker, D. R. *Capillary Electrophoresis*. New York: John Wiley and Sons 1995. ISBN: 0-471-11763-3.

Beaven, C. *Fingerprints*. New York: Hyperion 2001. ISBN: 0-7868-8528-9.

Bell, S. *Crime and Circumstance: Investigating the History of Forensic Science*. Westport, CT: Praeger 2008. ISBN: 978-0-313-35386-4.

Bell, S., and K. B. Morris. *An Introduction to Microscopy*. Boca Raton, FL: Taylor and Francis/CRC Press 2010. ISBN: 978-1-4200-8450-4.

Bevel, T., and R. M. Gardner. *Bloodstain Pattern Analysis*. Edited by V. J. Geberth. 3rd ed, *Practical Aspects of Criminal and Forensic Investigation*. Boca Raton, FL: Taylor and Francis/CRC Press 2008. ISBN: 1-4200-5268-3.

Bohan, T. J. *Crashes and Collapses*. Edited by S. Bell, *Essentials of Forensic Science*. New York: Facts-on-File 2009. ISBN: 978-0-8160-5513-5.

Cairns, D. *Essentials of Pharmaceutical Chemistry*. 3rd edn. London: Pharmaceutical Press 2008. ISBN: 978-0-85369-745-9.

Cole, M. D. *The Analysis of Controlled Substances*. West Sussex, UK: John Wiley and Sons 2003. ISBN: 0-471-49253-1.

Cole, S. A. *Suspect Identities: A History of Fingerprinting and Criminal Identification*. Cambridge, MA: Harvard University Press 2001. ISBN: 0-674-00455-8.

Conkling, J. A., and C. J. Mocella. *Chemistry of Pyrotechnics: Basic Principles and Theory*. 2nd edn. Boca Raton, FL: CRC Press/Taylor & Francis Group 2011. ISBN: 978-1-57444-740-8.

Dass, C. *Fundamentals of Contemporary Mass Spectrometry*. Edited by D. M. Desiderio and N. M. Nibbering, *Wiley-Interscience Series on Mass Spectrometry*. Hoboken, NJ: John Wiley and Sons 2007. ISBN: 978-0-471-68229-5.

Eiceman, G. A., and Z. Zarpas. *Ion Mobility Spectrometry*. 2nd edn. Boca Raton, FL: Taylor and Francis/CRC Press 2005. ISBN: 978-0-849-32247-1.

Emsley, J. *The Elements of Murder*. Oxford, UK: Oxford University Press 2005. ISBN: 0-19-280599-1.

Fisher, B. A. J. *Techniques of Crime Scene Investigation*. Boca Raton, FL: CRC Press 2004. ISBN: 0-8493-1691-X.

Goldstein, J., D. Newbury, C. Lyman, P. Echlin, E. Lifshin, L. Sawyer, and J. Michael. *Scanning Electron Microscopy and X-Ray Microanalysis*. 3rd edn. New York: Springer 2003. ISBN: 978-0-306-47292-3.

Heard, B. J. *Handbook of Firearms and Ballistics*. Edited by N. Nic Daeid. 2nd edn., *Developments in Forensic Science*. Oxford, UK: Wiley-Blackwell 2008. ISBN: 978-0-470-69460-2.

Hoffmann, E. D., and V. Stroobant. *Mass Spectrometry: Principles and Applications*. 3rd edn. Chichester, UK: John Wiley and Sons 2007. ISBN: 978-0-470-03311.

Karch, S. B. *A Brief History of Cocaine*. 2nd edn. Boca Raton, FL: Taylor and Francis 2006. ISBN: 0-8493-9775-8.

Kelly, J. *Gunpowder*. New York: Basic Books 2004. ISBN: 0-465-03718-6.

Kenkel, J. *A Primer on Quality in the Analytical Laboratory*. Boca Raton, FL: Lewis/CRC 2000. ISBN: 1-56670-516-9.

Kimothi, S. K. *The Uncertainty of Measurements: Physical and Chemical Metrology: Impact and Analysis*. Milwaukee, WI: ASQ Press (American Society for Quality) 2002. ISBN: 978-0-873-89535-4.

McMaster, M. *LC/MS: A Practical User's Guide*. New York, NY: John Wiley and Sons 2005. ISBN: 0-471-65531-7.

Meyer, R., J. Kohler, and A. Homburg. *Explosives*. 6th edn. Weinheim, Germany: Wiley-VCH Verlag. Original edition, 1977 2007. ISBN: 978-527-31656-4.

National Academy of Sciences. *Strengthening Forensic Science in the United States: A Path Forward*. Washington, DC: National Research Council of the National Academy of Sciences 2009. ISBN: 978-0-309-13135-3.

Noon, R. K. *Forensic Engineering Investigation*. Boca Raton, FL: CRC Press, Inc. 2001. ISBN: 0-8493-0911-5.

Taylor, H. E. *Inductively Coupled Plasma-Mass Spectrometry: Practices and Techniques*. San Diego, CA: Academic Press 2001. ISBN: 0-12-683865-8.

Thomas, R. *Practical Guide to ICP-MS: A Tutorial for Beginners*. 2nd edn. Boca Raton, FL: Taylor and Francis/CRC Press 2008. ISBN: 978-0-4200-6786-6.

Wheeler, B. P., and L. J. Wilson. *Practical Forensic Microscopy*. West Sussex, UK: John Wiley and Sons 2008. ISBN: 978-0-470-03176-6.

Zollinger, H. *Color Chemistry: Syntheses, Properties, and Applications of Organic Dyes and Pigments*. 3rd edn. Zurich: Verlag Helvetica Chimica Acta 2003. ISBN: 3-906390-23-2.

Appendix 5 The Electromagnetic Spectrum

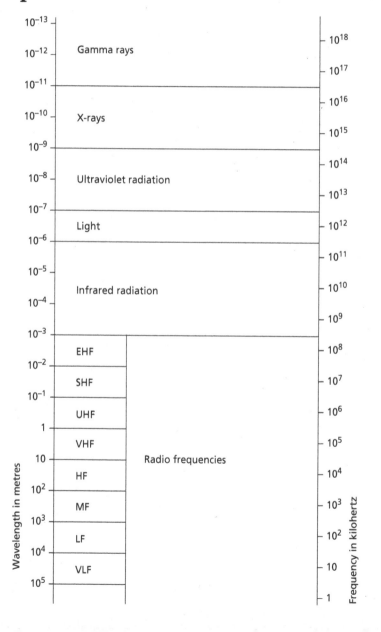

Appendix 6 The Chemical Elements

R.a.m. values with asterisk denote mass number of the most stable known isotope. a.n.: atomic number. r.a.m.: relative atomic mass

Element	Symb	a.n.	r.a.m.	Element	Symb	a.n.	r.a.m.
actinium	Ac	89	227*	germanium	Ge	32	72.59
aluminium	Al	13	26.98	gold	Au	79	196.967
americium	Am	95	243*	hafnium	Hf	72	178.49
antimony	Sb	51	121.75	hassium	Hs	108	265*
argon	Ar	18	39.948	helium	He	2	4.0026
arsenic	As	33	74.92	holmium	Ho	67	164.93
astatine	At	85	210*	hydrogen	H	1	1.008
barium	Ba	56	137.34	indium	In	49	114.82
berkelium	Bk	97	247*	iodine	I	53	126.9045
beryllium	Be	4	9.012	iridium	Ir	77	192.20
bismuth	Bi	83	208.98	iron	Fe	26	55.847
bohrium	Bh	107	262*	krypton	Kr	36	83.80
boron	B	5	10.81	lanthanum	La	57	138.91
bromine	Br	35	79.909	lawrencium	Lr	103	256*
cadmium	Cd	48	112.41	lead	Pb	82	207.19
caesium	Cs	55	132.905	lithium	Li	3	6.939
calcium	Ca	20	40.08	lutetium	Lu	71	174.97
californium	Cf	98	251*	magnesium	Mg	12	24.305
carbon	C	6	12.011	manganese	Mn	25	54.94
cerium	Ce	58	140.12	meitnerium	Mt	109	266*
chlorine	Cl	17	35.453	mendelevium	Md	101	258*
chromium	Cr	24	52.00	mercury	Hg	80	200.59
cobalt	Co	27	58.933	molybdenum	Mo	42	95.94
copper	Cu	29	63.546	neodymium	Nd	60	144.24
curium	Cm	96	247*	neon	Ne	10	20.179
darmstadtium	Ds	110	271*	neptunium	Np	93	237.0482
dubnium	Db	105	262*	nickel	Ni	28	58.70
dysprosium	Dy	66	162.50	niobium	Nb	41	92.91
einsteinium	Es	99	254*	nitrogen	N	7	14.0067
erbium	Er	68	167.26	nobelium	No	102	254*
europium	Eu	63	151.96	osmium	Os	76	190.2
fermium	Fm	100	257*	oxygen	O	8	15.9994
fluorine	F	9	18.9984	palladium	Pd	46	106.4
francium	Fr	87	223*	phosphorus	P	15	30.9738
gadolinium	Gd	64	157.25	platinum	Pt	78	195.09
gallium	Ga	31	69.72	plutonium	Pu	94	244*

Element	Symb	a.n.	r.a.m.	Element	Symb	a.n.	r.a.m.
polonium	Po	84	210*	tantalum	Ta	73	180.948
potassium	K	19	39.098	technetium	Tc	43	98*
praseodymium	Pr	59	140.91	tellurium	Te	52	127.60
promethium	Pm	61	145	terbium	Tb	65	158.92
protactinium	Pa	91	231.036	thallium	Tl	81	204.39
radium	Ra	88	226.0254	thorium	Th	90	232.038
radon	Rn	86	222*	thulium	Tm	69	168.934
rhenium	Re	75	186.2	tin	Sn	50	118.69
rhodium	Rh	45	102.9	titanium	Ti	22	47.9
roentgenium	Rg	111	272*	tungsten	W	74	183.85
rubidium	Rb	37	85.47	ununbium	Uub	112	285*
ruthenium	Ru	44	101.07	ununhexium	Uuh	116	292*
rutherfordium	Rf	104	261*	ununpentium	Uup	115	288*
samarium	Sm	62	150.35	ununquadium	Uuq	114	289*
scandium	Sc	21	44.956	ununtrium	Uut	113	284*
seaborgium	Sg	106	263*	uranium	U	92	238.03
selenium	Se	34	78.96	vanadium	V	23	50.94
silicon	Si	14	28.086	xenon	Xe	54	131.30
silver	Ag	47	107.87	ytterbium	Yb	70	173.04
sodium	Na	11	22.9898	yttrium	Y	39	88.905
strontium	Sr	38	87.62	zinc	Zn	30	65.38
sulphur	S	16	32.06	zirconium	Zr	40	91.22

Picture Acknowledgements

The publishers are grateful to the following for their permission to reproduce the images in this book. Every effort has been made to contact the copyright holders and we apologise for any that have been omitted. Should the copyright holders wish to contact us after publication, we would be happy to include an acknowledgement in subsequent reprints.

Baeyer, Friedrich William Haynes Portrait Collection, Courtesy of the Chemical Heritage Foundation Collections

Balthazard, Victor Suddeutsche Zeitung/Mary Evans Picture Library

Bertillon, Alphonse Library of Congress

Blandy, Mary Mary Evans Picture Library

Chamot, Emile Courtesy of the Division of Rare and Manuscript Collections, Cornell University Library

Crippen Bain Collection Library of Congress

Galton, Francis Public Domain

Kirk, Paul Leland © Bettmann/CORBIS

LaFarge, Marie Mary Evans Picture Library

Locard, Edmund Gamma-Keystone via Getty Images

Lucas, Alfred © Illustrated London News Ltd/Mary Evans

Marsh test Public Domain Courtesy of NLM

Orfila, Mathieu Joseph Bonaventura Public Domain Courtesy of NLM

Paracelsus istockphoto.com

Sacco and Vanzetti Case © Photos 12 / Alamy

Taylor, Alfred Swaine Public Domain Courtesy of NLM

Oxford Quick Reference

Concise Medical Dictionary

Over 12,000 clear entries covering all the major medical and surgical specialities make this one of our best-selling dictionaries.

'"No home should be without one" certainly applies to this splendid medical dictionary'

Journal of the Institute of Health Education

'An extraordinary bargain'   *New Scientist*

A Dictionary of Nursing

Comprehensive coverage of the ever-expanding vocabulary of the nursing professions. Features over 10,000 entries written by medical and nursing specialists.

A Dictionary of Dentistry
Robert Ireland

Over 4,000 succinct and authoritative entries define all the important terms used in dentistry today. This is the ideal reference for all members of the dental team.

A Dictionary of Forensic Science
Suzanne Bell

In over 1,300 entries, this new dictionary covers the key concepts within Forensic Science and is a must-have for students and practitioners of forensic science.

Oxford Quick Reference

A Dictionary of Chemistry

Over 4,700 entries covering all aspects of chemistry, including physical chemistry and biochemistry.

'It should be in every classroom and library ... the reader is drawn inevitably from one entry to the next merely to satisfy curiosity.'

School Science Review

A Dictionary of Physics

Ranging from crystal defects to the solar system, 4,000 clear and concise entries cover all commonly encountered terms and concepts of physics.

A Dictionary of Biology

The perfect guide for those studying biology — with over 5,500 entries on key terms from biology, biochemistry, medicine, and palaeontology.

'lives up to its expectations; the entries are concise, but explanatory'

Biologist

'ideally suited to students of biology, at either secondary or university level, or as a general reference source for anyone with an interest in the life sciences'

Journal of Anatomy

Oxford Quick Reference

The Kings and Queens of Britain
John Cannon and Anne Hargreaves

A detailed, fully-illustrated history ranging from mythical and pre-conquest rulers to the present House of Windsor, featuring regional maps and genealogies.

A Dictionary of World History

Over 4,000 entries on everything from prehistory to recent changes in world affairs. An excellent overview of world history.

A Dictionary of British History
Edited by John Cannon

An invaluable source of information covering the history of Britain over the past two millennia. Over 3,000 entries written by more than 100 specialist contributors.

Review of the parent volume
'the range is impressive ... truly (almost) all of human life is here'
Kenneth Morgan, *Observer*

The Oxford Companion to Irish History
Edited by S. J. Connolly

A wide-ranging and authoritative guide to all aspects of Ireland's past from prehistoric times to the present day.

'packed with small nuggets of knowledge'　　　　　　*Daily Telegraph*

The Oxford Companion to Scottish History
Edited by Michael Lynch

The definitive guide to twenty centuries of life in Scotland.
'exemplary and wonderfully readable'

Financial Times

Oxford Quick Reference

The Concise Oxford Companion to English Literature
Dinah Birch and Katy Hooper

Based on the best-selling *Oxford Companion to English Literature*, this is an indispensable guide to all aspects of English literature.

Review of the parent volume:
'the foremost work of reference in its field'

Literary Review

A Dictionary of Shakespeare
Stanley Wells

Compiled by one of the best-known international authorities on the playwright's works, this dictionary offers up-to-date information on all aspects of Shakespeare, both in his own time and in later ages.

The Oxford Dictionary of Literary Terms
Chris Baldick

A best-selling dictionary, covering all aspects of literature, this is an essential reference work for students of literature in any language.

A Dictionary of Critical Theory
Ian Buchanan

The invaluable multidisciplinary guide to theory, covering movements, theories, and events.

'an excellent gateway into critical theory'

Literature and Theology

Oxford Quick Reference

The Oxford Dictionary of Art & Artists
Ian Chilvers

Based on the highly praised *Oxford Dictionary of Art*, over 2,500 up-to-date entries on painting, sculpture, and the graphic arts.

'the best and most inclusive single volume available, immensely useful and very well written'

Marina Vaizey, *Sunday Times*

The Concise Oxford Dictionary of Art Terms
Michael Clarke

Written by the Director of the National Gallery of Scotland, over 1,800 entries cover periods, styles, materials, techniques, and foreign terms.

A Dictionary of Architecture and Landscape Architecture
James Stevens Curl

Over 5,000 entries and 250 illustrations cover all periods of Western architectural history.

'splendid ... you can't have a more concise, entertaining, and informative guide to the words of architecture.'

Architectural Review

'excellent, and amazing value for money ... by far the best thing of its kind.'

Professor David Walker

Oxford Quick Reference

The Concise Oxford Dictionary of English Etymology
T. F. Hoad

A wealth of information about our language and its history, this reference source provides over 17,000 entries on word origins.

'A model of its kind'

Daily Telegraph

New Oxford Rhyming Dictionary

From writing poems to writing birthday cards, and from composing advertising slogans to music lyrics, this dictionary has what every writer (or budding writer) needs. It contains rhymes for over 45,000 words, including proper names, place names, and foreign terms used in English.

'All wordsmiths are bound to enjoy feeling indebted (fetid, minareted, rosetted...)'

Julia Donaldson (author of *The Gruffalo*)

The Oxford Dictionary of Slang
John Ayto

Containing over 10,000 words and phrases, this is the ideal reference for those interested in the more quirky and unofficial words used in the English language.

'hours of happy browsing for language lovers'

Observer

Oxford Quick Reference

A Dictionary of the Bible
W. R. F. Browning

In over 2,000 entries, this authoritative dictionary provides clear and concise information about the important people, places, themes, and doctrines of the Bible.

The Oxford Dictionary of Saints
David Farmer

From the famous to the obscure, over 1,400 saints are covered in this acclaimed dictionary.

'an essential reference work'   *Daily Telegraph*

The Concise Oxford Dictionary of the Christian Church
E. A. Livingstone

This indispensable guide contains over 5,000 entries and provides full coverage of theology, denominations, the church calendar, and the Bible.

'opens up the whole of Christian history, now with a wider vision than ever'   Robert Runcie, former Archbishop of Canterbury

The Oxford Dictionary of Popes
J. N. D. Kelly and M. J. Walsh

Spans almost 2,000 years of papal history: from St Peter to Pope Benedict XVI.

'well-researched, extremely well written, and a delightful exercise in its own right'   *Church Times*

Oxford Quick Reference

The Concise Oxford Dictionary of Quotations
SIXTH EDITION
Edited by Susan Ratcliffe

Based on the highly acclaimed seventh edition of *The Oxford Dictionary of Quotations*, this dictionary provides extensive coverage of literary and historical quotations, and contains completely up-to-date material. A fascinating read and an essential reference tool.

Oxford Dictionary of Quotations by Subject
Edited by Susan Ratcliffe

The ideal place to discover what's been said about what, the dictionary presents quotations on nearly 600 areas of special interest and concern in today's world.

The Oxford Dictionary of Humorous Quotations
Edited by Ned Sherrin

From the sharply witty to the downright hilarious, this sparkling collection will appeal to all senses of humour.

The Oxford Dictionary of Political Quotations
Edited by Antony Jay

This lively and illuminating dictionary from the writer of 'Yes Minister' presents a vintage crop of over 4,000 political quotations. Ranging from the pivotal and momentous to the rhetorical, the sincere, the bemused, the tongue-in-cheek, and the downright rude, examples include memorable words from the old hands as well as from contemporary politicians.

'funny, striking, thought-provoking and incisive ... will appeal to those browsing through it at least as much as to those who wish to use it as a work of reference'
Observer

OXFORD